"That the People Might Live"

"That the People Might Live"

Loss and Renewal in Native American Elegy

Arnold Krupat

Cornell University Press
Ithaca and London

Copyright © 2012 by Cornell University

All rights reserved. Except for brief quotations in a review, this book, or parts thereof, must not be reproduced in any form without permission in writing from the publisher. For information, address Cornell University Press, Sage House, 512 East State Street, Ithaca, New York 14850.

First published 2012 by Cornell University Press
Printed in the United States of America

Library of Congress Cataloging-in-Publication Data

Krupat, Arnold.
  That the people might live : loss and renewal in Native American elegy / Arnold Krupat.
      p. cm.
  Includes bibliographical references and index.
  ISBN 978-0-8014-5138-6 (cloth : alk. paper)
  1. Indian literature—United States—History and criticism. 2. Folk literature, Indian—History and criticism. 3. American literature—Indian authors—History and criticism. 4. Elegiac poetry, American—Indian authors—History and criticism. 5. Indians of North America—Funeral customs and rites. 6. Loss (Psychology) in literature. 7. Death in literature. 8. Grief in literature. I. Title.
  PM157.K78 2012
  810.9897—dc23   2012022193

Cornell University Press strives to use environmentally responsible suppliers and materials to the fullest extent possible in the publishing of its books. Such materials include vegetable-based, low-VOC inks and acid-free papers that are recycled, totally chlorine-free, or partly composed of nonwood fibers. For further information, visit our website at www.cornellpress.cornell.edu.

Cloth printing   10 9 8 7 6 5 4 3 2 1

For Ralph Salisbury

Contents

List of Illustrations	ix
Acknowledgments	xi
Introduction	1
1. Oral Performances (i)	19
The Iroquois Condolence Rites	19
The Tlingit *koo.'eex'*	29
Occasional Elegy	38
Some Ghost Dance Songs as Elegy	44
2. Oral Performances (ii)	60
"Logan's Lament"	60
Black Hawk's "Surrender Speech"	69
Chief Sealth's Farewell	73
Two Farewells by Cochise	87
The Surrender of Chief Joseph	95

3. Authors and Writers	108
Black Hawk's *Life*	108
Black Elk Speaks	116
William Apess's *Eulogy on King Philip*	122
The Elegiac Poetry of Jane Johnston Schoolcraft, John Rollin Ridge, and Others	125
4. Elegy in the "Native American Renaissance" and After	134
Prose Elegy in Momaday, Hogan, and Vizenor	134
Elegiac Poetry	152
Appendix: Best Texts of the Speeches Considered in Chapter 2	171
Notes	183
Works Cited	213
Index	233

Illustrations

1. Tlingits in ceremonial regalia for 1904 potlatch · 32
2. Sitting Bull, Arapaho, 1885 · 48
3. Indian chiefs and U.S. officials at Pine Ridge, January 16, 1891 · 49
4. Arapaho ghost dance, 1900 · 52
5. Big Foot's camp after the Wounded Knee Massacre, 1891 · 58
6. Múk-a-tah-mish-o-káh-kaik, Black Hawk, 1831 · 71
7. Chief Seattle · 82
8. Chief Joseph, Nez Perce, before 1877 · 97
9. Black Elk and Elk in dance costume, 1880 · 119
10. Kiowa drawing of people bringing in the center pole for the Sun Dance ceremony, 1875–1878 · 137

11. Lone Wolf, Guipago, 1868–1874   140

12. White Bear, Sa-tan-ta, 1869–1874   141

Acknowledgments

I first offer thanks to my colleagues and friends Nina Baym, Bella Brodzki, Harald Gaski, Patricia Penn Hilden, Michael Hittman, Virginia Kennedy, Scott Lyons, David Murray, Duane Niatum, Ralph Salisbury, Brian Swann, Jace Weaver, and Shamoon Zamir for many different sorts of help and support over a long period of time. I most particularly thank Professor Weaver for allowing me to borrow the title of one of his books for this one. I owe J. Gerald Kennedy thanks for his invitation to participate in a small conference on Black Hawk at Louisiana State University in 2008 that led to my further work on Black Hawk's *Life*. I am also grateful to Granville Ganter for help with the rhetoric and history of Native oratory.

To Jack Campisi, Richard Dauenhauer, Michael Foster, Ives Goddard, Marianne Mithun, Eunice Schlichting of the Putnam Museum in Davenport, Iowa, Edwin Sweeney, Debbie Vaughan of the Chicago Historical Museum, George Venn, and Gordon Whittaker, I express my gratitude for the generous responses each offered to the inquiries of a stranger. I also want to express a very special thanks to Professor Karen Weisman of the

University of Toronto. As I note in the introduction, this project would not have been undertaken without her request that I contribute to her edited volume the *Oxford Handbook of the Elegy*. My editor at Cornell University Press, Peter J. Potter, has been supportive of this project from the first and patient with me when I sometimes grew impatient. I am grateful to him, as I am especially grateful to the two readers Peter chose to evaluate this manuscript for the Press. Both readers offered attentively detailed, insightful, and generous comments as well as acutely critical suggestions for revisions, almost all of which I have followed. I can't think of any time in my long career that "peer review" was as valuable and important to me as it was on this occasion.

As I have regularly noted in prior publications, because I teach at a small, liberal arts college, not at a major research university, my work could not have been done without the generous and diligent help of the Sarah Lawrence College librarians. My chief benefactor has been Geoffrey Danisher, sure-handed master of the Inter-Library Loan system, along with Bobbie Smolow. Janet Alexander has also and regularly provided much support. My undergraduate research assistants, Brigid Conroy and Alexander Mutter, deserve thanks for their help as well.

A slightly different version of chapter 2, section 3, "Chief Sealth's Farewell," first appeared in *American Indian Quarterly* 35 (2011) as "Chief Seattle's Speech Revisited"; and some of chapter 3, section 1, "Black Hawk's *Life*," appeared in *American Literary History* 22 (2010) as "Patterson's *Life;* Black Hawk's Story; Native American Elegy." I am grateful to both journals for permission to reprint. This book was completed with the help of a grant from the National Endowment for the Humanities, and I offer my sincere thanks to the Endowment for its generosity.

"That the People Might Live"

Introduction

This book attempts to provide the first broad treatment of Native American elegiac expression over a range of time and across the space of the contiguous United States and Alaska. The project arose from a request from Professor Karen Weisman, editor of the *Oxford Handbook of the Elegy,* to submit an essay on Native American elegy. My initial response was that there was no such thing, no correspondence between a genre originating in classical Greece and Rome and the oral expressive forms of the indigenous peoples of the Americas. The term "elegy" conventionally serves to categorize a very great number of Western poems that address death and loss. But there are no indigenous oral equivalents of the elegy as a genre, as there are also few formal elegies in the written work of Native authors, although I have indeed found some poems with "elegy" in their titles. I regretfully told Professor Weisman that I could not provide the essay she had requested. She patiently suggested I give the matter further thought.

I did, and as I was thinking, I came upon Bruce Robbins's observation that "genre categories impose an onerous and misleading set of expectations on national literatures that are not European. Non-European literatures are forced to compete in a marketplace whose values, defined by established European genres, put newcomers at a systematic disadvantage" (1646). Although Native American national literatures are hardly "newcomers" to American literature, they do continue to suffer the "marketplace disadvantage" to which Robbins alludes; comparing non-European performances and texts to the dominant European genres can indeed work to the detriment of these minority literatures. This observation by Robbins seemed only to confirm my initial response to Professor Weisman. But Robbins went on to observe that, nonetheless, "it's hard to imagine that incomparability is in the long-term interest of any national literature" (1649).

That seemed correct, but the question still remained, How might it be possible to make comparisons among European or Euramerican genres and the traditional genres of Native nations when, as Dan Ben-Amos noted, "ethnic genres are cultural modes of communication, [while] analytical categories are models for the organization of texts" (275)? Western genre theory—"analytical categories...for the organization of texts"—does not account very well for "ethnic genres" that are "cultural modes of communication" of an oral-performative rather than textual kind.

For example, the anthropologist Keith Basso has counted "four major...genres" of narrative among the Western Apache. He calls these "'myths'...'historical tales'...'sagas'...and stories that arise in the context of gossip" (1984, 34). The first three of these are indeed more or less familiar to the textual critic, but the fourth has no close or formal parallel among the "major" genres of Western literature. Robert Brightman writes that "Rock Crees class oral narratives either as aca ohkiwin or acimowina" (6). While the former are "said to be *true* accounts of events that transpired in an earlier condition of the world," the latter "are temporally situated in a kind of 'historical' time possessing continuity with the situation of narration" (7). We might call the tales in the first category "myth"—although we don't consider myths to be "true"—and call those in the second category more nearly historical—although Brightman notes that even the historical narratives "may contain events and characters which are supernatural or non-factual *from a non-Indian perspective*" (7; my emphasis). These observations pertain to most traditional Native American stories.

Donald Bahr's studies (1994, 1997) of T'ohono akimel (Pima) oral performances consider creation stories, a narrative genre familiar to the West, but also Oriole and Airplane songs. Oriole and Airplane songs are traditional dream songs (although the latter date only from the 1940s) that have no close parallels among Western lyrical genres. In the same way, strictly speaking, there are no traditional, oral elegies.

It seemed that one route to comparability might be found in John Frow's observation that whereas "the elegy as a genre remains...specifically concerned with the act of mourning a particular person," the elegiac *mode*, "is a matter of tone—of reflective melancholy or sadness" (132). Frow quotes Morton Bloomfield's view that since the early romantic period, elegy "is not a genre but a mode of approaching reality" (qtd. in Frow 132). Bloomfield may or may not be correct, but we can certainly study the ways in which Native peoples expressively approach the reality of death and loss.[1] As I increasingly discovered, they approach it very differently from what is to be found in Western elegy.

Of course the Native nations occupying what are now the contiguous forty-eight states and Alaska spoke many different languages and had many different cultures, so one would not expect to find anything like a Pan-Indian uniformity of expressive response to death and loss. But all of these nations were traditionally kin-based and relatively small-scale societies—*tribal,* as I will explore the matter further, in the broadest sense of that term—and these facts importantly influence their approach to the reality of death and loss. My research has found a substantial consistency of response among several different Native nations,[2] in particular, the fact that while death and loss were inevitably felt personally, they were intensely felt socially: someone who had contributed to the People's well-being was now gone. Native American elegiac expression traditionally, orally, and substantially in writing as well offered mourners consolation so that they might overcome their grief and renew their will to sustain communal life.

In an afterword to a collection of essays on "the politics of mourning," Judith Butler has written:

> The presumptions that the future follows the past, that mourning might follow melancholia, that mourning might be completed are all poignantly called into question...as we realize a series of paradoxes: the past is

irrecoverable and the past is not past; the past is the resource for the future and the future is the redemption of the past; loss must be marked and it cannot be represented; loss fractures representation itself and loss precipitates its own modes of expression. (467)

These powerful, even troubling remarks bear differently on the traditions of Native American elegy than they do on the Western elegiac tradition. So, too, do a number of the observations offered by other strong theorists of Western elegy reverberate differently in any consideration of Native elegiac expression.

Thus, Max Cavitch's statement that "the traditional task of the elegist is individuated mourning—to describe...the person and personality of the deceased, to reckon what is unique and irreconcilable about *this loss*" (2010, 227), may well be accurate for the Western elegist, but it has things altogether backward for the traditional Native American elegist—more usually elegists—whose task is to show how *this loss* is very much like other losses the People have suffered and to which elegiac performance has reconciled them in the past, as it may yet do again. For Native American communities, the irrecoverable personal uniqueness of any person is less important than his or her socially recuperable function. Indeed, William Bevis many years ago (1987) insisted on the "*insufferability* of individuality" to traditional Native people (590; my emphasis). Ralph Waldo Emerson's dictum "'Thou art unto thyself a law'," Bevis wrote, "is the exact opposite of Native American knowledge" (597). Traditional, oral elegiac performance offers consolation to the community so that it may recover and flourish. I have found that much written elegiac expression by Native Americans does so as well.

In these respects, Dylan Thomas's insistence in the last line of his powerful "A Refusal to Mourn..." (1945) that "After the first death there is no other" will very rarely find an equivalent in Native elegiac expression. Native American elegists more usually work from the fact that since death came into the world long, long ago—this may have been Coyote's doing—there have always been deaths and there always will be deaths. Certainly one must mourn, but one must do so, as I will explain further, in such a way that the People might live despite their loss; no loss has the uniqueness Thomas seemingly attributes to "the first death." In the same way, Native elegiac expression would not attempt to comfort a mourner, as in

John Milton's "Lycidas," by displacing "affection from the dead friend," as Tammy Clewell observes, "to a fiction in which the lost other 'lives and spreads aloft in heaven'" (48). Milton consoles himself through the conviction that *"Lycidas* sunk low, but mounted high, / Through the dear might of him that walk'd the waves" (lines 172–73). Having assimilated the young Edward King's death to Christian history, Milton may imagine for himself a release from grief, a passage "to fresh fields and pastures new."[3] But no such movement will be found in traditional indigenous elegy, which works to make it possible for the bereaved to *stay where they are,*[4] sustaining and continuing the collective life that has been threatened by loss. To cite Bevis once more, "tribal reality is profoundly conservative; 'progress' and 'a fresh start' are not *native* to America" (587).

In much the same way, the Native American mourner will not find solace when "Lilac and star and bird twine . . . with the chant of [his] soul," as in Walt Whitman's "When Lilacs Last in the Dooryard Bloomed."[5] Whitman's Emersonian placement of the I or ego at the center of things, as quoted above by Bevis, has no equivalent in traditional Native thought. To the contrary, lilacs and stars and birds have always been "twined"— codependent—with the individual "soul" in sustaining the ecosphere and the People who live in close relation to everything in it.

The elegies by Milton and Whitman provide illustrations of successful mourning as theorized by Sigmund Freud in his classic essay "Mourning and Melancholia" (1917); there, Freud wrote, when the work of mourning is "completed the ego becomes free and uninhibited again" (244). Freud differentiated mourning from melancholia, a pathological condition in which the ego cannot become free because it refuses to let go of the lost object of its affection. Freud revised this view in 1923, in *The Ego and the Id,* which was strongly influenced by his experience of World War I. That revision has enabled contemporary critics to elaborate a much more complex relation between mourning and melancholia than the simple binary of successful/normal as opposed to failed/pathological. Thus David Eng and David Kazanjian have commented that "in describing melancholia as a confrontation with loss through the adamant refusal of closure, Freud also provides another method of interpreting loss as a creative process" (2003b, 3). They note that "unlike mourning, in which the past is declared resolved, finished, and dead, in melancholia the past remains steadfastly alive in the present," and the mourner engages in "an ongoing and open relationship with the past" (3–4). It may be, they continue, that melancholia's "continued and open relation to the past...allows us to gain new perspectives on and new understandings of lost objects," providing an opportunity for a "rewriting of the past as well as the reimagining of the future" (4). This permits what David Eng and Shinhee Han have called the "depathologizing [of] melancholia" (363), a "depathologizing" implied by Jahan Ramazani's apparently oxymoronic conception of "melancholic mourning," which dilutes "Freud's overly rigorous distinction between 'mourning' and 'melancholia' to a matter of emphases within mourning" (ix, 29). These revisions of Freud's initial paradigm have significance for Native American elegiac expression.

The work of mourning for traditional Native Americans is performed not so that the *ego* but rather so that the *People* may become free and uninhibited again. It is precisely this sort of work that is achieved, for example, by the Iroquois Condolence Council and the Tlingit *koo.'eex'* (roughly, "potlatch"), as we will see in the first two studies in chapter 1 of this book. It is only in response to *exile*—I will explain what I mean by this term just below—that "melancholic mourning" becomes necessary that the People might live. This comes into play in some of the nineteenth-century Ghost Dance songs that I will examine as elegy in chapter 4.

In an essay on William Apess, a Pequot minister and writer in exile, Eric A. Wolfe summarizes some of this revisionist thought on mourning and melancholia in order to suggest that "melancholia is a more politically active stance than mourning." What Wolfe calls melancholia insists "upon the significance of past losses and upon the connections between present and past" (3),[6] in the interest of imagining an American future that may be productively different from the past. Whether it is more nearly mourning or melancholia, Native elegiac performance and much elegiac writing offer consolation to the People in order that they may survive and thrive despite their loss.

In a little-known but powerful essay entitled "Out of Chaos," Vine Deloria Jr. claimed that *exile* is the condition common to all indigenous tribal nations since the arrival of the Europeans regardless of whether any nation was actually forced from or allowed to remain on its ancestral lands. Deloria shows that from the first permanent settlements of Europeans in the Southwest and on the East Coast in the seventeenth century to the colonization of territory west of the Mississippi in the late 1830s and 1840s to the final conquest of the Western Plains by 1890, each and every tribal nation suffered a disruption in the enabling conditions of its ongoing ceremonial and ritual life—an exile. In order fully to understand this we must recognize that Native Americans think of the land very differently from Europeans.

Europeans conceive of land as property, a commodity that can be bought or sold and permanently owned. But, as Deloria notes, "when an Indian thinks about traditional lands he always talks about what the people did there, the animals who lived there and how the people related to them... and the ceremonial functions it was required to perform to remain worthy of living there" (1989, 261). The Houma law professor N. Bruce Duthu offers commentary that parallels Deloria's. Duthu writes: "From the Indian perspective, the relationship with their ancestral lands operates in the form of a sacred covenant between the community and the land, in which Indian peoples regularly minister to the land as stewards and the land reciprocates by supporting, nurturing, and teaching the community to live in proper balance with its surroundings" (79).

American restrictions on Indian land use, appropriations of sacred lands, and the imposition of a calendar based on agriculture (rather than hunting, fishing, root-digging, berry- or nut-gathering) made it difficult or impossible to perform ceremonies at the appropriate times, in the appropriate places, using materials that could be gathered only in those places, thus disrupting the traditional harmony between the People and the land. The "real exile of the tribes," Deloria writes, "occurred in the destruction of ceremonial life" (1989, 265).

This disruption was pervasive and persistent. As we will see, Native American writers from the nineteenth century to the present, both those from a traditional background as well as many from the cities or from lands far from those of their ancestors, also often express a deep sense of exilic loss in their work.[7] Theirs is a collective melancholic mourning that will not release the palpable *presence* of what is *absent*, that will not *mourn* in the classic Freudian sense. Land loss and ceremonial loss, as Deloria shows, are foremost. But there is also language loss, culture loss; loss of the young to the Indian boarding schools, and, later, to drugs, alcohol, and suicide. Then there is the loss of names, both the names of ancestors, so important to the condolence ceremonies of the Iroquois and Tlingit People, as we will see, and the names of significant places.

In Leslie Marmon Silko's novel *Ceremony,* the narrator explains how the indigenous "world had become entangled with European names: the names of the rivers, the hills, the names of the animals and plants—all of creation suddenly had two names: an Indian name and a white name" (68). This begins when Columbus bestows the name San Salvador on an island he *knows* its inhabitants call Guanahani; then, abducting six natives of the island, he gives them Spanish names.

The consequences of this sort of renaming persist. Simon Ortiz writes of visiting Pueblo Indian students at Laguna Elementary School and asking them if they know where Deetseyamah—his home at Acoma Pueblo—is. When no one responds, he asks, "Who knows where McCartys is?" Then, "many of the children quickly raised their hands." Ortiz explains that the place known for generations as "Deetseyamah in their own language" has been renamed McCartys. As "a writer, teacher, and storyteller," Ortiz writes, one of his tasks is "to demystify language," to untangle the names and, in the interest of a different future, to hold onto the old ones rather than merely mourn their passage (1992, 3). Of course, some of the names bestowed by the whites were not merely "entangling" or "mystifying" but painfully derogatory: names like Squaw Valley, Squaw Peak, and Squaw Creek. Squaw, as William Bright has noted, "belongs to a rather special semantic set... 'buck, squaw, papoose' [that] is unusual among terms for ethnic groups... this pattern seems to group Indians with animals (e.g., horse: stallion, mare, colt) rather than with other human groups" (ms. 5). It is also "unusual... for ethnic groups" still to be called by names the group finds offensive: names like Washington Redskins in football and Atlanta Braves in baseball. This practice is unimaginable today with regard to blacks or Jews.

The experience of exile, the disruption of ceremonial life, affected the People in innumerable ways, all of them baleful. In the sixteenth and seventeenth centuries, the nations of the Southeast and Southwest resisted the Spanish invasion militarily; the great Pueblo revolt occurred in August 1680. In the seventeenth century the northeastern nations, too, fought back against invasions by the English, the French, and the Dutch. What was called King Philip's War ended in 1676 with the defeat and death of Metacomet—Philip—but not before "more than half of all the colonists' settlements in New England had been ruined and the line of English habitation... pushed back almost to the coast" (Lepore xii). Indigenous military resistance continued through the eighteenth century, both before and after the American Revolution—the majority of Native people supported the British—and intensified in the nineteenth century.

But even before the Cherokees were driven onto the "Trail of Tears" in 1838, en route to Indian Country from their homes in Georgia and South Carolina, Black Hawk's Sauk People had already been driven into exile. Nor did it matter, as Deloria has made clear, that this particular exile did not involve as great a geographical displacement as it did for the Cherokees. And there were many other "removals" as well.[8] Much the same—exile to places far away or not so far from traditional homelands—would be the case for Cochise's People and the peoples of Sealth, Chief Joseph, and Black Elk in the second half of the nineteenth century. Indeed, the various Ghost Dance movements arose as a form of cultural and ceremonial resistance to the experience of exile.

Having found that Native American elegiac expression differed from Western elegy in the ways I have sketched—what I have sketched does not, of course, amount to a complete picture of Western elegy—I thought it useful to borrow the title for this book from a book published by Jace Weaver in 1997: *That the People Might Live: Native American Literatures and Native American Community*. I borrowed the first part of Professor Weaver's title, with his permission, as an effective way of indicating that a great deal of what can be considered indigenous elegiac expression—Native American oral performances and written texts generally concerned with death and loss—is, as I have said, strongly oriented toward the community rather than the individual, a community that must be consoled in the interest of what Gerald Vizenor has called "continuance" and "survivance," that the People might live.[9] Most of the traditional, oral performances I will consider, and many of the written texts as well, proceed from what Weaver has called a "communitist" perspective (303 and passim). What is lost—persons, to be sure, but, as we have seen, also land, names, and traditions[10]—affects not only a particular individual or family but the larger community—clan, moiety, tribe, nation—as a collective entity.

The "theory" of Native American elegiac expression that I propose is, thus, theory of a Jeffersonian, inductive kind. It is not, that is to say, an abstract logical deduction, but rather a set of generalizations that arose from a wide sampling of specific examples. This is *theory* of a social-scientific and humanist kind; it is not *law* of the kind posited by the hard sciences.[11]

The theory makes the strong descriptive claim that *most* Native oral performances concerned with death and loss function to console and sustain the community. It in no way claims that *all* Native elegiac oral performances do so. Similarly, the theory affirms that elegiac *writing* by Native Americans, in what struck me as a surprising degree, also takes a "communitist" (Weaver) perspective. It in no way claims that *all* Native elegiac writing does so.

It should also be understood that this theory of Native American elegiac expression is *descriptive* and in no way *prescriptive*. It neither states nor in any way implies that Native oral performances (e.g., those I later call "occasional elegies") *should* work for the collective continuance and survivance of the People, nor does it state or imply that those that do not do so are somehow "not-Indian" or not "authentically" Native. We will see this in Native American elegiac writing as various as the elegies of Jane Johnston Schoolcraft and John Rollin Ridge, among other nineteenth-century Native poets, and the twentieth-century text *The Way to Rainy Mountain* by N. Scott Momaday, along with the work of several contemporary Native poets. Without invoking the cliché that exceptions prove the rule—I don't know that they do—the particular exceptions I will offer do not invalidate the theory of Native American elegiac expression I have posited. Rather, they point to what I will reemphasize, its status as a descriptive *theory*, not a determining or prescriptive *law*.

Important as it is to be clear about the distinction between a general theory and a law, so, too, is it important to be clear about a number of other terms that will come up in this book. Among these are pairs such as traditional-modern, oral-written, authentic-inauthentic, and communitist-individualist. It is important to state that these terms are useful insofar as they name *distinctions* (or emphases), not *oppositions*. To speak of traditional peoples or cultures is not to speak of unchanging entities or values fixed in time.[12] Traditional cultures, as many have remarked, inevitably *change*, although the emphasis is always on sameness not difference. As Bevis notes (above), tribal reality is profoundly conservative. For Native peoples of the contiguous United States and Alaska, the traditional means of expression (for the practice of "science," "philosophy," curing, "literature," and every sort of pedagogical enterprise) was, and in important measure still is, *oral*. But at least since the seventeenth century some indigenous persons have chosen to appropriate the medium of writing (see Meserve; and Parker 2011).

The adoption of the technology of alphabetic writing eventually tips the balance between sameness and difference in the direction of difference. But this does not make Indian writers—who, by writing, inevitably become modern in some measure[13]—somehow inauthentic, not the real thing, nor does it totally and irrevocably sever them from "tradition." Traditionality and modernity are, once more, names for different sorts of emphases and possibilities; the terms do *not* name an opposition. My brief discussion of elegies by the Ojibwe writer Jane Johnston Schoolcraft, the Cherokee John Rollin Ridge, and N. Scott Momaday in *The Way to Rainy Mountain* will attempt to negotiate the complex interactions of various aspects of what could be called "traditionality" and "modernity" in their texts. Some measure of the latter, let me repeat, does not—as the fact of their writing does not—make them any less *Native American*.

This is to emphasize that the appropriation of the technology of writing by Native authors—this is the very nature of writing—grants them somewhat more latitude in their expression than does oral performance (which also, it must be recognized, allows in different degrees at least *some* latitude). In particular, writing allows the writer to engage with a variety of cultural perspectives. But this engagement need not, and in practice usually does not, obliterate a residual and often quite powerful communitism—again, in varying degrees. These "theoretical" matters will be developed in the specific studies that follow in this book.

As I have previously written about the way in which the criticism of Native American literatures has proceeded from the three perspectives of *nationalism, indigenism,* and *cosmopolitanism*,[14] and as my own perspective has been largely cosmopolitan, a few words about the dominant perspective in this particular book—so far as I am aware of it—may be in order. Most of the studies in this book are *nationalist* in perspective. This came about not as a conscious decision on my part, but rather as a consequence of the type of work I was trying to do: examining the ways in which indigenous peoples and individuals expressively responded to death and loss. What I found, as I have said, was a strong emphasis on community and collectivity, that is to say, on the nation-people. In that my conceptions of nationalism, indigenism, and cosmopolitanism had long seen these three perspectives as inevitably—and fruitfully—overlapping, I see the nationalist orientation of this book as basically a shift in emphasis; my nationalist perspective here, I believe, remains consistent with an ethnocritical and comparative cosmopolitanism.

There is another important difference between traditional Native elegiac performance and Western elegy to note here. Although, as we will see further, Native oral elegy, along with much of the written work relating to grief and mourning, powerfully includes what the West would call a "religious" dimension, referring to supernaturals and worlds other than the immediate and material "real"—this is more usually the case with the oral materials, although often true of the written texts as well—neither appeals specifically to God or an overarching Creator Spirit. Further, these performances and texts *never*, so far as I have found, interrogate God, the Great Spirit, or Supreme Being concerning the *reasons* for any particular death or loss. "Why, Lord, why?"—a question often asked in Western elegy—has almost no equivalent in Native elegiac expression.

This is to say that we will find nothing resembling, for example, Tennyson's "In Memoriam," where, after 131 stanzas, the speaker in that great poem at last resigns himself to the loss of his dear friend by situating that death in the narrative framework of Christian history. (As I have noted, something like this was more economically the case in Milton's "Lycidas.") Tennyson's speaker says:

> the man, that with me trod
> This planet, was a noble type
> Appearing ere the times were ripe,
> That friend of mine who lives in God,
>
> That God, which ever lives and loves,
> One God, one law, one element,
> And one far-off divine event,
> To which the whole creation moves.

Why did the young Arthur Henry Hallam have to die? Ultimately, the speaker answers that question by imagining his friend living "in God," to whose law all "creation moves."[15] But Native American elegiac expression, consistent with Native American religious thought generally, is focused on creation and re-creation in this world, not salvation in the next. Different tribal peoples imagine the dead to dwell in a variety of places, but death does not result in a different sort of living—with God or some regal or imperial deity whose mysterious purpose somehow requires this particular death. In this regard as well, Native American elegiac expression views and responds to loss very differently from the West.

Like the speaker in Tennyson's poem, the speaker in Allen Ginsberg's "Kaddish" also questions God, although he never does arrive at an acceptance of the loss he has suffered. Ginsberg's elegy for his mother ends in a standoff between God and the poet's ego: "Lord Lord O Grinder of giant Beyonds my voice in a boundless / field in Sheol."[16] But nowhere in Native elegiac expression will we find the mourner alone, crying in the wilderness, and certainly not in an individualistic relation, oppositional or otherwise, to a universal yet personal God. To cite Bevis once more, "the first assumption of tribalism is that the individual is completed only in relation to others...and the group which must complete his 'being' is organized in some meaningful way" (587). Many other differences between Western elegy and Native elegiac expression will be apparent in the studies that follow.

Ben-Amos writes that the differentiating characteristics among indigenous ethnic genres are, broadly, "prosodic, thematic, and behavioral" (287). In terms of prosody, oral poetry is distinguishable from prose narrative or oratory in that it exhibits a regular "metric sub-structure" (288), such as is found in songs or chants.[17] Genres can be distinguished *thematically* in regard to what they are *about,* and *behaviorally* in terms of what they *do* or functionally seek *to bring about.* The ritual and ceremonial songs and speeches about death and loss of which there are records behaviorally function to help bring about the appropriate "feeding," placating or "releasing" the spirits of the dead, aiding their journey to the spirit land, commemorating or, indeed, helping the living to forget them. They also and very importantly, as I have several times pointed out, function to console the living, raise their spirits, and restore healthy communal relations, that the People might live. Again, this is also true of a good deal of Native American elegiac writing.

With these many things in mind, I have structured this book in four chapters. Chapter 1, "Oral Performances (i)," treats a variety of oral performances, beginning with the Condolence Rites of the Iroquois. Well documented since the sixteenth century and to some extent still practiced today, the Rites of Condolence take place upon the death of one of the fifty chiefs of the League. They include, among other elements, chants rehearsing the history of the Iroquois League (founded perhaps in the fifteenth century), and "Requickening" oratory in which the tears of the mourners are symbolically dried so that they may see clearly again, their ears and their throats freed of obstacles so that they may hear and speak fully once more. The Rites conclude with the appointment of a replacement for the deceased chief, someone who will bear his name and carry on his work, that the People might live.

Section 2 of chapter 1 moves to the Pacific Northwest to examine the memorial *koo.'eex'* of the Tlingit People of what is now southeastern Alaska and British Columbia. Once called a "potlatch," and for a long time badly described as predominantly oriented toward the establishment or confirmation of rank and status, the Tlingit ceremony is a mortuary and commemorative ritual in which one of the two Tlingit moieties, the Ravens or the Eagles, performs to assuage the grief of the moiety that has lost one of its own. As with the Iroquois Condolence Rites, oratorical performance—whose imagery I analyze—and also, here, the display of clan property, restore the vitality of the People.

Section 3 of chapter 1 looks at a number of more informal, occasional oral performances responding to loss, from several different Native nations. So far as I can tell, these do indeed seem to be more nearly personal or individualistic than social or communitist. This is to say that they are expressive in a manner *not* so far distant from Western lyric of an elegiac sort. I've gathered song-poems from Alaska, California, and the Great Basin that approach loss in a variety of ways.

The final section of the chapter considers songs of the religious resistance movement known generally as the Ghost Dance. The songs accompanying the Ghost Dance constitute the first major genre of oral, elegiac expression in response to exile. Syncretic compositions, they innovatively combine traditional and culture-specific materials with new elements, either Native (e.g., one People's borrowings from other tribal nations) or Euramerican (e.g., from Mormons, Shakers, or other Christian denominations), to acknowledge loss and to grieve, but also to imagine renewal, that the People might live. The songs thus mourn, but they also serve as symbolic attempts at restoration, expressing a collective, melancholic, and therefore political relation to the past.

Chapter 2, "Oral Performances (ii)," treats oral performances of a single kind, the Indian "farewell" speech. Indian farewells have been printed at least since the seventeenth century, when Christian ministers recorded (or perhaps sometimes wrote) the pious deathbed speeches of their Indian converts. From the late eighteenth to the late nineteenth century, however, the speeches of greatest interest to the American public were those attributed to prominent Indian leaders who had—with the exception of Chief Sealth—resisted the whites militarily. Indeed, the speeches attributed to Chief Sealth and Chief Joseph continue to be celebrated today

In 1774, at the end of "Lord Dunmore's War," the Mingo chief Logan was said to have made a farewell speech that was brought to international attention by its publication in Thomas Jefferson's *Notes on the State of Virginia* (1784). When he surrendered to General Joseph Street at the end of the "Black Hawk War," in the summer of 1832, Black Hawk was also said to have delivered a "farewell" speech—not one that achieved the renown of Logan's, but one that was often reprinted. Farewell speeches were also attributed to the Apache leader Cochise and to the celebrated Chief Joseph of the Nez Perce, both prominent fighters against the Americans in the 1870s. A speech published in 1887, said to have been delivered in 1854 by Chief Sealth—who had *not* fought against the whites—became the most famous of them all.

Section 1 of chapter 2 introduces the subject of the "farewell speech" and offers a study of Chief Logan's speech. Section 2 offers a study of Black Hawk's "surrender speech"; section 3 of Sealth's "farewell"; section 4, two speeches attributed to Cochise; and section 5, Chief Joseph's address, once again presumably a "surrender" speech. As the reader will have noted, I have spoken in terms of speeches "attributed" to or "said to have been" made by one or another of these Native leaders; this is because there are substantial questions about who may or may not have actually said what. Because I have found the historical record to be full of errors—different dates and occasions given for one or another speech, different texts, and so on—I have included an appendix that provides the most accurate texts of these speeches as possible.

Although the Ghost Dance songs demonstrated the vitality of oral performances as late as the last decade of the nineteenth century, they had already been preceded by varieties of Native written expression that may be read in the context of elegy, which are the subject of chapter 3, "Authors and Writers." The first section of chapter 3 considers Black Hawk's autobiography, published in 1833 by the young newspaperman John Barton Patterson. Black Hawk did not write, but he may well be considered among the first Native American *authors*. His *Life* was long read as elegiac in the Western sense, mourning what was irrevocably gone, as in Black Hawk's early lament, after describing the customs of his People: "But these were the times that were!" (2008, 48). I will make the case that Black Hawk's narration is more nearly elegiac in the Native American sense, a performance that can be seen as a symbolic act intending the continuance of Sauk traditional life; it is not Western mourning but indigenous "melancholic mourning" of a particularly creative kind.

Section 2 of chapter 3 is a study of *Black Elk Speaks,* published in 1932, almost a hundred years after Black Hawk's *Life*. *Black Elk Speaks* is the work of a later, prominent Native *author* whose autobiography was produced in collaboration with the Nebraska poet John G. Neihardt. Also long read in the Western sense as an elegy for times and lifeways long dead, Black Elk's book is better read in much the same vein as Black Hawk's. In a manner consistent with traditional Native American elegiac practice, it is very much a symbolic act acknowledging what has been lost to exile, while seeking to enact by narrative means the continuance and survivance of Black Elk's People.

Section 3 of chapter 3 turns to Black Hawk's contemporary the Reverend William Apess, a Pequot minister and the first Native American to write his own extended autobiography, *A Son of the Forest,* published in 1829.[18] My focus, however, is Apess's final work, the *Eulogy on King Philip* (1836), in which he memorializes the seventeenth-century Wampanoag leader Metacomet. In a radical revision of the American master narrative of tragic and inevitable Indian "vanishment," Apess's *Eulogy* refuses to mourn Philip as dead and gone forever; rather, in an act of "melancholic mourning," he claims Philip lives on, and he uses Philip's legacy precisely as an opportunity for a "rewriting of the past" in a way that can serve as a "reimagining of the future" (Eng and Kazanjian 2003b, 4). Consistent with Native American traditional elegy, however, the most immediate *function* of Apess's *Eulogy* is to forestall the "removal" of the Cherokee Nation of Georgia to lands west of the Mississippi by President Andrew Jackson, so that ultimately the Cherokees, Indian people more generally, and indeed, all persons of color might live full and free lives.

Section 4 considers some nineteenth-century contemporaries of Apess and Black Hawk, the Ojibwe writer Jane Johnston Schoolcraft and the slightly younger Cherokee writer John Rollin Ridge. It also includes a few lesser-known nineteenth-century Indian poets, as well as some who published early in the twentieth century. Schoolcraft wrote a number of formal English elegies on the death of her young son, William, along with an elegy for her Irish aunt, Mrs. Kearny. Although Schoolcraft also wrote in and translated from Ojibwe (in which she was fluent), her perspective in these particular poems is entirely and conventionally Christian. I see no way to place them in relation to any tradition of Native elegiac expression. This is also the case for the elegies of Ridge and the other poets we will examine in this section.

Before offering a brief description of the studies in chapter 4, the final chapter in this book, I need to warn the reader that the studies up to this point—and, indeed, after—offer a great deal of historical and cultural material in addition to literary analysis of the performances or texts they consider. Both readers of the manuscript of this book for Cornell University Press urged me to be careful not to let this material overwhelm the literary analysis, and I have tried to heed their advice. But whereas one can simply say, John Milton published "Lycidas," an elegy on the death of his friend the young Reverend Edward King, in 1638, or Walt Whitman published "When Lilacs Last in the Dooryard Bloomed," an elegy on the death of President Abraham Lincoln, in 1865, and move quickly on from there, one can't just say, "The Iroquois Condolence Council is…" or "Tlingit potlatch oratory is…" or "The Ghost Dance songs were…," and simply go on from there. Nor can one say, Logan's speech was supposedly delivered in 1774 or Sealth's in 1854 or Chief Joseph's in 1877, and simply go on from there. A reader who isn't sure just who Milton or Whitman was can Google them and the titles of their elegies and gain some minimal context for understanding in very little time. It isn't possible—or, more exactly, it's definitely not easy—to do this for Iroquoian or Tlingit condolence oratory or for the farewell speeches attributed to the several chiefs. Nor is it possible to do so for the Ghost Dance songs or, for that matter, for the ostensibly elegiac autobiographies authored by Black Hawk and Black Elk or for other Native American elegiac work. Although I have tried not to let the historical and cultural materials get out of hand, they are fairly dense nonetheless. Any reader so inclined can skim or skip as he or she wishes. I hope few will choose to do so. Further, although our understanding of Native American history and culture has improved enormously in the last decade and advances continue to be made, a great number of basic *facts* important to Native American studies have simply not yet been firmly established. In relation to the materials relevant to this book, I've tried to establish some of these facts as best I could.

Chapter 4, "Elegy in the 'Native American Renaissance' and After," contains just two studies. The first considers three works: the elegiac autobiographical text *The Way to Rainy Mountain* (1969), by the presumptive initiator of the so-called Native American Renaissance, N. Scott Momaday; the "Prologue" from Linda Hogan's novel *Solar Storms* (1995), which vividly depicts an improvised condolence ceremony organized by a Chickasaw woman living among Cree people of the north; and a series of prose elegies for a red squirrel by Gerald Vizenor. The second study looks at elegiac work in a wide range of Native American poets: Sherman Alexie, Jim Barnes, Kimberly Blaeser, Jimmie Durham, Lee Francis, Lance Henson, Maurice Kenny, Adrian Louis, Simon Ortiz, Carter Revard, Ralph Salisbury, and others. Although I don't at all claim to have "covered" the field—there may indeed be poetry of an elegiac kind in other Native writers active in this period—I have tried to range widely enough that my generalizations can serve, as I noted earlier, as a "theory" of a social-scientific and humanist sort.

1

Oral Performances (i)

The Iroquois Condolence Rites

> Hail, Grandfathers,
> Isn't this what you decreed:
> In the far future this institution shall
>   be carried on,
> that the law shall be continued
> by our grandchildren?
> Hail, Grandfathers!
>   Peter John (Fenton 1946, 117)

"The League of the Iroquois, or Confederation of Five Iroquois Tribes," William Fenton writes, "had already been formed by the year 1570 A.D." (1944, 80; see also Hewitt 1977, 163). But Fenton elsewhere, and others (e.g., Daniel Richter: the League was "established sometime late in the fifteenth century" [1992, 31]), suggest it may well have been in place a hundred years earlier, yet an exact date for its origin is not likely ever to be established. Originated by Deganawidah, and an associate named Hiawatha,[1] historical figures with mythic attributes, the League or Confederation—in Mohawk, the "*Kaienerekowa* ('the great law of peace')" (Alfred xvi)—was established to promulgate the "principles of reason, righteousness, law, and peace" (Fenton 1944, 81; 1998, 95). Taiaiake Alfred, the contemporary Kanien'keha (People of the Flint) or Mohawk scholar and activist, notes that his book *Peace, Power, Righteousness: An Indigenous Manifesto* (1999) "is inspired by and draws its structure from the ritual songs of the Rotinoshonni ['people of the long house' (xxvi)] Condolence ceremony" (xvii). "The Condolence ceremony," he writes, "represents a way of bringing people back to the power of reason" (xix) after they have sustained a loss. Deriving from Hiawatha's "concern to find a proper way to console mourners of the dead and to restore individuals, families, and nations to society" (Fenton 1998, 95; also Richter 1992, 32), the full Condolence ceremony was traditionally performed three days after the death of one of the fifty chiefs of the League.[2] The loss Alfred addresses, however, is the more general loss to the People resulting from five hundred years of colonialism. "The Condolence ritual pacifies the minds and emboldens the hearts of mourners by transforming loss into strength," he writes. "It revives the spirit of the people and brings forward new leaders embodying ancient wisdom and new hope." "His book," he affirms, "embodies the same hope" (xii). In Jace Weaver's terms, Alfred hopes "to promote communitist values...to participate in the grief and sense of exile felt by Native communities and the pained individuals in them" (xiii).[3] But Alfred's book, consoling the People so that they might live, is a "manifesto." Although the form of the Condolence ritual, he states, "is central" to his book (xvii), it is not strictly elegiac expression. Here I will examine the Iroquois Condolence Council or Rites of Condolence as a form of Native American elegiac expression.

The death of one of the fifty high chiefs assigned by Deganawidah long ago is a loss which threatens the health and vitality of the grand polity of the Six Nations.[4] The Condolence Council, as Fenton describes it, "was in no sense a funeral ceremony, since the dead officers had already been buried with fitting rites; but it was rather a memorial service for the honored dead....[5] When all sorrow had been wiped away, the new candidate [for the office vacated by the deceased] was shown and the antlers of office were placed on his head" (1944, 66).[6] Fenton notes that "in the civil polity of the Iroquois peoples an office never dies; only its bearer dies. The name is one; the bearers are many" (66; also Hewitt [1916] 1977, 165). Gunther Michelson also remarks the continuance of the names of the chiefs: "This procedure," he writes of the Condolence ceremony, "was devised by the ancient Iroquois law givers to ensure that the position and title name of a hereditary chief would be passed on from one generation to the next" (62), that the People might live.[7]

The Six Nations are divided into two moieties. The first, usually referred to in the literature as the Elder Brothers, consists of the Mohawks, the Onondagas, and the Senecas; and the second, the Younger Brothers, is made up of the Oneidas, Cayugas, and, as I have noted, since the eighteenth century, the Tuscaroras (some Tutelo, Delaware, and Nanticoke people were also later included).[8] When a chief dies, a warrior of the bereaved moiety "spreads the news of the death throughout the League. Intoning the mourning call, '**kwaa, kwaa, kwaa**'," he carries "invitation wampum to a member of the 'clearminded' moiety," his Brothers across the fire (Woodbury xxxi). These "clearminded" (their minds are less clouded by grief) or "unscathed" Brothers (relatively speaking—the loss affects all of the People) then "journey across the forest," or "journey on the trail," chanting "the Eulogy, or Roll Call, of the Founders of the League" (Fenton 1998, 137),[9] and reciting all fifty of the chiefly names. The auditors regularly respond—here and elsewhere—with *Haie!* or *Hai!* variously spelled; this signifies assent and approval and is usually translated as "Hail! Hail!" The condoling guests arrive "at the thorny bushes" or "at the woods' edge," where the mourners, having kindled a fire, welcome them.[10] There is then a "Requickening Address," accompanying "the *Rubbing Down Ceremony*" (Woodbury xlii), in which both the condolers and the mourners dry the tears from each others' eyes and also clear each others' ears and throats choked with grief. As the condolers perform this "pivotal ritual of the Condolence" (xl) they chant what have been called either the three *bare* or the three *rare* words of Requickening.

In most of his work on the Condolence Council, Fenton, for example, speaks of the three "*bare* words" of Requickening. But in his 1946 essay describing the Condolence Council he had observed a year earlier, he calls them the three "*rare* words" (114; my emphasis). Alfred spoke of the "rare" words of Condolence (xx), as did Anthony F. C. Wallace (11) and Michael Foster (195) in their contributions to a volume of Iroquoian studies called *Extending the Rafters* (1984). But Foster, in an essay that appeared only a year later,[11] would say of the "*three rare words* of the Condolence Council" that "some uncertainty exists as to whether this phrase should be 'The Three *Bare* Words'" (1985, 124; second emphasis mine). Dr. Jack Campisi, an editor of the 1984 volume, thought "that the use of the word 'rare' is an error, probably made by [an] over-zealous copy editor." "It seems unlikely," he writes, "that had these mistakes been sent to [Wallace and Foster] they would not have corrected the copy editor" (personal communication). Campisi, in his own contribution to the volume, refers to the "three words of *action*" (97; my emphasis). Hanni Woodbury, speaking to the "uncertainty" mentioned by Foster, "provide[s] the proper context to decipher the terminology" in the introduction to her Onondaga text of the Condolence Rites, where she makes clear that the Native language version most literally translates to "they will console them / [with the] *'few* words'"—in that sense rare *or* bare "words of action" (xlii; my emphasis).[12]

The mourners then conduct their visitors to the council house, and "the singer for the clearminded" again "chants the Roll Call (or Eulogy) of the Founders, naming all fifty founders" of the League (Fenton 1998, 137). Wampum strings are once more passed between the mourners and the condolers. Inside the council house, a curtain is drawn between the two moieties, and the clearminded sing six songs of farewell to the dead chief; taken together, these are "said to be the most sacred of all Iroquoian rituals" (1946, 116). Later, with the curtain removed, "the clearminded perform part two of Over the Forest, reciting the laws of the League," along with the "remainder of the Requickening Address" (1998, 139). The mourners then reciprocate, also with six songs, "return[ing] the words of condolence and [some] wampum strings" to their visitors (139). After the condolers perform the second part of "Wiping their Tears," they call on the mourners to present the new candidate for the chiefly office that has become vacant (Woodbury xxxii; Fenton 1998, 728). The clan matron on the mourners' side presents the new chief to the assemblage, and a speaker for the clearminded reminds him and all those in attendance of his duties. Finally, the "horns" of authority—deer antlers, represented by wampum—are bestowed on the new leader, who, as I have several times noted, "inherits not only the position but also the name" of the deceased chief (Bierhorst 112). The ceremonies conclude with a feast and "Rubbing Antlers: the celebration dance. Society is restored" (Fenton 1998, 139).

There are records of at least parts of these rites, as I have noted, from as far back as the sixteenth century, and comparing those records to later observations, it seems clear, as Dennis Foley affirms, that for the most part "the ceremony does not change through time" (50). The pioneering Iroquoian scholar Lewis Henry Morgan wrote briefly of the Condolence Council in his *League of the Iroquois* (1851), and Fenton's research has found records of "some seventy-nine condolence events taking place between 1645 and 1805" (1998, 181). Later, in essays published in 1895 and 1907, the Reverend William Beauchamp described Condolence Councils he had attended. It was also in 1895 that Horatio Hale published an account of a Condolence Council he had witnessed in 1883. "On that occasion the principal celebrant was Chief John Arthur Gibson," a man we will meet again (Fenton 1998, 135). The Reverend Asher Wright had attended a Condolence much earlier, in 1839, at the Onondaga Longhouse at Buffalo Creek, New York, although his account did not appear in print until 1916. Also important are William Fenton's descriptions of Condolence Councils he had attended in 1945 (1946) and in 1951 (1998). The anthropologist Annemarie Shimony attended a Condolence Council on the Six Nations Reserve in Ontario, Canada, sometime between 1953 and 1958. It is briefly described (although not specifically dated) on pages 256–60 of her book. And Gunther Michelson published an account of a Condolence he had observed in 1962 (1988). All of these include bits of text and descriptions that vary in their comprehensiveness and detail.

The fullest records of the Condolence, however, do not derive from any actual performance, but rather from the dictation of one or another Iroquois traditionalist. (These traditionalists had participated in and observed Condolence Councils, but their dictations do not represent any specific performance they had experienced.) Foremost among these are those of Chief John Arthur Gibson, mentioned above. Gibson (1849–1912) was a Seneca (his father was Onondaga) from the Six Nations Reserve in Ontario, Canada. He had met Horatio Hale as early as 1883 and dictated a version of the Condolence Council in Onondaga to J. N. B. Hewitt, a Tuscarora ethnologist, in 1899. A year later, Chief Gibson was a principal contributor to what has been called the "Chiefs' Version" of the Condolence Council

(Scott 1912).[13] In 1912, the last year of his life, he made one final attempt to document the League Tradition, narrating to the anthropologist Alexander Goldenweiser a complete account of the founding of the League. Representing, as Hanni Woodbury writes, "his most mature understanding of the subject," Chief Gibson's 1912 text includes "a complete set of rituals of the Condolence Council" (Woodbury xix, xi).

Gibson's early dictation to Hewitt (1899) was reviewed by Abram Charles, a Cayuga chief, and John Buck, an Onondaga chief, before Hewitt published it in 1916 as "The Requickening Address of the League of the Iroquois." Hewitt later revised that account, giving his revision the lengthy title "The Requickening Address, or Fifteen Burdens, the Third Ritual of the Convocation to Condole the Dead Federal Chieftains...and Install Candidates for Chiefship in the Council of the Iroquois League" and submitting it for publication shortly before his death in 1936 (Fenton 1944, 65). Perhaps because, as Fenton wrote, Hewitt's style late in his life "had become so involved that many of his sentences needed recasting for reading," the essay was not published. In 1939, Hewitt's manuscript was turned over to Fenton. Working with John Arthur Gibson's sons Simeon and Hardy Gibson, and his nephew Howard Sky (Fenton 1944, 65; 1998, 135), Fenton edited Hewitt's text and published it in 1944.[14] The Gibson/Hewitt/Fenton text was, for some forty years, the fullest account of the Condolence available in English.

Yet ten years earlier, in 1934, Fenton had also been given Gibson's 1912 dictation to Goldenweiser. It was not until some fifty years later that Fenton presented "an analysis of [it]...at the Iroquois Conference in 1986," although he did not publish a translation (1998, 725). He had probably made one, however, because Woodbury—to whom Fenton had, around 1978, given the Gibson-Goldenweiser manuscript—writes that she compared her own translation of Gibson's dictation to Fenton's; her citations of it are to pages in his (Fenton's) manuscript (Woodbury xiii). Parts of Fenton's translation of the Gibson-Goldweiser text did eventually appear in his last published work in 1998, mostly in his chapter 5, called "Chief Gibson's Account," and in an appendix where he provides a summary of the Condolence Council based on the Gibson-Goldenweiser manuscript (Fenton 1998, 726–32).

Working with four speakers of Onondaga in the years 1978–90, Woodbury "re-elicited" Goldenweiser's 1912 manuscript of Gibson's dictation.[15] Woodbury's *Concerning the League: The Iroquois League Tradition as*

Dictated in Onondaga by John Arthur Gibson (1992) contains the fullest and most detailed account of the Condolence Rites.[16] Her book offers "Each word of the text... in five versions," the first four of which will be comprehensible only to those with formal linguistic training (I say this as someone with no formal linguistic training) (Woodbury xvii). "The fifth version," however, "at the bottom of the page is a freer translation of the text" in which Woodbury sought to "remain close to the text and to provide as much as possible of the formal qualities of the Onondaga original without letting the translation sound stilted or strained" (xvii, xvi).

But there is another recorded tradition of the Condolence Council worth noting.[17] Horatio Hale wrote that in 1879 he received two copies of a manuscript of the "Condoling Councils" from Chief John "Smoke" Johnson, "who for many years had held the high office of Speaker of the Great Council," and from Chief John Buck, an Onondaga councilor and "the official keeper of the 'wampum records' of the confederacy, an important trust" (Hale 1883, 27, 28). (This is the same John Buck who would later work with Gibson and Hewitt.) Hale supposes the text originally to have been transcribed just past the middle of the eighteenth century by a Mohawk chief, David of Schoharie. Hale's English translation comes mostly from Chief George H. M. Johnson, John "Smoke" Johnson's son. "A second or supplementary part of the book," Hale writes, was "obtained from the interpreter Daniel La Fort,"[18] and it was La Fort "and another educated member of his tribe" who translated this supplement (31, 33).

The Reverend William Beauchamp also knew the Daniel La Fort manuscript used by Hale, and his account of the Rites of Condolence (1907) is largely based upon it. Yet another account comes from Hewitt, who, in 1928, published "A Mohawk Form of Ritual Condolence, 1782," this from a manuscript by the Canadian Mohawk John Deserontyon, dated April 9, 1782, which he (Hewitt) had acquired at a sale in New York in 1925. The translation includes mentions of clearing the eyes and the throat, and also cleansing the bloody mat, apparently of a chief who has died violently, but little else of the Requickening materials. Hewitt provided an interlinear Mohawk-English version and also photographically reproduced the pages of the manuscript.

I will offer commentary on the parts of the "Requickening Address" called "Wiping their Tears" (Woodbury xxxii; Fenton 1998, 725 and

728). As I have noted, this address occurs twice: first, early in the ceremony "At the Wood's Edge" or "Near the Thorny Bushes," where the mourners wipe the tears of the arriving condolers, and then the condolers reciprocate, wiping the tears of the mourners and also clearing their ears and their throats. As the reader may know or by now have well guessed, *reciprocity* is a principle central to Iroquois ritual and social life just as it is central to the ritual and social life of most, if not all, Native nations.[19] These Rites occur again later, in the council house of the mourners, as part of the ceremony for the installation of the new chief, as the condolers now comfort the mourners (Fenton 1998, 138; Woodbury xxxii), after which the mourners again wipe the tears of the condolers and address the many concerns or "burdens" occasioned by the loss of a chief.[20]

In what follows, I'll cite Chief Gibson in the Hewitt-Fenton translation (Fenton's 1944 version of Hewitt's 1936 revision of his 1916 publication) because despite its archaisms—which may indeed, as I've said, accurately reflect the style of the original—it seems to me the most satisfactory balance of the literal and the literary. The literal accuracy of the Hewitt-Fenton translation has been fairly well established; its literary quality represents a judgment on my part alone. For purposes of comparison, however, in the notes I'll cite passages from Hanni Woodbury's 1992 translation of Chief Gibson's 1912 dictation to Alexander Goldenweiser—this is, as I've said, the fullest and most literal translation of all—as well as passages from Hale (1883) and Beauchamp (1907). The two latter versions differ somewhat stylistically from the other translations, and, in particular, they derive from sources other than Chief Gibson.

Fenton sets the stage as follows: "When the closing words of the Chant of Welcome, solemnly congratulating the visiting cousin phratry for its safe arrival At-the-woods-edge, have been intoned by the appointed chanter on behalf of the bereaved tribal phratry,[21] then the chosen speaker for the *unscathed* tribal phratry...intones the first three articles or burdens of the Requickening Address, called "The Tears," "The Ears," and "The Throat" (Hewitt 1944, 69–70). The chosen speaker calls on his tribesmen, the clearminded, who are, in this particular case, the Three Elder Brothers (Mohawk, Seneca, Onondaga), to "pass our hands through thy tears in sympathy; now, we wipe away the tears from thy face, using the white fawn-skin of pity," so that "thou wilt continue to look around thyself, enjoying again the light of the day.... Now, therefore, verily, thou wilt again do your thinking in peace" (70).[22]

The speaker then notes a further matter: "It comes to pass where a great calamity has befallen one's person that the passages of the ears become obstructed and the hearing is lost. One then hears not the sounds made by mankind, nothing of what is taking place on the earth." At this point the condolers will "proceed to restore thy person[23] by removing the obstacles obstructing the passages of thy [sic] ears.... Now thou wilt again hear all things, also all that is taking place on the earth, all these things thou wilt again hear." But "there is still another matter to be considered." For "it comes to pass where a great misfortune has befallen a person, where the Great Destroyer has been harshly cruel, that the throat of the flesh-body becomes sorely obstructed." The Three Brothers "remove from [the afflicted Four Brothers'] throat...the throttling obstructions." Thus, "again thou wilt breathe with ease and comfort.... Now, too, thou wilt again speak with pleasure" (Hewitt 71).[24]

While the eyes of the mourners may literally fill with tears, while their hearing may indeed become less acute than usual, and they may actually feel a lump in their throats, the references to the eyes, the ears, and the throat are also strongly metaphorical. In the three words—the few, the bare, or rare words—of the first part of the Requickening Address, we find grief represented as having baleful physical effects, effects that solicitous care may assuage. The metaphorical transformation of grief from a set of feelings to a set of concrete conditions, which may be altered or alleviated, is something we will find in other traditional elegiac performances.[25] This process continues in the second and longer part of the Requickening Address, which "concludes the main features of the Condolence Council" with the installation and charge to the new chief, leaving only the celebratory feast and a social dance still to come (Hewitt 1944, 69; Fenton 1998, 727). I'll consider just a few of the remaining eleven sections of the second part of the Requickening Address.

The first article of the second part of the Requickening Address, the "Water of Pity," addresses the fact that Death, "the Faceless One...the Great Destroyer," can disorder the organs and produce gall spots on the body, an affliction Iroquois people were especially concerned to avoid. Thus, "it shall be the duty of him whose mind is left *unscathed*" to take up the Water of Pity, and "pouring it down the throat of the one on whom the great affliction has fallen... it will at once begin the work of reorganizing all the many things there which have been disarranged and disordered by the shock of the death, not only in his body but also in his mind (Hewitt 1944, 72).[26]

The third article addresses the "darkness of grief": "That where a direful thing befalls a person, that person is invariably covered with darkness, that person becomes blinded with thick darkness itself." Therefore it will be the work of the Three Brothers to "make it daylight again for thee... when again thou wilt look about thee whereon is outspread the handiwork of the Finisher of our Faculties on the face of the earth" (Hewitt 1944, 73).[27]

The eighth article is called "The Council Fire" and addresses the fact that death, "the Being of Darkness... goes about menacing with its couched weapon—with its uplifted hatchet—eagerly muttering its fell purpose, 'I, I will destroy the Work—the Common Wealth'"—in other words, the League itself (Hewitt 1944, 75). Now, "at this very moment, there is in that lodge of bark a vacant mat because of this stroke," a chief has been taken. In "striking this cruel blow... the Great Destroyer has danced exultingly stamping that hearth [the one untended because of the death of a chief] under foot" (75), thus threatening the wholeness and health of the Great Peace. This article makes especially clear the threat to the polity as a whole posed by death, the Great Destroyer, whose attack on a single chief is an attack on all the People. In response to this, the Three Brothers say, "Now we gather again the scattered Fire-Brands... we rekindle the (Council) Fire for thee.... Now, again, indeed, we raise thee up to full stature among thy people.... Do thou again transact the business upon which thou wert hitherto engaged promoting the welfare of the prosperity of thy families" (76).[28]

The tenth article recognizes that "the mind of him who has suffered from a grievous calamity" may "become insane," and the Three Brothers urge the mourners to "let not the minds of thy people become insane from grief...[but] instead, remain in perfect peace" (77).

Finally, the twelfth article, "Loss of the Torch," works to regain the torch for the People by means of "the appeal for the candidate," the one who will take the name and the office of the deceased. "Do thou now point out to us the one who shall be our co-worker," say the Three Brothers.[29] Announcing that "we... have completed the ceremony" (78), they pass a string of black wampum back to the mourners they have consoled. It remains for the new chief to take the name and place of the one who has passed on, that the People might live.

Considering this great ceremony, Hewitt, in "an unusual burst of enthusiasm," as John Bierhorst notes, wrote: "The psychological insight of the framers of this wonderful ritualistic address is without question unsurpassed in any other composition of its kind in any other literature of the world" (qtd. in Bierhorst 117). Extensive in its attention to the most complex details of individual and collective grief, rich in metaphor, mixing discursive modes (chant, roll call, oratory, song), the Iroquois Condolence Council performs a successful act of mourning that the People might live. The Council exhibits both similarities to and differences from the great Tlingit memorial *koo.'eex'* or potlatch ceremony, to which I now turn.

The Tlingit *koo.'eex'*

> We put these names as medicine on their wounds in times of sorrow.
> Tlingit elder (Kan 1983, 53)

In *Haa Tuwunaagu Yis, for Healing Our Spirit: Tlingit Oratory,* Nora and Richard Dauenhauer present, in Tlingit and in English, thirty-two condolence speeches by twenty Tlingit elders, delivered between 1968 and 1988. These speeches are an important part of the Tlingit *koo.'eex'* or "potlatch."[30] A considerable body of anthropological writing on the potlatch has focused on it as a ritual primarily to affirm or contest status and rank in the intensely hierarchical societies of the Native nations of the Northwest Coast and southeastern Alaska.[31] Much of this writing has viewed all potlatch ceremonies through the classic descriptions—that is, from Boas forward—of Kwa'wa'ka (formerly Kwakiutl) potlatching. But Frederica de Laguna, Sergei Kan, and the Dauenhauers, among others (e.g., Catharine McClennan) have shown that this focus tends to distort the Tlingit potlatch.[32] While the Tlingit potlatch does involve exchanges of words and property for "maintaining or changing the social order" (Kan 1989, 201) it is more importantly "the central ritual in traditional Tlingit ceremonial life for spiritual healing and removal of grief" (Dauenhauer and Dauenhauer 1990, xi). Thus, the Dauenhauers "do not dispute" the "social dimensions of potlatch" but insist as well on "the spiritual dimensions—at least as they are explicit in the oratory" (xi, xii). Frederica de Laguna had also affirmed that "the primary purpose of the potlatch was to mourn and honor the dead" (1972, 606) in order "to reunite the community after the tragedy of death, by reaffirming the kinship bonds between the members" (1952, 5). Kan adds that the potlatch's "most explicit function is removing grief from the souls of the mourners/hosts and helping them to return to normal life" (1983, 53). Thus, "despite the prevalence of hierarchy and competition, Tlingit mortuary rites were also characterized by a strong emphasis on equality, unity, and cooperation between matrikin as well as balanced reciprocity between member of the two moieties one acting as hosts and the other as guests" (Kan 1989, 10), much as was the case with the Iroquois Condolence Rites. "Death," Kan continued, "threatens the basic assumptions of order on which society rests," so—again like the Iroquois—the Tlingit "in their mortuary rites...transformed death from a threat to the social order into the major opportunity for strengthening and enhancing it" (15, 289). The condolence oratory central to the Tlingit *koo.'eex'* is an important example of traditional Native American elegiac expression, that the People might live.

Whereas the Iroquois Condolence Rites are based on the social division between the Older Brothers and the Younger Brothers, the moiety division for the Tlingit *koo.'eex'* is that between the clan distinctions of Ravens and Eagles, who gather as hosts and guests, the bereaved and their condolers.[33] The moieties as such have "no political organization or power" (Dauenhauer and Dauenhauer 1990, 6), but between them they include "approximately 50 clans" (Tollefson 53), and "political organization rests at the clan level.... Clans have traditional leaders" (Dauenhauer and Dauenhauer 1987, 5).

The term *koo.'eex'* is made up of the Tlingit stem *-eex'*, "to invite," "as to a banquet or feast," while the "prefix *ku-* [*koo-*] refers to action involving people," thus, "*ku.eex'*—'people invitation,'" with feasting implied (Dauenhauer and Dauenhauer 1987, 421, 422).[34] The ceremony takes place about a year after the death of a community member (see fig. 1). It is hosted by the clan of the deceased (as was the case with the Iroquois Condolence Council) and typically lasts four days. Kan regards the *koo.'eex'* as a "ceremonial exchange of words of condolence for words of gratitude between the guests and the hosts" (1983, 48)—again, with similarities to the Iroquois Condolence Rites.

The ceremony begins with the "Cry" or "taking up the drum" by the bereaved hosts, who may indeed cry and wail, as they also perform "a series of mourning songs" (Kan 1983, 49). The guests then stretch out their arms in a show of sympathy, and the hosts respond "that the love and respect shown them by the guests is making their pain subside" (49–50).[35] This is followed by the "Widow's Cry" (it is called that regardless of whether the deceased is male or female), which consists of songs, speeches, and displays of *at.oow*.

The Dauenhauers explain that *at.oow* is "the fundamental concept [that] underlies all dimensions of Tlingit social structure, oral literature, and ceremonial life," and that "it is the spiritual, social, and rhetorical anchor for the oratory in [their] book" (1990, 14), as it was for the book of traditional oral narratives they had earlier published in 1987. The term *at.oow* refers to "'an owned or purchased thing,'" (14), where "the 'thing' may be land...a heavenly body, a spirit, a name, an artistic design...an image from oral literature,...a story or song about an event in the life of an ancestor" (1987, 25). *At.oow* also and importantly consists of material goods such as tunics, hats, crests, sashes, blankets, and staffs owned by a moiety and its clans. Strongly invoking the presence of departed ancestors to whom they once belonged, *at.oow* of various kinds are prominently displayed in potlatch ritual. As the ceremony progresses, the glum "general mood of the participants gradually change[s] to a more optimistic one"; there is a "transition from sadness to joy or from social death to life" (Kan 1983, 50). In the final part of the ceremony, the hosts offer short speeches thanking the guests for helping to restore their spirits, that the People might live.

"In the speeches of the Widow's Cry," the Dauenhauers write, "the guests perform a ceremony to remove the grief of the hosts to whom they are usually related through marriage or paternity" (1990, 47). The second section of the Dauenhauers' volume on Tlingit oratory provides the texts of "a set of seven speeches,...delivered during a traditional memorial in Hoonah in October, 1968, in memory of Jim Marks" (xii).[36] Although they are referred to as "speeches," these performances, like those of the Iroquois Condolence Rites, are chanted rather than spoken, with the voice pitched several notes or an octave higher than normal (Kan 1983, 51; Dauenhauer and Dauenhauer 1990, 76). The diction of the speeches is "heavy," in the sense that the language treats of weighty matters, and also in that "the

32   Chapter 1

Figure 1. Tlingits in ceremonial regalia for 1904 potlatch. Alaska State Library, Elbridge Warren Merrill Photograph Collection, P57–021.

metaphorical language [employed]…differ[s] greatly from…everyday" speech (Kan 1983, 50).

Jim Marks was of the Eagle moiety; thus it is the Ravens, as guests, who will speak to condole their Eagle hosts. In the "Widow's Cry" for Jim Marks, Jessie Dalton's speech was "the longest and most complicated,…the oratorical climax of the set" of speeches offered (Dauenhauer and Dauenhauer 1990, 78). Dalton (Naa Tlaa) performed in Tlingit, which the Dauenhauers print on the page facing their English translation; line numbers are given for both the Tlingit and the English texts. The Dauenhauers indicate the general response *aawe* on the part of audience members, which means "something like 'amen'" (Dauenhauer and Dauenhauer 1994, 153). These responses roughly parallel the *Hai! Hai!* response of the auditors as the Iroquois Condolence Rites proceed. The Dauenhauers also indicate individual responses offered by individual participants—for example, "thank you" expressed in one or another form on the part of the hosts—and they identify the responder by name so far as possible. I will omit those identifications and indicate line numbers of the English translation only occasionally.[37]

Dalton begins by establishing a genealogy of clan relatives:

> Does death take pity on us too
> my brothers' children,
>> *Aawe* [thank you.]
>
> my fathers.
> It doesn't take pity on us either,
> this thing [death] that happens.
>> *That's how it is.*

At line 18, she invokes the dead ancestors of her T'akdeintaan clan by pointing to their *at.oow* or treasured clan possessions currently being worn by persons in attendance. The *at.oow* conjures the ancestors' presence to condole their Eagle hosts:

> Here someone stands wearing one,
> this Mountain Tribe's Dog [hat].
> it's barking for your pain is how I'm thinking about it,
>> *Thank you.*
>
> my fathers, my brothers' children
> my father's sisters,
> yes.

Here someone is standing next to it, next to the *at.oow* she has just mentioned. In line 27, she speaks of

> ...Raven-Who-Went-down-along-the-Bull-Kelp,
> Someone is standing closer, next to it.

"It" is also *at.oow,* "a shirt one of the T'akdeintaan is wearing, formerly owned by Weiha, Jim Fox"; its "motif is taken from an episode in the Raven cycle," a myth of the earliest times (Dauenhauer and Dauenhauer 1990, 388).

Kan describes "the structure of a typical condolence speech" as made up essentially of reference to a "mythological tragedy" that parallels "the suffering experienced by the addressees mourning the death of their kinsman," and also reference to "a mythological protagonist...likened to the helping actions and comforting words of the guests" (1983, 52). (There is also, as I have noted, the establishment of genealogical relations, and a third element Kan mentions that I'll consider just below.) The story from the Raven cycle would seem to operate as the mythological reference.[38] Further, "use of this shirt," with its representation of an episode from the Raven myths, as the Dauenhauers write, "is a good example of the connection between visual art, verbal art, ceremony, and the kinship system. Tribal art is worn or brought out by certain people at certain times; the art usually quotes, commemorates, or otherwise alludes to songs, stories, or history" (1990, 388), and Jessie Dalton will allude to other myth stories as she continues.

Here, however, she continues to invoke the ancestors' presence by means of their *at.oow*. In line 29, Dalton speaks of "Lyeedayeik's robe," worn now by a relative, and in line 35 she points to another:

>Lutakl [Jim Lee, deceased]
>your father
>it was once his blanket,
>once his Chilkat robe.
>>*Ho, Ho* [thank you].

As she points to *at.oow* she recites either the names of those who formerly were their owners or of those who possess them now. In particular, she names her clan mother, *Saayina.aat* (line 45), or Irene Young, wearing "the Tern robe" (line 46). As Richard Dauenhauer kindly reminded me (personal communication), Dalton's T'akdeintaan clan has the tern as its main crest, and Dalton herself is the designated clan mother. Reference to the Tern robe leads to an extended metaphor with mythic reference (line 50):

>A person who is feeling [grief] like you
>would be brought by canoe,
>yes,
>to your fathers' point,

> Gaanaxaa.
> That is when
> the name would be called out, it is said,
> of the person who is feeling grief.

And in lines 57–75 she does indeed call out the names of many of the grieving Eagle clan hosts, putting "these names as medicine" on the "wounds" of the bereaved (Kan 1983, 53).[39]

Gaanaxaa is "a point near Lituya Bay,...a tern rookery." Dalton's earlier pointing to the Tern robe makes "Ganaaxa...literally and figuratively present" (Dauenhauer and Dauenhauer 1990, 390). She continues:

> These terns I haven't completely explained,
> yes,
> these terns.

She chants,

> Your fathers' sisters would fly out over the person
>   who is feeling grief.
>   *Aawe* [thank you]
> Then they would let their down fall
> like snow
> over the person who is feeling grief.
>   *Your brothers' children are listening to you.*
>   *Thank you.*
> That's when their down
> isn't felt [*sic*].
> That's when
> I feel it's as if your fathers' sisters are flying
> back to their nests
> with your grief.
>   *Thank you indeed.* (lines 128–40, 251)

The image is of the terns flying "out over the person who is feeling grief, and let[ting] their down shower like snow over him or her. The down is soothing." The speaker presents her sense that it "feels as if the terns are removing the grief"—*drying* it—"by absorbing it into their down and flying back to their nests with it" (Dauenhauer and Dauenhauer 1990, 390). Kan identifies this as the third element of a typical condolence speech, in which a contrast is posited "between *grief* and the *absence of grief*... expressed by the following oppositions: darkness/light; wet (rain)/dry (sunshine) hunger/eating; lack of sleep/sleep," among others (1983, 52). The "emotional states (sadness, grief, sense of loss)" in these speeches are presented metaphorically "as physical ones (being cold, hungry, wet, etc.). Once the emotions had been concretized, depicted as physical afflictions, the speaker was more capable of 'eliminating' them by 'warming,' 'feeding,' or 'drying' the mourners" (53). This parallels the Iroquois Requickening Address, where, as I've noted, although the mourners may literally have tears in their eyes, a lump in their throats, and a sense of deafness to the world, the tears and the obstruction to the throat and ears are largely metaphorical.[40] They are "emotional states presented as physical ones" (53),[41] and as such they are susceptible to elimination, leading to the restoration of normalcy.

Dalton offers yet another powerful image of drying grief. She says:

> Yes.
> And here,
> yes,
> is the one this brother of mine explained a while ago:
> how that tree rolled for a while on the waves.
> Then when it drifted to shore
> the sun would put its rays on it.
> Yes.
> It would dry its grief
> to the core.
> At this moment this sun is coming out over you,
> my grandparents' mask.
> > *That's it.*
> > *Thank you.*
> > *Ho, ho* [thank you]. (lines 198–208, 255)

The mask is the Sun Mask; as the Dauenhauers observe, "The sun that is drying the grief is again the at.oow" (1990, 395), in the form of what Dalton calls the "grandparents' mask," now in the possession of George Mills. The brother Dalton refers to is David Kadashan, her clan brother, not her biological brother. He had spoken earlier and used an extended image of an uprooted tree—I am condensing the Dauenhauers' analysis—which he "compared both to the grieving survivors as well as to the deceased" (395). Falling into the river and tossed by the waters, the tree would eventually come up on land where the sun's rays "would begin to dry it out" (qtd. in Dauenhauer and Dauenhauer 1990, 237, line 48). David Kadashan had said: "My hope is that you become like this / from now on" (qtd. in Dauenhauer and Dauenhauer 1990, 237). Jessie Dalton repeats this image, in what the Dauenhauers point to as "the line that extracts the sorrow" (396). Dalton chants:

> At this moment
> my hope is that your grief
> be like it's drying to your core.
> *It shall be.*
> Thank you. It shall be. (lines 208–11, 256–57)[42]

As Kan puts it, "The oratory admitted...the inevitability of death but, at the same time, denied its power to affect the collective destiny of basic kinship groups" (1983, 560), that the People might live.

My account of Iroquois and Tlingit condolence oratory has sought, following Ben-Amos, to identify its *thematic* concern with death and loss and its behavioral *function* of memorializing the dead and consoling the living, successfully mourning the deceased and thus providing assurance that the clans and the People will live. I've also identified the *prosodic* nature of this oratory in two regards. First, I've indicated that these speeches, although chanted, are oral prose, not poetry; they do *not* possess "an underlying metric sub-structure."[43] And, second, I've indicated that although they are prose, not poetry, their organization and their use of metaphor and simile are such as to require the critical attention the West usually applies to *literature*. The Dauenhauers sum up Jessie Dalton's oratorical work as "binding, or uniting...at least three levels: rhetorical, spiritual, and social" (1990, 104), of which their analysis engages, perhaps most fully, the rhetorical or literary level. Having examined Jessie Dalton's speech, with reference to David Kadahsan's, one might well agree with the Dauenhauers' assessment, offered on the very first page of their preface, that "the central images" in these speeches are "among the most beautiful in world literature" (ix). As ritual and ceremonial expression, Tlingit potlatch oratory functions as symbolic action, to mourn, to heal and console, by a process of naming and pointing (to *at.oow*), and by the metaphorical invocation of positive states dispersing or overcoming negative ones, with reference to communally familiar myth stories. It is possible that oral performances of these condolence speeches in Tlingit may not last much longer, for the younger generation is, unsurprisingly, less fluent in the language than the elders—yet the tradition was still alive and well in the latter half of the twentieth century.

Occasional Elegy

> I thought I'd be that way forever
> But now my strength is gone.
> Dan Hanna

In this section I consider several examples of oral elegiac expression that largely exist apart from communal ritual and ceremony. Unlike the Iroquois Condolence Rites and Tlingit *ƙoo.'eex'* oratory, these performances do not take place at fixed times, nor are they addressed to a public greater than a group of family members or friends (Hinton 1984, 6). It is also the case that—again, unlike Condolence or potlatch oratory—they are substantially improvisational. In Ben-Amos's terms, all are *about* death or loss, and all have an underlying *metric sub-structure* (they are oral *poems*). But the examples I have found are too few and indeed too various for me to generalize with any confidence about what they *functionally* seek to *bring about*. Some, much like Western elegies, function simply as expressions of strong feelings of grief deriving from any one of several different occasions of loss. Still others, however, like the short song with which I begin, do not, at least explicitly, express any emotion at all.

From the Tsimshian People of the Northwest Coast, near neighbors to the Tlingit, there is a very short text that has been given the title "Little Boy's Mourning Song" by Jean Mulder, who recorded and transcribed it in British Columbia sometime between 1979 and 1981. Mulder provides musical notation, a phonetic rendering of the original, a literal word-for-word translation, and a freer, literary translation, which is what I give here:

> Mother was in the wave,
> My mother did not see the big one.
> My dear one is lost in the kelp. (108)

Another song Mulder titles "Old Woman's Mourning Song" is, in her literary translation, no more than a single line:

> I gather the bones of my dear ones, my
> dear ones. (112)

In both of these songs emotion is implied—by the use of "dear one" and the repetition of "dear ones"—but it is not directly stated.

Some of the poems collected in Tom Lowenstein's *Eskimo Poems from Canada and Greenland,* however, express a great deal of emotion. "The Widow's Song," sung by Qernertoq, asks:

> Was the agony I felt so strange,
> when I saw the man I loved
> thrown on the earth
> with bowed head?
> Murdered by enemies....

She continues:

> He was not alone
> in leaving me.
> My little son
> has vanished
> to the shadow-land. (19)

Qernertoq also mourns for herself:

> Long will be my journey
> on the earth.
> It seems as if
> I'll never get beyond
> the foot-prints that I make....

She concludes:

> A worthless amulet
> is all my property:
> while the northern light
> dances its sparkling steps in the sky. (20)

Only the amulet remains to her, an amulet she deems "worthless." Yet the northern light still "dances...in the sky."

Uvlunuaq, a Netsilik woman from Pelly Bay, mourns her son, who, after killing his hunting companion in a fit of rage, has "left the settlement." She sings:

> I ought, I suppose, to be ashamed
> of the child I once carried on my back....
>
> But far from being
> properly ashamed,
> I'm envious of others
> when they break up
> after feasts, and set off
> with crowds of friends
> behind them, waving on the ice....
>
> ...when the news
> about the murder came,
> and that he'd fled,
> the ground heaved under me
> like a mountain,
> and I stood on its summit,
> and I staggered. (41–42)

Here one can readily feel the strong emotion of Uvlunuaq as she staggers on ground heaved up like a mountain.

Powerful feelings are also expressed in some Eskimo songs that mourn the singer's lost strength or youth, like Ivaluardjuk's "A Hunting Memory" (25), Akjartoq's "An Old Woman's Song" (33), and Ulivfak's "The Spring of Youth," which begins: "Sadly I recall / the early spring of my youth," and concludes:

> Thus I still re-live
> the early spring of youth.
> Old men seek strength
> in the thaw of younger days. (37)

This poem brings to mind the comment of one of anthropologist Morris Opler's Chiricahua Apache consultants: "Many years ago I saw an old man sitting by the fire working. He sang [a] song then, and, as he sang it, the tears rolled down his cheeks. He was thinking back to the good times he had when he was a young man. It's really an old man's song" (qtd. in Opler 471). Opler could only learn a few lines of that "old man's song":

> When I was young, I took no heed;
> Old, old I have become!
> Because I knew that age would come
> To me, I took no heed. (471)

Curiously, the heedlessness is said to come from the knowledge that old age *would* come, but there is no "reliving" the heedless time when the singer was young, and tears roll down the old man's cheeks as he sings.

Neither is there consolation to be had in old age from the strength of one's youth in Dan Hanna's moving "Farewell Song"—although in this song, the singer states that he did *not* "know that age would come." Dan Hanna, a Havasupai man (the Havasupai are a Yuman-speaking tribal nation in Arizona), performed his song for Leanne Hinton around 1964.[44] The "Farewell Song" is an example of an ethnic genre among the Havasupai known as "old men's songs" (there are also "old women's songs"), specifically "composed to express a deeply felt emotion" (Hinton 1994, 690). In this regard, Hinton points out, the *songs* differ from traditional Havasupai *tales* in which "the emotions of the characters are *not* described" (691; my emphasis). Central to understanding the "Farewell Song" is the Havasupai People's deeply held belief—one, as I have noted, shared by all Native American peoples—that "the land is always treated as sentient." In the words of a Havasupai woman quoted by Hinton, "the land knows you're there, and it misses you when you're gone" (693).

Dan Hanna begins (in translation):

> I thought I'd always be that way,
> I'd be that way forever.
> But now my strength is gone,
> ha na.[45]

The singer then asks the specific places he knew ("Thicket of bushes, / that place," "Fallen logs.../ that place," "Trail lying there / that I once followed," etc.) to "forget about [him]":

> Trail lying there
> that I once followed,
> once followed.
> That place.
> Listen to me.
> Forget about me;
> forget about me,
> ha na.

After many verses, he concludes:

> I'd always be with the mountains,
> it seemed;
> that's how I was,
> that's what I believed.
> I felt
> so proud.
> I thought I'd be that way forever.
> But now my strength is gone.
> I thought I'd be that way forever.
> That's how I was,
> how I was,
> how I was,
> ha na. (Hinton 1994, 702–3)

A feeling similar to that which Dan Hanna expressed appears—wittily—in a much shorter song-poem from the Swampy Cree by John Rains, translated by Howard Norman:

> I am the poorest one.
> I cook bark.
> I have bad luck in hunting.

A duck caught my arrow
and used it for her nest.

I am the poorest one.
I sit in mud and weep.
A goose caught my arrow
and broke it
in two.

I am old, old.
Don't bring me pity,
but food
yes. (93–94)

This section concludes with a song performance from 1998, Mabel Wright's "Prayer for Pyramid Lake."[46] Pyramid Lake, an important source of fish for the Northern Paiutes, and the subject of a good deal of litigation, is, as Mrs. Wright laments, going dry:

Where the Water goes to?
Which way the Water goes to?
White people—
White people—
They turn the water to their side.
They use it for themselves.
They forget about us!
They forget about our Lake
To fill 'em up again.

"Now," she sings:

Now my poor Lake is getting dry
Every year, my poor Lake getting dry!

Now I feel sorry, I feel bad,
When I see my Lake going down.
Oh, make me feel so bad,
I feel like to cry....

I sit around over there by the Lake, and sing ...
I take my drum, sing away, about this Lake.

> And I say:
> My beautiful Lake,
> That God made for us,
> Is going down.
> Everything's going down,
> My poor Lake ...
> I feel like to cry all the time,
> When I don't eat no fish any more,
> Like used to be. (n.p.)

Mrs. Wright's song, like songs cited earlier, is an example of occasional elegy—an elegy for a lake[47]—expressing personal feelings of loss. But it is more than that, for it is also a response to what Vine Deloria Jr., as noted in the introduction, calls the experience of exile, an experience he sees as defining, in varying degrees, the postcontact life of all Indian tribal nations. I turn now to the songs of the Ghost Dance movement, a major response to exile by several tribes in the nineteenth century.

Some Ghost Dance Songs as Elegy

> Thus the Father saith,
> Lo, he now commandeth
> All on earth to sing,
> To sing now.
> Thus he hath spoken,
> Thus he hath spoken.
> Tell afar his message,
> Tell afar his message!
> Sung by Tatanka-Ptecila, Short Bull (N. Curtis 47)

The Native American religious movement known as the Ghost Dance had a long history and many antecedents before 1890, the date most usually associated with it. James Mooney, the earliest and perhaps still the greatest chronicler of the Ghost Dance, draws attention to the movement's long history and precursors in the opening chapters of his monumental *The Ghost-Dance Religion and the Sioux Outbreak of 1890* (1896). These chapters have unfortunately been omitted from the edition most often cited today, Anthony F. C. Wallace's abridged version of Mooney's work (1965). Mooney's full text opens with a chapter titled "The Narrative: Paradise Lost" (1973, 657).[48] This reading of the Ghost Dance movement's "narrative" accords quite well with the dominant society's *tragic* view of Native decline as the obverse of its own *comic* narrative of "progress" and ascent to "civilization."[49] But this reading also contests the dominant society's view that the Ghost Dance movement was a unique and unprecedented phenomenon, one that came from nowhere and, in the end, led nowhere.[50]

Mooney's sixteenth and final chapter, "Parallels in Other Systems" (1973, 928)—also omitted in Wallace's abridgement—rebuts such a view by placing the Ghost Dance movement in the broadest cultural and historical context, comparing it to developments in "The Biblical Period," to the founding of "Mohammedanism," to the fervor surrounding "Joan of Arc," and to other radical religious movements. These comparative generalizations across many periods and cultures also work in two ways. On the one hand, they blur any number of local, particular, temporal, and culture-specific differences between the Ghost Dance and other movements. On the other, they accord it a stature equivalent to that of parallel phenomena of great importance.

Words Mooney was to write many years later well express the central premise of the "Narrative" he offered: "While all goes well with the tribe the religious feeling finds sufficient expression in the ordinary ritual forms of tribal usage, but when misfortune or destruction threaten the nation or the race [*sic*], the larger emergency brings out the prophet, who strives to avert the disaster by molding his people to a common purpose through insistence upon the sacred character of his message" (qtd. in Blair 2: 272). When "paradise" is in fact or in effect "lost," and the People suffer exile, they may turn to a prophet whose teachings offer possibilities of condolence and renewal, performing a sort of "melancholic mourning" (Ramazani) that both grieves and seeks renewal. Mooney names some of these Native prophets, active roughly from the years around 1812 to the period of the Civil War, the 1870s, and, of course, 1890. Although he recognized that elements of the 1890 Ghost Dances had been part of various Peoples' traditional culture for many years, Mooney took them largely to be responses to the "relative deprivation" caused by white pressures, or what I have called, with reference to Vine Deloria Jr., the exile of the tribes; Mooney saw them, that is, as "revitalization movements."[51] Although some form of the Ghost

Dance—what Leslie Spier called the "Prophet Dances"—flourished "at least as early as the opening of the nineteenth century" (1935, 7).[52] I will look only at the Paiute Ghost Dances of 1870 and 1890, the latter inspiring the Ghost Dances on the Northern Plains.

Shortly before 1870, a prophet arose among the Paiutes whose vision would influence their later Ghost Dance. The prophet, Wodziwob, or Fish Lake Joe, had moved north to the Walker River Reservation from his home in Fish Lake Valley, Nevada. He had experienced a vision in which he saw the dead and learned from them that they "would return within three to four years time from 1869" (Hittman 1973, 251). Because the Northern Paiutes had recently lost many of their number to "ague, bilious, and typhoid fever" (255), this might have seemed very good news—but, as we will see, the matter is more complicated. Hittman discusses the 1870 movement as in part an "Increase Rite" (259). He also considers the Paiute Ghost Dance of 1870 to be very much a response to "a series of deprivations caused by Euro-American expansion. Not only did these Paiutes lose their native lands and valued resources, they suffered from starvation and epidemics upon...the very land area set aside for their exclusive use" (248).

Given the population decline I have noted, an increase in their numbers achieved by means of the return of the dead might indeed have seemed appealing to the Paiutes. But the Paiute People, like other southwestern peoples, strongly exhibited what Hittman calls "ghost fright" (1992, 180) or ritual avoidance of the dead. This set of beliefs was marked by "immediate burial of the dead; destruction of all personal belongings; a 'talker' who at the gravesite pleaded with the dead not to return...and bother the living; prohibition against mentioning the name of the dead person, [and] relocation of [the] campsite" (Hittman 1973, 265; 1990, 80). Thus it does not seem likely that this salient feature of Wodziwob's doctrine would have appealed to the Paiutes.

But Wodziwob, as I have noted, was from Fish Lake Valley, and, as Hittman notes, "Fish Lake Valley Paiute culture contrasted with the culture of the Northern Paiute...in the treatment of the dead. Whereas the Northern Paiute hastily disposed of the dead and never again mentioned their names, the...Fish Lake Valley Paiute held an annual mourning ceremony...([the] "cry dance")...at intervals from one to four years following a death" (1973 266). Thus, in view of the decimation of their numbers, the Northern Paiutes for a short time at least—Wodziwob's Ghost Dance ended in 1871, when it became clear that the dead had not, in fact, returned—were willing to accept the imminent return of the recently deceased. Something similar would be the case for the Paiute Ghost Dance of 1890.[53]

On January 1, 1889, during a total eclipse of the sun, another Northern Paiute man, named Wovoka (Wood Cutter) or Jack Wilson, lost consciousness, perhaps as the result of a fever. While unconscious, he had a vision in which he found himself transported to heaven. There he saw the dead—Paiutes, other Indians, and whites as well—and received instruction about how to proceed so that the living would be reunited with the dead in heaven. The People were to be honest, work hard, and adopt a generally accommodating relation to the whites. They were also to perform a series of dances based on the traditional, Paiute round dance.[54] The People were to dance for five nights and to sing songs that would be revealed to dancers who fell into trances.[55] "Wovoka's religion," Hittman writes, "was all the more remarkable insofar as it projected a racially-integrated life to come" (1990, 98).[56]

Word of the Ghost Dance spread. On the Southern Plains, where the buffalo herds had been extinct since 1881, the Arapahos, hearing of the Ghost Dance, sent emissaries to visit Wovoka. On their return, the Arapahos became, as Mooney wrote, "the first great apostles of the [Ghost Dance] doctrine among the prairie tribes" (1965, 51). Indeed, the Arapaho Sitting Bull (see fig. 2) came to be regarded by the southern tribes "almost in the same light as the messiah [Wovoka] himself" (150).[57]

The Kiowas learned of the Ghost Dance from the Arapahos around 1890, just about the time they suffered the loss of their Sun Dance;[58] the largest Kiowa Ghost Dance took place in October 1890. Shortly thereafter, one of their prominent men, A'piaton (Wooden Lance), took it upon himself to pay a visit to Wovoka. Upon his return, he announced to his Kiowa People that there was no power at all in the Ghost Dance. Nonetheless, after the tragedy at Wounded Knee (see below) the Kiowa revived the Ghost Dance and practiced it from 1894 to 1916 (see Kracht; I note below other continuations of the Dance well into the twentieth century).

Figure 2. Sitting Bull, Arapaho, 1885. National Archives and Records Administration.

The Sioux or Lakotas also learned of the Ghost Dance from the Arapahos, and in November 1889, they sent a delegation made up of "Good Thunder, Flat Iron, Yellow Breast, and Broken Arm from Pine Ridge; Short Bull...from Rosebud, and Kicking Bear from Cheyenne River agency" to visit Wovoka (see fig. 3). Also visiting around that time were three Cheyennes, one of whom was named Porcupine. The Lakotas returned in March 1890 and a month later "made their report at Pine Ridge" (Mooney 1965, 64) It confirmed many wonderful things that had been heard about the Paiute messiah. In the spring, "Short Bull, on Rosebud reservation, at once began to preach to his people the doctrine...of the messiah" (88). In the fall of that year, Sitting Bull invited Kicking Bear, now considered "the chief high priest of the Ghost dance among the Sioux," to Standing Rock reservation to inaugurate the dance, and "Red Cloud himself, the

Figure 3. Indian chiefs and U.S. officials at Pine Ridge, January 16, 1891.
Among those in the photo are Short Bull and Kicking Bear.
Library of Congress Prints and Photographs Division.

great chief of the Ogalala, [at Pine Ridge] declared his adhesion to the new doctrine" (92, 65).

Kicking Bear, born an Oglala, was the nephew of Sitting Bull and a cousin of Crazy Horse; he had married the daughter (or niece) of the Minneconjou leader, Big Foot. He and Short Bull had demonstrated—and would continue to demonstrate—strong resistance to the whites, and it is their understanding of the Ghost Dance doctrine that has often been cited as altering, or indeed "perverting," Wovoka's peaceful message.[59] There is no doubt that these Lakota emissaries reported, contrary to what Wovoka seems most often to have said, that the whites would *not* be present in the new world order when the living and the dead were united.[60] But it would be a mistake to take this—as many reservation agents, military men, and journalists of the time did—as necessarily a threat or a forecast of aggression. Hittman points out (1990, 98) that Wovoka's own understanding of his revelation may have changed over time; indeed we know of several statements he made that contradicted other of his statements.[61] Raymond DeMallie asserts that "Lakota accounts of visits to the prophet clearly show that his teachings were not formulated into a creed; each man went away from meeting Wovoka with a personal interpretation of the ghost dance religion" (1982, 387). Absent a fixed text to cite, there could be no orthodoxy for an orally transmitted religious message.

Thus Porcupine of the Cheyenne, a nation often allied with the Lakota, reported that Wovoka had told his delegation "that the whites and Indians *were to be all one people*" (qtd. in Mooney 1965, 40; my emphasis). But, Kuwapi, a Lakota from Rosebud agency, in answer to the question "Do you mean to say that all mankind except the Indians will be killed?" replied: "Yes." When pressed to say "how, and who is going to kill the white people," Kuwapi responded: "The father [Wovoka] is going to cause a big cyclone or whirlwind, by which he will have all the white people perish" (qtd. in Mooney 43). It is surely the case that some Indians still believed that the whites could be made to leave by force, but that belief seems not to have been sanctioned by any People's understanding of the message of the Ghost Dance. Dance and song were the ritual, ceremonial, religious means to mourn the persons and practices that had been lost and also to console and renew the People. They were also the means to make the whites disappear—if, indeed, that was necessary to restore the world as it had always been.

The songs that accompanied these dances, like the dances themselves, adapted older forms to new conditions; they were at once entirely traditional and creatively innovative oral performances. Mooney printed 161 Ghost Dance songs from seven different tribal nations in bilingual versions, and his collection remains the chief source for the years just before and after 1890. Mooney's compilation consists of seventy-three songs from the Arapahos, nineteen from the Cheyennes, four Comanche songs, nine from the Paiutes, twenty-six from the Lakotas, fifteen Kiowa songs, and fifteen Caddo songs. The Plains bias here is obvious. Among other collections of Ghost Dance songs are the 130 *naraya* songs of the western Shoshones collected by Judith Vander (1997); only a few of these might be said to have been influenced by Wovoka—and even this influence appears to be slight. William Powers (1999 provides sources for all the Lakota Ghost Dance songs that have been published, and he retranslates fifty-five of them. Powers includes the three Lakota Ghost Dance songs that had been published by Natalie Curtis (1907), who also printed four Pawnee songs, and one Arapaho song by Sitting Bull, all accompanied by musical transcriptions. Additionally, Jeffrey Anderson (2005) has retranslated twenty-five Arapaho songs, and I will examine a few of these.

Not all of the Ghost Dance songs are elegiac in the manner I have been discussing. Paiute Ghost Dance songs, for example, like the Ghost Dance songs of the Shoshone *naraya* or those of the related Havasupai dance called the *yimaaje,* do not have human actors nor is there much action. Leanne Hinton's observation of the Havasupai songs, that they "are mostly about the things that are basic to Havasupai life, the rocks, the crops, baskets, mention of mythical beings, even topics such as hard luck, and many songs about the dance itself" (1984, 18), seems true as well of Paiute Ghost Dance songs. Mooney describes the following (in his translation) as "one of the favorite songs of the Paiute Ghost dance":

> The snow lies there—*ro'rani'!*
> The snow lies there—*ro'rani'!*
> The snow lies there—*ro'rani'!*
> The snow lies there—*ro'rani'!*
> The Milky Way lies there,
> The Milky Way lies there. (1965, 289)

Mooney writes that *"ro'rani'* serves merely [*sic*] to fill in the meter" (1965, 290); it is what we now refer to as a vocable (see note 65 below). He remarks that for the Paiute as for "many other tribes, the Milky Way is the road of the dead to the spirit world" (290), but he offers no further interpretation.[62] Other Paiute songs are similar to the one I have quoted. The songs I discuss below all come from the Plains. I've chosen them for no reason other than that they seem more clearly to work in the particular manner of Native American elegiac expression I have been describing than Ghost Dance songs from elsewhere. In Ben-Amos's terms, they are *prosodically* oral poetry in that they possess "an underlying metric sub-structure" (288). They are *thematically* concerned with mourning the dead and the old ways of life in such a way as to enable their return; the songs *functionally* seek to bring this about as they are sung in accompaniment to the dances.

Anderson notes (450) that the Ghost Dance songs of the Arapaho were especially highly regarded by Mooney, as they were also esteemed by other tribes, in particular the Lakota, who adopted some of them for their own Ghost Dances. My account of them is substantially indebted to Anderson's introduction to his retranslation of twenty-five Arapaho Ghost Dance songs.

Figure 4. Arapaho ghost dance, 1900. Based on photograph by James Mooney. National Archives and Records Administration.

Arapaho Ghost Dance songs were composed as part of a communal religious ritual, but, as Anderson notes, there was a "unique poetic creativity circulating in the dance" (459) and in the songs that accompanied them (see fig. 4). Traditional Arapaho rituals, Anderson writes, concentrated on suffering or "life-negating" conditions in order to "release or discard them for lighter, life-generating movements" (453). In relation to our discussion thus far, they may be seen as operating in a manner parallel to what we have remarked in Iroquois and Tlingit condolence oratory. "The songs," Anderson notes, "were not necessarily direct expressions of sorrow for the historical moment, but really a means of transvaluing that state into a ritualized sorrow and thus a condition that could be discarded and from which release is possible" (453), that the People might live. Mooney called the Arapaho song he numbered 28 "the most pathetic of the Ghost-dance songs" (1965, 226). I cite it in Anderson's retranslation:[63]

> Father, have pity on me!
> Father, have pity on me!
> Now, I am wailing-fasting-thirsting.
> Now, I am wailing-fasting-thirsting.
> There is no food.
> There is no food. (468)

The Father referred to is Wovoka, who is thought of here as a prophet or indeed the Messiah,[64] although Anderson comments that Arapaho addresses to the Father are "not unambiguous" (454), since the Father also invokes an overarching Creator Spirit. Mooney described this song as being "sung to a plaintive tune, sometimes with tears rolling down the cheeks of the dancers as the words would bring up thoughts of their present miserable and dependent condition" (1965, 226). But, as I have earlier quoted Anderson, the focus on grief and loss is very specifically meant to transform this "miserable...condition" into something more positive. As Anderson writes, "The promised or prophesied new world was *really already experienced* in the movements of dance, songs, and visions they engendered" (460; my emphasis).

This seems especially evident in the second of the Arapaho songs published by Mooney. Again, I cite Anderson's translation:

> Flat Pipe is telling me. Eiyohei'eiyei.
> Flat Pipe is telling me. Eiyohei'eiyei.

> Our Father. Yohei'eiyei.
> Our Father. Yohei'eiyei,
> We shall surely be put together again. Eiyohei'eiyei!
> We shall surely be put together again. Eiyohei'eiyei! (463)

"Flat Pipe" is not a proper name. Mooney translates the Arapaho as "The sacred pipe tells me," and he notes that the pipe is "the sacred tribal medicine of the Arapaho" (1965, 207). (The repeated "Eiyohei'eiyei" are vocables that have no specific semantic meaning; they serve to fill out the rhythm.)[65] Mooney's translation of the last lines is "We shall surely be put again (with our friends)—E'yahe'eye!" (207). Mooney added the words in parenthesis to clarify the meaning of the song. Because they do not appear in the song text itself, Anderson's translation does not include them.

The desire to be reunited with friends and other beloved persons who have died is evident in the following song sung by Short Bull, a Lakota whom we have already encountered. Short Bull's song was first published by Natalie Curtis in *The Indians' Book* (1907):

> Mother, oh come back,
> Mother, oh come back,
> Little brother calls as he seeks thee, weeping,
> Little brother calls as he seeks thee, weeping.
> Mother, oh come back,
> Mother, oh come back!
> Saith the Father,
> Saith the Father. (48)[66]

The Father referred to is, again, Wovoka, at one and the same time father of the Ghost Dance and the Messiah himself; but here, too, I would guess aspects of the Creator Spirit are interwoven in the reference to the Father as well.

If Short Bull sang to be reunited with his mother, there are also many songs in which grieving mothers sing to be reunited with their children. One example is the Cheyenne song composed by Mo'ki, "Little Woman," the wife of Grant Left-hand, an Arapaho "and the son of Nawat, or Left-hand, the principal chief of the southern Arapaho" (Mooney 1965, 278):[67]

> The crow woman—
> The crow woman—

> To her home,
> To her home,
> She is going,
> She is going.
> She will see it,
> She will see it,
> Her children,
> Her children.
> She will see them,
> She will see them. (278)

Mooney explains that this couple lost a first child soon after birth, and then another child at the age of four. Both parents grieved deeply. Then, writes Mooney, "came the Ghost dance and the new doctrine of a reunion with departed friends" (279). When the mother attended a Ghost Dance, she fell into a trance and met her children in the spirit land. She encouraged her husband to attend, and he, too, experienced a trance enabling him to visit with his children. An observation of Loretta Fowler's seems applicable here. She writes: "A community may perceive innovations as expressions of their identity and as cultural *continuities*" (qtd. in Kracht 454; my emphasis)—that is, as not really innovations at all. This is something we have already noted, and something common to oral societies. Mo'ki's song expresses intensely personal emotion by means of an identification with "the Crow Woman, i.e., the woman messenger from the spirit world" (Mooney 1965, 278), a familiar character in Cheyenne ritual and ceremony. Mo'ki uses similar imagery in another song:

> The crow—*Ehe'eye'*!
> The crow—*Ehe'eye'*!
> I saw him when he flew down,|
> I saw him when he flew down.
> To the earth, to the earth.
> He has renewed our life,
> He has renewed our life.
> He has taken pity on us,
> He has taken pity on us. (275)

Here, Mooney writes, "the Crow is...considered as the lord of the new spirit world," a variant, I would speculate, of the Crow Woman mentioned above.

There are also a number of Ghost Dance songs that vividly represent not only individuals who have passed away but also some of the traditional practices of the People. As Thomas Overholt observes, "The two most frequent themes in the songs are the return of the dead and the restoration of the game, both of which are central to Wovoka's original teaching. Beyond that, their most striking feature is the recounting of the old-time activities, particularly games that the dancers witnessed during their visionary trips to the spirit world. This focus on the old way of life, *which was soon to be realized again,* is but an elaboration of the prophet's message" (56; my emphasis).

Thus there are songs that contain a vision in which the singer saw herself making *wasna* or pemmican, "made from buffalo meat, lard, and chokecherries pounded together" (Powers 1990, 69), such as the following Lakota song:

> Give me my knife,
> Give me my knife,
> I shall hang up the meat to dry—*Ye'ye'!*
> I shall hang up the meat to dry—*Ye'ye'!*
> Says grandmother—*Yo'yo'!*
> Says grandmother—*Yo'yo'!*
> When it is dry I shall make pemmican,
> When it is dry I shall make pemmican,
> Says grandmother—*Yo'yo'!*
> Says grandmother—*Yo'yo'!* (Mooney 1965, 301)

"This song," Mooney writes, "brings up a vivid picture of the old Indian life" (301), a life the singer mourns while melancholically refusing to let it go; she wishes still to "hang up the meat to dry." Other such songs recall setting up the tipis, playing games and gambling, traditional activities that have disappeared or are currently threatened. These things are remembered with pleasure and with the hope that the singer and the People will experience them again; indeed, in some measure, as Anderson noted, they experience them in the singing of the song. From the Arapahos, for example, there is the following:

> The ball, the ball—
> You must throw it swiftly,

> You must throw it swiftly.
> I want to win,
> I want to win. (Mooney 1965, 251)

And this:

> With the *ba'qati* wheel I am gambling,
> With the *ba-qati* wheel I am gambling.
> With the black mark I win the game,
> With the black mark I win the game. (245)

Mooney comments that this was a game "which was practically obsolete among the prairie tribes, but which is being revived since the advent of the Ghost Dance" (245).

The singing of these songs and the performance of the dances were troubling to the government Indian agents on the various reservations, particularly those of the Lakotas. Sitting Bull, who, as I have noted, encouraged the ghost dancers, was shot and killed (along with his seventeen-year-old son, Crow Foot) by Indian police who had come to arrest him on the morning of December 15, 1890. After Sitting Bull's death, only Big Foot of the Minneconjous was considered a possible instigator of hostilities. But Big Foot, ill with pneumonia in the middle of winter, agreed to surrender to federal troops, moving his People "to Wounded Knee Creek, about 20 miles northeast of Pine Ridge agency" (Mooney 1965, 114). On the morning of December 29, his warriors were ordered to surrender their weapons. When only a few older rifles were turned in, troops—these were men of the Seventh Cavalry, George Armstrong Custer's former division—entered the tipis and searched for arms, upsetting the women. Yellow Bird, a medicine person, had been urging the warriors to resist, assuring them that the Ghost Dance shirts many of them wore would protect them from the soldiers' bullets. At some point, a young man named Black Fox or Black Coyote "drew a rifle from under his blanket and fired at the soldiers, who instantly replied with a volley directly into the crowd...that must have killed nearly half the warriors" (118). Then the big Hotchkiss guns trained on the camp opened fire, killing mostly women and children. Those who survived fled and were pursued and massacred (see fig. 5). Although he finds that "the answering volley and attack by the troops was right and justifiable," Mooney nonetheless judges the subsequent "wholesale slaughter of women and children...unnecessary and inexcusable" (119).

Ever since Mooney titled his monumental study *The Ghost-Dance Religion and the Sioux Outbreak of 1890* (my emphasis) the two have been inextricably but perhaps unfortunately linked. That is to say that despite the latter part of Mooney's title (and a substantial portion of his text), there was, in fact, *no* "Sioux outbreak" in 1890. Even Valentine T. McGillycuddy—whom DeMallie calls "the former *dictatorial* agent of Pine Ridge" (1982, 386; my emphasis)—concludes a lengthy statement (part of which DeMallie quotes) with the following postscript: "P.S. I neglected to state that *up to date there has been neither a Sioux outbreak nor war*. No citizen in Nebraska or Dakota has been killed, molested, or can show the scratch of a pin, and no property has been destroyed off the reservation" (qtd. in Mooney 1965, 78; my emphasis).[68]

Figure 5. Big Foot's camp three weeks after the Wounded Knee Massacre, 1891. Library of Congress Prints and Photographs Division.

After the massacre at Wounded Knee Creek, the Ghost Dance, for obvious reasons, lost many adherents, but it in no way ceased to exist. The Kiowas, for example, practiced the Ghost Dance from 1894 to 1916 (Kracht), and Judith Vander has traced the ongoing performance of Shoshone *naraya* songs at least into the 1980s (Vander 1988). Leanne Hinton writes that "the songs sung" by the Havasupai People "in the presentday [1980s] festival were all inspired by the Ghost Dance of 1890" (1984, 17). Ake Hultkrantz reported seeing a Ghost Dance performed at Wind River after World War II (Anderson 451), and Alice Kehoe has traced the "New Tidings" movement among the Lakota of Saskatchewan as a continuation of the Ghost Dance into the 1950s. "New Tidings, (*Woyaca Teca* in Dakota)," she writes, "is the name applied to Fred Robinson's version of Wovoka's teachings" (46). Mr. Robinson learned these from none other than Short Bull somewhere around the turn of the twentieth century.

Discussing Wounded Knee with Ace (or Asa) Daklugie (d. 1955), son of the renowned Apache chief Juh (Jo or Whoa), the translator of Geronimo's autobiography, Eve Ball asked: "And that is where the Ghost Dance ended?" Daklugie responded: "Ended! Who says it has ended? In every reservation in the United States today it is observed at least once a year. And it is not too late yet for the White Eyes to get just what they inflicted upon the Indians—this genocide" (Ball 2000, 85). A younger Apache consultant later confirmed to Ball his belief that the day would yet come when "everyone would die but that after four days the Indians would be restored to life. The buffalo would return to the plains, the antelope to the hills, and the deer to the mountains" (313).[69]

As the Ghost Dancers were responding to their experience of exile by innovatively adapting traditional, oral-performative means of continuance and survivance, melancholically mourning, in the nineteenth century other Native American people were responding to exile by engaging with the nontraditional technology of writing, either as writers or authors, that is to say, initiators of narratives that would become texts. We turn now to several examples of Native American oratorical performances responding to loss.

2

Oral Performances (II)

"Logan's Lament"

> I think he did more good by his death then he could have done by his life.
> John Eliot on the death of Wampora (Murray 34–35)

Indian people have been saying good-bye for more than three hundred years. As David Murray notes, John Eliot's *Dying Speeches of Several Indians* (1685)—from which I've taken the quotation above—inaugurates a long textual history in which "Indians...are most useful dying"(35) or, as in the speeches I will consider, bidding the world farewell as they embrace an undesired but apparently inevitable exile or demise. Unlike the Iroquois and Tlingit condolence oratory we have examined, these elegiac speeches are addressed by Indians not to other Indians but to whites, and, it would seem, exclusively to whites (this is not to say that they haven't been overheard by other Indians), who have shown themselves to be keenly interested in preserving and circulating them (although they represent only a small percentage of Native oratory).

Whereas the speeches of dying Indians were useful in the seventeenth century for the purpose of advancing the Gospel, by the eighteenth century, Murray writes, "dying Indians offered comfort within a different frame of reference, that of inevitably doomed nobility. The focus, therefore changes from ordinary Indians to Indian *leaders*" (35; my emphasis) to "chiefs," eventually, as J. B. Paterson insisted regarding Black Hawk (see below), to Native American "heroes." Murray goes on to show how after the American Revolution, "in an increasingly bourgeois society," the "*popularity* of surrender...speeches by Indians," is "acted out [as] the renunciation of power by a nobility" (35, 36).[1] By the nineteenth century, this conflict of classes is largely overridden by the discourses of scientific racism and "manifest destiny,"[2] instantiating a national narrative of progress in the comic mode, as I have described it. "Noble" or not, the "savage," comically—or, from his perspective, tragically—had to go. The farewell speeches I will consider here, with one exception—"Logan's Lament" of 1774, with which I begin—all date from the nineteenth century. These are Black Hawk's farewell, and the two ascribed to Cochise, along with the better-known good-byes presumably articulated by Sealth and Chief Joseph. Like the protest speeches Murray noted, all of these are also contextually overdetermined, but unlike them, "what" they say is as important as the fact and manner of their saying.

This type of Native American elegiac oratory comes into being, like the Indian autobiography, as a consequence of Indian defeat, mostly in warfare although not exclusively (e.g., Sealth's speech). These farewell speeches, like the Indian autobiographies, are original, bicultural, composite compositions produced at the urging of whites in the ideological service of progressive expansionism. But to a degree far greater than Indian autobiographies, these farewell speeches have no prior model in traditional oral expression.[3] This is to say that I have never encountered any mention of warriors defeated in battle delivering speeches to their tribal conquerors.[4] Thus, even if it should be the case that these farewell addresses have some fair degree of authenticity(and, as I will show, all but one of them is highly suspect), they are largely an innovation, a performance produced—coerced is perhaps too strong a term, although one that readily comes to mind—by the occasion of actual or imminent (Sealth, once more) Indian defeat. I suggest that it is this occasion and its contexts that explain the disparity between the apparent resignation to loss expressed in these farewell speeches and the determination to overcome loss in the interest of continuance and survivance expressed in most other Native elegiac expression. (But, as we will see further, there were most certainly moments when the stated acknowledgment of defeat was the best available means of continued survival.)

In "Query VI: Productions Mineral, Vegetable, and Animal" of his *Notes on the State of Virginia* (1784), Thomas Jefferson wrote: "I may challenge the whole orations of Demosthenes and Cicero, and of any more eminent orator, if Europe has furnished more eminent, to produce a single passage, superior to the speech of Logan, a Mingo chief, to Lord Dunmore" (444). He then quotes the brief *message* apparently sent by Logan to Dunmore in 1774, treating it as a *speech*.[5] Although both its authenticity and its excellence have been questioned on occasion from Jefferson's time to our own,[6] Logan's speech, which became known as "Logan's Lament" for its mournful, elegiac nature, has had broad cultural influence. It attracted the attention of Diderot and was several times translated into French in the eighteenth century.[7] In the United States, it served as the basis for poems, plays, and works of fiction from about 1790 to 1902, was reprinted in the fourth and fifth editions of the popular "McGuffey Readers" in the 1850s and 1860s, and drew the approving notice of President Theodore Roosevelt.[8] It continues to be reproduced in our own day.[9] But what do we know of Logan, and how shall we understand the "speech" attributed to him in relation to Native American elegiac expression?[10]

Logan's father, a man named Shickellamy, was either "an Oneida who lived along the Susquehanna River from the late 1720s until the late 1740s" (Merrell 227) or a Cayuga—possibly a Frenchman by birth who had been adopted by one or the other of those tribes.[11] The identity of Shickellamy's son, Logan the orator, is also not entirely clear, for Shickellamy had two sons,[12] one named Tahgahjute and known as James Logan, and one named Tachnedorus (various spellings) or John Logan. I believe that Tachnedorus/John Logan is Logan the orator.[13]

Daniel Richter explains that when "agents of Virginia governor Lord Dunmore provoked a war between Virginians settled at Pittsburgh and the Shawnees" in 1774 "to pre-empt the competing [land] claims of Pennsylvanians," a "brief but brutal conflict counted among its victims the family of the Mingo Tachnedorus, or John Logan" (2001, 213).[14] A particularly brutal event of that war occurred when "a party led by Daniel Greathouse killed and scalped nine Indians, including Logan's kin, at Baker's Tavern,...across from the mouth of Yellow Creek" (Wallace 1999, 3). Among Logan's murdered kin was his pregnant sister, who was mutilated along with her unborn child. At the end of Lord Dunmore's War, Logan was asked to attend a treaty meeting with Dunmore. He refused but apparently sent a message through General John Gibson that eventually was transformed into a speech in English. Gibson, although married to Logan's sister, had fought against the Indians (and lost his wife and unborn child). He would have understood Logan's Cayuga—if indeed that was the Iroquoian language Logan spoke—although it has also been conjectured that the English version of the message presented in writing to Lord Dunmore might possibly have been the work of Simon Girty, a well-known, mixed-blood Indian trader.[15]

To transform a *message* into a *speech* is to perform a particular kind of ideological work, ennobling the "savage," as Jefferson did, for whatever purposes.[16] To demote Native speeches to mere messages, as we will see further in regard to Chief Joseph's surrender oratory, performs a different sort of ideological work. In an impassioned defense of Cresap—Logan stated that it was he, not Greathouse, who killed his kin—that misses no occasion to disparage Logan, Brantz Mayer in 1851 wrote of two communications by Logan. According to Mayer, in July 1774, after killing the family of a man named John Roberts, Logan forced a white prisoner named Robinson to write a brief note in "gunpowder ink" that began: "What did you kill my people on Yellow Creek for?" It also is said to have included the phrase "Then I thought I must kill too" (56). This note was said to have been attached to a war club and left in Roberts's house. Later, in October 1774, General Gibson visited Logan on Lord Dunmore's behalf and, returning to the British camp, had Logan's words "committed to paper" (Mayer 61). To Mayer, Logan's words are "neither a speech, a message, nor a pledge of peace" (61). Citing Jefferson's version of the "speech," Mayer sneers: "Thus the famous 'speech of Logan' which has been so long celebrated as the finest specimen of Indian eloquence, dwindles into a reported conversation with, or *message* from, a cruel and blood-stained savage" (61; my emphasis). Mayer's account is picked up by M. Louise Stevenson in 1903, who further seeks to disparage the "speech" by noting that the sentence beginning "I appeal to any white man…" is very much like Matthew 25:35–36 in the New Testament. But "how many believe," she asks, that "Logan was familiar enough with Matthew 25th chapter, to quote it thus literally?" (156).[17] It "is high time," Stevenson continues, "that this 'conversation' *should be eliminated from the school books*" (159).

Attempting to recuperate Logan's reputation in 1965—and garbling the accounts in Mayer and Stevenson—Louis Jones writes of a *message* to Dunmore sent by Logan that was "pinned to the head of his war club" (49). Although "by no means a formal oration," this nonetheless "may well be ranked" not only with the *speeches* of Demosthenes, but also with "William Jennings Bryan's 'The Cross of Gold'" (50; my emphasis). Had Jefferson lived to know of Bryan, perhaps he might have concurred.

Jefferson, however, wanted a speech and not a message. Anthony Wallace writes that Jefferson said he'd "heard [Logan's] *speech* at Lord Dunmore's in 1774 [from] General John Gibson to whom Logan had delivered his *speech* and who had translated it into English for Lord Dunmore" (1999, 4; my emphasis). But Edward Seeber had many years earlier quoted a 1797 letter of Jefferson's that complicates the matter. In it, Jefferson confirms that he "*learned*" the speech "[he] *believe*[s] at Lord Dunmore's," as he finds "in [his] pocket-book of that year (1774) an entry of the narrative, as taken from the mouth of *some person,* whose name, however, is not noted or recollected" (qtd. in Seeber 1947, 146; my emphasis).[18]

However Jefferson may have learned of it, Logan's speech had been in print for several years before Jefferson's 1784 publication of it brought it to international attention. Like Jefferson's account of how he got the speech, its early publication history is not completely clear. The "earliest known version" (Seeber 1947, 146) of it occurs in a letter dated January 20, 1775, from James Madison to William Bradford, who published it in his *Pennsylvania Journal* for February 1, 1775. The editors of Madison's papers admit that "by what means JM secured a copy [of Logan's speech] is unknown" (Hutchinson and Rachal 137–38). The Madison version appeared that same month in three other newspapers (see Seeber 1947, 146). But another "slightly different version," Seeber writes, "had appeared at Williamsburg in the *Virginia Gazette* of February 4, 1775" (1947, 146). Ray Sandefur notes "two letters published in the *American Archives* in

1837," one of which "was written in Williamsburg, Virginia, February 4, 1775," and may be "the one *reported to have appeared* in Dixon and Hunter's *Virginia Gazette* of that same date" (291; my emphasis). The editors of Madison's papers also refer to that issue of the *Gazette* as having contained a version of Logan's speech (Hutchinson and Rachal 137). But the second reader of this book for the Cornell University Press, with diligence well above and beyond the call of duty, obtained a copy of the *Virginia Gazette* for that date—something I had not been able to do—and writes that there is no mention of a speech by Logan in it! My best guess is that there are three early versions of Logan's speech in print: the one sent by Madison to Bradford, who was first to publish it; then, a version in a letter written in Williamsburg dated three days after Bradford had published the speech, which was "reported"—erroneously, it would seem—"to have appeared in ... [the] *Virginia Gazette*"; and, finally, Jefferson's version in his *Notes on the State of Virginia*. Jefferson's text is almost identical to the Madison version, and the variations among all three of these early versions are minor.

In the *Notes on the State of Virginia,* Jefferson quoted and praised Logan's speech for two reasons, only one of which he makes explicit. Intending to rebut the conclusions of the Count de Buffon that the "productions" of the New World were in every way inferior to those of Europe, Jefferson pointed to the "genius" of the American Indians as demonstrated in their capacity for noble oratory. He quotes Logan's speech to illustrate that point.[19] But Logan's "Lament" is, of course, an Indian farewell. Although it is—quite unusually for Native elegiac expression, a matter I will return to below—largely personal—Logan laments his own condition not that of his People—Jefferson's offering it more generally, as an elegy for a vanishing race, suits his project of acquiring, and aiding others to acquire, Indian lands.

As Wallace writes in the introduction to his book *Jefferson and the Indians,* "I have tried to be fair in assessing Jefferson's conduct in Indian affairs, but viewed from the late twentieth century, some of his actions appear to be hypocritical, arbitrary, duplicitous, even harsh" (1999, viii). "Harsh" seems rather weak, following as it does on words like "arbitrary" and "duplicitous." I would suggest in its place terms like "unscrupulous" and "shamelessly self-interested." "Jefferson's story of Logan," Wallace continues, "serves as a rationalization of the past and a vision of the future, a paradigm of destiny, a parable of fate" (2). It functions, that is to say, as a justification for dispossessing the "savages" of lands they soon will not need. Let us examine the speech not in relation to noble savagism, to Cicero, Demosthenes, or William Jennings Bryan, but rather in relation to what we have thus far discovered about Native American elegiac expression in general.

After an initial "I," the translation of Logan's remarks shifts to third-person self-reference, something we will find quite frequently in the English translations of other Indian farewell speeches. This form of self-reference "does not," as Thomas McElwain asserts, "reflect an Iroquoian speech pattern, which used personal pronouns" (2001, 118). I strongly suspect that it also does not reflect Algonkian, Apachean, Salishan, Sahaptian, or other Native-language speech patterns. Nonetheless, the great majority of Logan's self-references in English are in the third person.

What Logan says at the beginning of his speech, as Stevenson noted long ago, parallels the twenty-fifth chapter of the Gospel of Matthew (Matt. 25:35–36): "For I was an hungered, and ye gave me meat:...I was a stranger, and ye took me in: Naked and ye clothed me" (Stevenson 156; qtd. in Seeber 1947, 142). Seeber points to other biblical parallels (142), and I have noted Sheehan's sense of the speech's eloquence as "Biblical rather than Indian" (351n). McElwain, who has published a line-by-line commentary on the speech as heard by his "West Virginia Mingo ears," finds that the "appeal to hospitality as evidence of goodwill toward 'white people'...could not have been made by a Native person...hospitality in the Iroquoian context does not imply goodwill" (2001, 113).[20] The implication that "giving food and clothing is an act of charity" is a Christian notion—something Stevenson had long ago noted—and "quite foreign [sic] to the Native American mentality" (114).

Logan claims to have been "an advocate for peace," and one who was regarded as "the friend of white men." This was also the stance, as we will see, of Chief Sealth and to some extent of Chief Joseph as well, although it was most certainly not that of Black Hawk and Cochise. Logan notes that his "*countrymen*" had remarked on his "love for the whites," and, using the term from which "countrymen" would derive, says: "For my *country*, I rejoice at the beams of peace" (my emphasis). "Countrymen," McElwain writes, "is not a natural translation of any Iroquoian term" (2001, 115).[21]

He points out that Logan "certainly had a clan identity inherited from his mother" (115), and he might have used specific terms to indicate Cayuga or Oneida tribal identity. "Countrymen" seems more likely to have come from Gibson, perhaps Logan's translator, who was, in 1774, a soldier of King George. Gibson would certainly have thought in terms of country and countrymen, terms with which Jefferson and Madison would have been comfortable. And "beams of peace" is an abstraction of a sort unlikely to appear in oral discourse.

Meanwhile, as I briefly indicated above, it is important to note that the speech isn't at all about Logan's "countrymen," nor is it about his band, tribe, clan, nation, or People. Rather, it is entirely about Logan, who—again, atypically for a Native person—in translation refers to himself in the first or third person some fourteen times ("I," "Logan") in a very short speech. Unlike Black Hawk, who, as we will see, claims that he "drank the blood of the whites" on behalf of his *nation,* Logan's vengeance serves only to assuage his own pain at the losses he has suffered. To cite McElwain once more, "Just redress is one of the features claimed as foundational to the establishment of the Iroquois League" (2001, 117) and includes "the adoption of [captured] people to replace lost relatives" (117–18), that the People might live. That is to say that Iroquois "vengeance," to let that word stand, is not a matter of personal revenge.

In much the same way, the statement that there is "not one" "to mourn for Logan" seems thoroughly inconsistent with traditional views of this matter. Didn't eighteenth-century Cayuga or Oneida Mingos, like League Cayugas and Oneidas, practice some form of the Condolence Rites we have examined? I suspect they did. If so, and if Logan was indeed a chief, he not only would have been communally mourned, but he would continue to live on in the role call of the chiefs, as the founders of the League had determined. I'll return to this point below.

Logan's apparent "love for the whites" changed, he says, as a consequence of the actions of Colonel Michael Cresap, who "in cold blood and unprovoked, murdered all the relations of Logan, not sparing even my women and children." Although Cresap had indeed "participated in two earlier attacks that resulted in the death of some of Logan's...relatives" (Wallace 1999, 5), the particular atrocities referred to by Logan here were perpetrated, as we have noted, by Daniel Greathouse and his men. In regard to Logan's claim that "I had even thought to have lived with you...,"

McElwain notes that, to the contrary, there is evidence that Logan was instead planning "to settle on the west bank of the Ohio...conspicuously beyond the reach of the settlers" (2001, 115).

In consequence of the wrongs done to his People and his blood relations, Logan, previously an advocate for peace, was, as I've noted, provoked to seek "revenge." Typically for a warrior (e.g., Black Hawk and Cochise, as we will see), he proclaims his valor: "I have killed many: I have fully glutted my vengeance." He then returns to the third-person self-reference he was earlier assigned, as he announces that "Logan never felt fear," moving to his climactic farewell, "Who is there to mourn for Logan?—Not one." This sense of individual isolation and finality runs counter to anything to be found in traditional Iroquoian condolence speeches, as well to all traditional Native elegiac expression. McElwain affirms that a sentence like the one ascribed to Logan entirely "neglect[s]...Iroquoian kinship perspectives," adding that "it is difficult to imagine a Native person...who could have felt so kinless as this speech makes him out" (2001, 117). If Tachnedorus articulated sentiments of this nature, they would almost certainly have been provoked by the cruel circumstances under which he was pressed to speak. But I think these sentiments do not actually come from Logan. Thus, despite Jefferson's strong defense of Logan's speech, there are good reasons to question whether it does, in fact, represent anything Logan may actually have said at the end of "Lord Dunmore's War." As we have the brief speech, there is nothing in it that stands securely as an example of Native American elegiac expression.

I will close with a return to Logan's claim that he was utterly without kin, in order to note that he did, in fact, have at least one blood relative, a nephew, for it was that nephew who killed him on his return from a visit to Detroit in 1780. It's possible that this was because Logan had become "increasingly intemperate and deranged," as Wallace remarked (1999, 12), and as Sheehan confirms in calling Logan an "unfortunate, culturally disintegrated Indian" (351).[22] Were Logan as far gone as Sheehan thinks, however, his People surely would not have arranged for his demise. Indeed, he may have been killed because, as the nephew that did the deed said later, "he was too great a man to live...he talked so strong that nothing could be carried contrary to his opinions" (qtd. in Wallace 1999, 12). If that is the case, then, as Wallace has remarked, "by a twist of fate, the eloquence that earned Logan immortality led also to his death" (13).

Black Hawk's "Surrender Speech"

> [Black Hawk] has done nothing for which an Indian ought to be ashamed. He has fought for his countrymen, the squaws and papooses, against white men, who came, year after year, to cheat them and take away their lands.
> Black Hawk (Drake 136–37)

Black Hawk (fig. 6), along with the prophet, Wabokieshiek, surrendered to Winnebago agent General Joseph Street on August 27, 1832, at Fort Crawford, Prairie du Chien, Wisconsin, ending the Black Hawk War. In his autobiography, as we will see, Black Hawk insisted that the decision to surrender was his, although two of the Winnebago Indians who accompanied him, Chaetar and a man known as One-Eyed Decorah (or Decorri; various spellings), insisted that they had captured Black Hawk.[23] Street's "Report of the Delivery of Black Hawk and the Prophet," sent to Lewis Cass, the secretary of war, records a brief speech by Decorah boasting of his contribution to Black Hawk's surrender—although, as Nancy Lurie notes, it would seem that "Decorah really had no part in the matter" (163). This was followed by Street's flowery response beginning: "My children, you have done well." Street concluded: "My children, I shall now deliver the two men, Black hawk [sic] and the Prophet, to the chief of the warriors here" (Whitney 1066)—that is, to Colonel Zachary Taylor, commander of Fort Crawford. Street's report goes on to reproduce the brief speech given by Taylor largely reiterating what Street himself had just said. After Taylor's address, Chaetar, somewhat inappropriately (he probably should have allowed Taylor the last word), asked for and was granted permission to speak. His speech is also recorded by Street. But there is no mention of a speech by Black Hawk.

The Illinois *Galenian* for September 5, 1832, printed a "paragraph [that] was part of a Sept. 4 story which reported the arrival of the steamboat *Winnebago*," carrying about a hundred Sauk prisoners, Black Hawk among them (Whitney 1103). The paragraph begins: "Black Hawk, this morning, desired to speak to General Street. The amount of what he said was..." (1103); and a brief paraphrase of what Black Hawk presumably said follows (see the appendix in this book). While the story's reportage of the steamboat's arrival was entirely current, the news of a speech by Black Hawk to Street of course was not.

In these years just before the invention of the telegraph (1837), news traveled by mail. If there had indeed been a speech to Street by Black Hawk on August 27—or possibly on some "morning" between that date and the departure of the steamboat *Winnebago*—word of it would very likely only have arrived when the steamer docked—although it could, conceivably, have arrived by means of messengers on horseback. Young J. B. Patterson (b. 1806) had become editor of the *Galenian* "when the war with Black Hawk began, and the publisher...went off to join the troops" (Jackson 27). Patterson obviously was interested in Black Hawk and the war, and it is possible that he had someone on the scene to observe the surrender at Fort Crawford, or perhaps just after. If he did, I wonder whether that person could have been the wide-ranging government interpreter Antoine LeClaire.

LeClaire and Black Hawk had known each other for years—indeed, Black Hawk had been unhappy with LeClaire for counseling him not to go to war—and they would collaborate in the production of Black Hawk's *Life,* his autobiography published in 1833. It was also LeClaire who served as interpreter for the Indians at the official "Black Hawk Treaty" or "Treaty with the Sauk and Fox" of September 21, 1832 (C. Snyder 95; Whitney 1185).[24] That LeClaire might have been present at the surrender on August 27 is pure speculation on my part. (There is nothing in the LeClaire papers at the Putnam Archive documenting any speech of Black Hawk's, nor, as I shall note further, is there any manuscript of their collaboration on the autobiography.)

The first text of a farewell speech attributed to Black Hawk appears in the third, enlarged edition of Samuel Drake's *Biography and History of the Indians of North America from Its First Discovery,* published in 1834.[25] Drake's account of the Black Hawk War concludes with material from Street's "Report" and quotes all of the speeches I have mentioned above (Street, Taylor, Chaetar; these are also given in Wakefield). After citing Chaetar's speech, Drake introduces Black Hawk's speech as follows:

> The following speech of Black-Hawk, on being taken prisoner, would have been introduced in its proper place, if it had been in our possession when

Oral Performances (ii) 71

Figure 6. Múk-a-tah-mish-o-káh-kaik, Black Hawk, 1831. Painting by George Catlin. Smithsonian American Art Museum. Gift of Mrs. Joseph Harrison, Jr. 1985.66.2.

that part of our manuscript was written [i.e., for the first edition]. If there be any who entertain skeptical notions in regard to its genuineness, they may feel as well satisfied to meet with it in this place. For ourselves, we confess there is room for doubts about it. Nevertheless we thought proper that it should appear, as it is in true Indian style, and we know nothing to the contrary but that it is genuine. (136)

Why would it be that "any who entertain skeptical notions in regard to its genuineness...may feel well satisfied as to meet with it in this place?" Is it simply that Drake's reputation as an authority on Indian history is such that the mere fact of his printing it means "that it is genuine"? In view of the fact that Drake confesses "there is room for doubts about it," this is hardly a ringing endorsement of the authenticity and accuracy of his text.

By the time of the 1841 edition of his very popular work, Drake's introductory remarks to the farewell speech add the comment that "the following *is said to be* the speech which *Black-hawk* made when he surrendered himself to the agent at Prairie du Chien [i.e., to Street]" (1841, 657; first emphasis mine). But the speech, as I've noted, is *not* in Street's "Report," and Drake gives no source, not even the *Galenian*—which in any case did not provide a text. What, then, is the source of Drake's text? We don't know.

Most of the subsequent publications of "Black Hawk's speech" derive from the 1841, or eleventh, edition of Drake's enormously popular work (which, as he wryly makes clear, is really the same as his eighth edition). In the text first given by Drake in 1834 (see the appendix in this book), Black Hawk refers to himself in the third person, something he does only very rarely in his autobiography. He remarks on the prowess of several of the American military men, something a warrior might well do, and he praises the better of the American fighters.[26] Acknowledging the superior power of the whites, Black Hawk testifies both to his ability to bear whatever hardships he may face (although he would surely have known that physical "torture" was unlikely) and to his present helplessness. He speaks of having "fought for his countrymen,"[27] and as well for the women and young children of his nation. The negative connotations of "squaws and papooses" would surely not have been present in any terms he might actually have used.

Black Hawk then offers criticism of the whites who lie, "carry false looks, and deal in false actions," who "deceive" the Indians and "ruin [their] wives," and coil themselves about the Indians "like the snake"—a reference, perhaps, to Genesis. Similar critiques appear in a great many Native addresses, as do attestations like Black Hawk's to the effect that he "is a true Indian," who "does not care for himself," but only for his "nation and the Indians" (Drake 1834, 137)—also with third-person self-reference. Black Hawk's assertion that he "drank the blood of some of the whites" is strictly metaphorical and would have been taken as such. Once more referring to himself in the third person, he concludes with the very recent fact that "he has been taken prisoner," and it is as a prisoner that he speaks. His "plans" to "save" his nation are "stopped. He can do no more. He is near his end. His sun is setting, and he will rise no more. Farewell to Black-hawk" (137).

But this is not at all the end of Black Hawk's story. As we will see in chapter 3 of this book, Black Hawk, in his autobiography, will go forward from this low moment to request the return of his medicine bag from Agent Street so that he might pass it on to his son and to his People, that they might live. Despite the words attributed to him here, there will be no "stop" to his "plans" to "save" his nation; indeed, the decision subsequently to narrate the story of his life, as I will show, is itself an attempt to save his nation. "Farewell to Black Hawk?" Perhaps on the dark day of his surrender; certainly those who had fought against him and his People hoped this would be the case, and it is quite possible that one of them—not, I think Samuel Drake, although I don't know this for sure—expanded on the paraphrase in the *Galenian*, putting words into Black Hawk's mouth in order to emphasize the pitiful, possibly "vanishing" state of the Sauk. Even today we do not have a source for the words ascribed to Black Hawk, so nothing beyond speculation can be offered. There is no question, as we will see below, that much of Black Hawk's *Life* did indeed come from the old warrior himself, and it is my sense, as I have already indicated, that the *Life* is far less a good-bye than the speech first printed by Drake.

Chief Sealth's Farewell

> The white man, he took over, see.... They came to this country looking for freedom of speech and to worship the way they wanted to. But when they got here they forgot when it came to the Indian.... They've taken everything.
> Unidentified Nisqually man in the 1960s (Davis 105)

Chief Sealth or Seattle was born about 1786 at Old Man House, the winter village of his Suquamish (the name means "people of the sheltered salt water") Nation, on Bainbridge Island in what is now Washington State.[28] His father, Schweabe, was Suquamish, and his mother, Scholitza, was a Duwamish woman from the area of present-day Kent, Washington.

Sealth is said to have attained chiefly status as a result of his actions in defending his People against an attack from upriver tribes,[29] the sort of career success expected at one time or another for a young man of his noble lineage. There are various monuments to him in Seattle and the state of Washington, but his national and international renown derives from a speech he is usually said to have given in 1854 or 1855. This speech was not published until October 29, 1887, when it appeared in the *Seattle Sunday Star* in a translation version by Dr. Henry A. Smith. It was reprinted a few years later in Frederic Grant's *History of Seattle, Washington* (1891). In 1931, Sealth's speech was reproduced in publications by Clarence Bagley and Roberta Frye Watt, and in 1932 by John Rich. All three of these authors added a thirteen-word conclusion—"Dead did I say? There is no death, only a change of worlds"—to the speech as it had been printed in 1887.[30] Sealth's speech was then "retranslated," "from the Victorian English of Dr. Henry Smith," by William Arrowsmith in 1969 (Kaiser 509) and subsequently rewritten and expanded by Ted Perry in the early 1970s for a film he had been commissioned to produce for the Southern Baptist Convention (Kaiser 513–15; Buerge 1991, 27). It was once again altered for the Spokane Expo of 1974 (Kaiser 530–32).[31] It is only the 1887 text that is relevant to our study of Native American elegiac expression.[32]

Sealth's speech, as I've noted, is frequently said to have been delivered in either 1854 or 1855 during meetings convened by Isaac Ingalls Stevens, the newly appointed governor of Washington Territory, with the aim of persuading the Puget Sound Indians to give up most of their lands in Kitsap County for a reservation at Port Madison. As the historian Carole Seeman explains, "Between Christmas Day, 1854 and January 26, 1855, Governor Stevens...made three treaties [Medicine Creek, Point Elliott, and Point No Point] with representatives of some of the six thousand or more Indians who inhabited Puget Sound" (24). Stevens began negotiations with the Indians at Point Elliott on January 22, 1855, and a treaty was signed the following day.[33] Sealth was in attendance at the Point Elliott meeting; indeed, his is the first signature to appear on the treaty. If the famous speech had been delivered at Point Elliott it would have been on one of those January days in 1855. But there is no one on record who claims actually to have heard Sealth deliver a *lengthy* address at Point Elliott.[34] Clarence Bagley's 1931 essay asserted that Dr. Henry Smith was present at Point Elliott (247), although other sources dispute Smith's presence (e.g., Clark: "The name of Dr. Smith does not appear among those listed as witnessing the Point Elliott discussions" [4]), and I tend to think he was *not* at Point Elliott.

But so far as Sealth's speech is concerned, speculations about Dr. Smith's presence or absence at Point Elliott are to no point whatever. This is because Dr. Smith himself stated very clearly that he did *not* hear the speech at Point Elliott. Rather, as he wrote in the prefatory remarks to his reconstruction of the speech, "when Governor Stevens first arrived in Seattle, and told the natives he had been appointed commissioner of Indian affairs for Washington Territory, they gave him a demonstrative reception in front of Dr. Maynard's office, near the water front on Main Street" (qtd. in Furtwangler 11). On that occasion, as Dr. Smith tells us, Dr. Maynard introduced Stevens to those assembled, and Stevens gave a brief speech. Then, Smith writes, "Chief Seattle arose...[and] commenced his memorable address in solemn and impressive tones" (11).

Stevens assumed his position as governor of Washington Territory and commissioner of Indian affairs in November of 1853,[35] and, according to Rudolf Kaiser, he visited Puget Sound after he "returned from a trip to the East," in December 1854. Kaiser believes that 1854 is the "most likely date for the address" (504); it is also the date earlier given by the historian of Seattle, Roberta Frye Watt (178). The Lushootseed linguist Vi Hilbert, citing Kaiser, accepts this date (259), although David Buerge believes that Stevens first met with Chief Sealth at a large public gathering attended by most of the city's residents and a great many Indians almost a year earlier, specifically on January 12, 1854 (1988, 28), a date much closer to Stevens's arrival.[36] Dr. Smith gave no date for Seathl's speech, and I tend toward Buerge's rather than Kaiser's guess. But the important thing to note is that whether the speech was delivered in January or December 1854, it was *not* delivered at Point Elliott but in Seattle, on Main Street, on an occasion when Stevens would have announced his intention to negotiate for Indian lands—negotiations that did not actually take place until approximately a year (or, it is possible, only a month) later.[37]

Why, then, in view of Dr. Smith's clear statement of where he heard the speech, have some scholars continued to set it at the Point Elliott treaty convention?[38] Apart from the possibility of some confusion (the many publications dealing with Sealth's speech, as should already be apparent, do not agree on some very basic facts), the reason is surely because Sealth's speech offers a number of specific responses to proposals made by Stevens for the sale or exchange of Indian lands—proposals, to repeat, that were *not* made when Stevens first met with the Indians of the Sound a year (or possibly only several weeks) earlier, the occasion on which Dr. Smith says he heard Sealth speak.

Briefly to recapitulate before moving forward: Dr. Henry Smith said that Sealth's great speech was delivered on Main Street, in front of Dr. Maynard's office, near the waterfront, on the occasion of Governor Isaac Stevens's first introducing himself to the Indian peoples of Puget Sound. Smith gives no date for this occasion, but it had to have been either January 1854 (my best guess, as I have said) or at the latest December that year. No actual negotiations for Indian land took place at that time, although Sealth's speech quite clearly responds to a number of proposals—which were not actually presented until the Point Elliott or Mukilteo treaty meetings that took place January 21–23, 1855.

Sealth was present at the Point Elliott talks, and he signed the treaty agreeing to a reservation for his People. But Smith was almost surely *not* present at those talks, and, moreover, he explicitly stated that he produced Sealth's speech from notes he took at the meeting in Seattle in front of Dr. Maynard's office. Those notes cannot have included responses that Sealth could only have made at a later time. Thus, it's my sense that Smith did indeed hear Sealth speak in January 1854 (or, again, possibly some time later, in December that year), and that he was impressed with Sealth's oratorical powers, took notes on what he heard, and, *later,* made further notes from hearsay or from the local papers reporting Seathl's remarks at Point Elliott, some of which, as I have said, are on the record, but others of which may have been lost. It is not hard to imagine that with the passage of more than thirty years, Smith might have consciously or unconsciously conflated his notes from different occasions, collapsing them into one grand speech.

It is also worth remarking that in 1887, Dr. Smith would have been aware of the considerable attention paid to the "farewell" speech of Chief Joseph of the Nez Perces (which we will look at next), said to have been delivered in 1877, and, very importantly, that he almost surely would have followed the ongoing congressional debate over the Dawes or General Allotment Act that was eventually passed into law on February 2, 1887. Dawes was explicitly intended to destroy the tribally held Indian land base and to turn American Indians into Indian-Americans who valued private property and a dollar in their trousers' pocket. An elegiac lament for a vanishing race may well have come from Sealth in 1854–55, but it may also take some of its tone from Dr. Smith's understanding of the events of 1887, a time when prospects for the continued tribal life of Indian peoples seemed dim.[39]

It's also possible that some measure of the fatalism voiced by Sealth may derive from Dr. Smith's sense of his own situation in the 1880s. Buerge notes that although "Smith and his pioneer compatriots had done very well, becoming middle-class landowners, a propertied elite that liked to call itself 'Old Seattle,'" nonetheless, "by the mid-1880's they were losing power to a growing working class and to a class of urbane professionals and entrepreneurs who styled themselves as 'New Seattle" (1991, 28). Ironically, as Buerge speculates, it is possible that "Smith and his pioneer colleagues felt themselves to be in much the same situation as the one they had put the Indians in in the 1850s" (29). This may further help us understand why Dr. Smith decided to construct and publish a valedictory speech by Sealth in 1887.

In much the same way, we may contextualize Roberta Watt's 1931 description of Sealth's speech as "the swan song of a dying race" (179) and John Rich's 1932 description of it as a "Funeral Oration of the Great Indian Race" (10) with another of Buerge's insights. He reminds us that these grandiose and mistaken pronouncements were made in "the depths of the Great Depression...as a possible prophecy of [American] social collapse" (29), yet another example of the projection of the settler-society's anxieties onto the Indians. But "the Great Depression" was also the nadir of the Dawes period, when the dire results of Dawes—its destructiveness to Native tribal nations—were thoroughly documented by the Merriam Report of 1928. Just as Dr. Smith in 1887 might have imagined *both* the end of tribal life *and also* the dominance of his own class, so, too, might Watt and Rich in the early 1930s have conflated *Indian* demise with *American* economic collapse. They could not have been aware that in just a very few years the Indian Reorganization Act (1934) would be passed precisely to enable the continued vitality of "the Great Indian Race" (although sometimes by less than fortunate means).

I will discuss two aspects of Sealth's "farewell" speech of 1854 in the context of Native American elegiac expression. First, I want to consider its status as a formal statement of exile and ending, one that may be compared to the valedictories apparently enunciated by Chief Logan and Black Hawk, which we have already examined, and to the speeches ascribed to Chief Joseph and Cochise, which we will soon consider. To do this requires an estimate—one I have offered in regard to other Indian farewells—of the degree to which the speech published in 1887 accurately represents things Sealth might have said in 1854 and perhaps 1855 as well. This is especially important because, as we have noted, there are three versions of Sealth's speech that are largely fabrications. Second, I want to consider whether the speech, in the manner of most Native American elegiac discourse, seeks to console the People and contribute to their continuance and survivance, so that they might live—or whether it takes a different tack.

If we were to judge the accuracy of Dr. Smith's rendition of Sealth's words strictly on the basis of his setting for them, the verdict would be mixed. In his comments framing the speech, Dr. Smith says that Sealth "was the largest Indian I ever saw, and by far the noblest looking. He stood nearly six feet in his moccasins, was broad shouldered, deep chested and finely proportioned" (qtd. in Furtwangler 10). Others have also described Sealth as a tall and noble red man.[40] Yet Fredric Grant, publishing only four years later than Smith, writes that "Seattle was short and heavy, weighing as much as 180 pounds. He was round-shouldered.... His face was refined and benevolent but not particularly strong" (62).[41] It was also Smith's sense that when Sealth spoke, "deep-toned, sonorous and eloquent sentences rolled from his lips like the ceaseless thunders of cataracts flowing from exhaustless fountains" (qtd. in Furtwangler 10). Sealth almost surely had a powerful voice, perhaps one that "could be heard a distance of half a mile," an often-repeated statement that probably derives from D. T. Denny, "who arrived at Alki point [Washington Territory] in 1851," and who is quoted to this effect by David Carlson in 1903 (7). Smith would probably have known Denny, although his sense of the matter, expressed, to be sure, in florid, Victorian language, might indeed derive from his own experience of Sealth's oratorical power. Jay Miller has made the point that "most [Puget Sound] chiefs had inherited power from Thunder and passed it along to their heirs for generations, giving each a booming voice and eye-catching flair" (1999, 31). We know that Sealth had Thunder power,[42] and thus a booming voice—and, perhaps, an impressive figure as well. Smith's sense of his vocal power and physical stature may well be accurate.

I suspect Smith is less accurate in stating that when "Governor Stevens sat down, Chief Seattle arose with all the dignity of a senator, who carries the responsibilities of a great nation on his shoulders. Placing one hand on the governor's head, and slowly pointing heavenward with the index finger of the other, he commenced his memorable address in solemn and impressive tones" (qtd. in Furtwangler 11). First, it seems to me extremely unlikely that Sealth would have put his hand on the head of any white man (or any Indian, for that matter), especially the head of an important government official whom he had probably never before met.[43] I also suspect that Stevens's head in rainy Seattle—and this was in winter, the rainiest season of the year—would have been covered by a hat. The "senator" reference invokes classical Rome, and perhaps it has something to do with Smith recalling Jefferson's references to Logan, whom he compared favorably to Roman orators.

In the speech attributed to him by Thomas Jefferson, Chief Logan presumably said that other Indians had *pointed* at him as a friend of the white. Thomas McElwain, some of whose discussion of Logan's speech I cited earlier, observes that pointing, in the sense of "throwing up a finger"—exactly what Sealth is said to do here—is a "non-Native behavior.... A Native person indicates with eyes or pursed lips" (115). Smith has painted a portrait of Sealth as both Roman senator and biblical patriarch—hand on the head in blessing, finger pointed to the heavens—one that is easy to imagine in an ornate frame, hung on a museum wall. This portrait is at the least highly suspect and perhaps historically and culturally impossible. What of the speech itself?

Sealth spoke in Lushootseed, the central coastal Salishan language of his Suquamish/Duwamish People.[44] His words would have been translated by one of the Indians into Chinook jargon—which Dr. Smith may well have understood. David Buerge (1988, 28) and Crisca Bierwert (1998, 284) suggest that George Gibbs, a surveyor for Stevens's party who sometimes served as his interpreter, might have been the one who translated the jargon into English for Governor Stevens and other of the white settlers of Seattle.[45] Bierwert sensibly concludes that "the language translation process puts whatever Smith heard at considerable remove from its literal origins, *although not, perhaps, its oratorical qualities*" (284; my emphasis). Buerge, on the basis of his examination of Smith's other writings, finds that "Chief Seattle's speech [is] easily the best thing Smith ever 'wrote'" (1988, 28). He therefore concludes that "its strength and imagery derive from what Smith *heard* rather than from his own talent" (29; my emphasis). Vi Hilbert put the matter both generously and usefully in her estimate that Dr. Smith "sensed the beauty of [Sealth's] speech.... He took notes of this impressive speech *and from them wrote the English version* published some thirty-three years later" (262; my emphasis). It is my belief that the oratorical power of the speech Dr. Smith published does indeed derive substantially from Sealth's performance on that January day in 1854, supplemented by responses the chief would later have made to propositions offered by Governor Stevens at Point Elliott.[46] While it surely does not represent a literal or linguistically accurate translation, I would nonetheless conclude that what Dr. Smith published in 1887 does convey some of what Sealth had said in 1854 and 1855.[47] We may turn now to it as an Indian farewell, elegiac expression.

Sealth begins his speech with a strong fatalism with regard to the social and political future of his People, a fatalism that carries through to the end of his address. Responding to the fact that the "white chief sends us word that he wants to buy our lands but is willing to allow us to reserve enough to live on comfortably," Sealth says that this "indeed appears just, even generous, for the Red Man no longer has rights that he need respect, and the offer may be wise also, as we are no longer in need of an extensive country" (qtd. in Furtwangler 13).[48] There is a strong temptation, today, to read these words ironically, but it is a temptation that is probably best resisted. Sealth's People had suffered considerable depopulation as a result of the introduction of Western diseases to which they had not developed any immunity, and Isaac Stevens was clearly determined to get lands for the railroad and expand white settlement exponentially. Acquiescence to Stevens's demands could well have seemed the best option that the People might live. And yet, as we will see further, Sealth fully engages the possibility that the People might *not* live.

Tulalip elder "Gram" Ruth Sehome Shelton, born sometime between 1855 and 1859, who heard of these matters directly from her relatives, tells us that Stevens was known as "the changer" (55), and in the short speech by Sealth at Mukilteo that she quoted from memory, she has him refer to the whites generally as "changers." In Vi Hilbert's English translation of Shelton's Lushootseed, she has Sealth say: "You folks observe the changers / who have come to this land" (qtd. in Hilbert 262). This does not simply indicate an awareness that from the first arrival of the whites things began to change, or even that this specific changer, Stevens, will carry that work forward. Rather, we must note that "Southern Coast Salish myths tell of a myth age when there were beings with both human and animal qualities. This age ended with the coming of the Transformer...who *changed* many of the myth age beings into animals, *changed* some dangerous creatures into stone, and gave human beings the rudiments of culture" (Suttles and Lane 496; my emphasis). Indeed, according to Suttles, "The central figure in Coast Salish mythology is the Transformer," who "is called [Dookweebathl] in the Puget Sound...languages" (1957, 379).[49] Stories about the Changer or Transformer, Bierwert notes (1996, 63), in "Lushootseed, as in other Northwest Coast literatures, constitute a genre" akin to Trickster stories. As she describes it, "At some point in Lushootseed time, the Changer...appeared, stalking through the world and asking everyone, 'What are you doing?' Depending on their responses, he then decided for them what their future characteristic activity in the world would be" (63). The Coast Salish Transformer appears as the purposeful creator of a new order" (Suttle 1957, 379). When Ruth Shelton says that Stevens was known as the "changer," the word she uses is indeed [Dookweebathl] (55), with the strong implication that the Puget Sound natives understood quite well that he might indeed have the power to decide for them "what their future characteristic activity in the world would be."

For Christian Indians like Sealth (as we will see further), Stevens's arrival might also represent something like a Second Coming—not of Christ, to be sure, but of the Transformer, one who would not resurrect the Indians' old traditional life but rather see to it that their "future...activity in the world" would be to become like white people. "Our progeny," Shelton has Sealth say, "will watch and learn from them now, / those who will come after us / our children. / And they will become / ...just the same / as the changers [] who have come / here to us / on this land" (qtd. in Hilbert 262). Dr. Smith would not have heard Sealth speak these words, although he may have heard of or read them *after* the great speech that he did hear. They are important to consider as we try to understand that speech.

By the time of Stevens's arrival, Sealth already had a substantial reputation as a friend of the whites (fig. 7). He claimed to have witnessed his People's first contact with Europeans, when, as a boy of about six, he saw

Figure 7. Chief Seattle (from a postcard).

"the British ship *H.M.S Discovery,* captained by George Vancouver, anchored off Bainbridge Island on May 20, 1792" (Buerge online).[50] Although he grew up in a traditional manner, engaging in a successful vision quest, gaining Thunder power, taking two wives, and participating in a number of military actions, one of which we have already noted, after the death of one of his sons in battle, he "sought and received baptism into the Catholic Church, taking the prophet Noah as his spiritual intercessor...and he appears as Noe Siattle in the Oblate Sacramental Register. His children were also baptized...and his conversion marked the end of his fighting days and his emergence as a leader seeking cooperation with incoming American settlers" (Buerge online).[51] Carole Seeman has noted of Isaac Stevens that "in spite of [his] professed objectives to incorporate the natives into white society, he was not much committed to this ideal. He and his followers found themselves, however, confronted with native people who approved of the idea" (26). Sealth seems to have been one of these people.

Ruth Shelton also noted that the treaty at Mukilteo was known as the "hooraying" treaty (17, 22, 26ff.), and what those who cheered were approving was indeed the fact that the Indians "will be taught to become like white people" (20). She also makes clear, however, that unlike Sealth, "there were lots of them [Indians at Mukilteo], there were more of them who said 'No' to the selling of their lands" (19). One of these was the Nisqually leader, Leschi. His X mark had appeared on the earlier Medicine Creek Treaty, but there is good reason to believe that it was placed there by someone else.[52] A leader in the Puget Sound War of 1855–56, he was "planning to sneak up on the white people at Seattle in order to kill them" (28). But Sealth had sent a Duwamish man named Kelly to eavesdrop on Leschi's deliberations. Upon Kelly's return, Sealth informed the whites at Seattle of Leschi's plans, allowing them to escape by boat. Shelton notes that "this is why (Chief Seattle) was so highly honored by the white people at Seattle because he saved them from being killed" (29). As she understands it, "It was not because he was a leader that you folks know about him. He was greatly honored by the white people at Seattle for saving their lives" (29).

Thus it seems clear that Sealth was a "progressive" rather than a "conservative" or "traditional" chief, as these terms have been applied to Native leaders who, for a variety of reasons, made the decision to accommodate the aggressive whites or even to try to become like them rather than to offer obdurate resistance, as Leschi did. But it is important *not* to equate "progressive" with terms like "bad," "traitorous," and "inauthentic," taking "conservative" or "traditional" to mean "good" or "authentic." The situation historically is far too complicated for such reductively facile judgments. Further, when we consider the testimony of such very different writers as the anthropologist Jay Miller, the Acoma poet Simon Ortiz, and the Muscogee critic and novelist Craig Womack (among others) to the effect that "traditional" broadly means "'anything that supports the continuity of the community'" (J. Miller 1999, 1), Sealth's "progressivism" may be seen as entirely a "traditional" and even a "nationalistic" response to the conditions facing his People.[53] I say this recognizing fully that Sealth's elegiac farewell ultimately does *not* seem to believe that *any* response his People can make will ultimately assure the "continuity of the community"—at least, as we will see further, as a *living* community of Indians—but this fatalism, as I have tried to show, may in itself be the consequence of a modern twist to tradition, what I have called the Second Coming of the Changer.

Having accepted the practical reasonableness (or, to repeat, the mythic inevitability) of the white man's proposition to his People, Sealth next offers the hope that "hostilities between the red man and his pale face brothers may never return," because the Indians "would have everything to lose and nothing to gain." Continuing the language of fathers and children that had become common in treaty negotiations since the eighteenth century, he notes that if the Indians accept Stevens's offer, "the great father Washington" will "be our father as well as yours." But Sealth then makes a quite extraordinary turn with the statement to Stevens that "your God loves your people and hates mine...he makes your people wax strong every day, and soon they will fill the land; while our people are ebbing away like a fast-receding tide, that will never flow again." If this is so, "How," asks Sealth, "can your father become our father and bring us prosperity and awaken in us dreams of returning greatness?" "No," says Sealth, "we are two distinct races and must ever remain so. There is little in common between us" (qtd. in Furtwangler 14). He then proceeds to illustrate the difference between the Indians and the Euramericans with reference to relations between the dead and the living.

Sealth remarks that while the "ashes of our ancestors are sacred and their final resting place is hallowed ground," the whites, to the contrary, "wander away from the tombs of [their] fathers seemingly without regret" (qtd. in Furtwangler 14–15).⁵⁴ Denise Low has observed that "the central purpose of [Sealth's] speech was the preliminary negotiations for rights of Suquamish and Duwamish people to visit their burial grounds, a prerequisite for practice of their religion" (408). Or, as Sealth himself put it to Stevens in Dr. Smith's publication, "We will ponder your proposition.... But should we accept it, I here and now make this the first condition: That we will not be denied the privilege without molestation, of visiting at will the graves of our ancestors and friends" (qtd. in Furtwangler 16). (Black Hawk was also so concerned, as I will note.) This "first condition" comes rather late in Dr. Smith's version of the speech, but it is, indeed, as Low has noted, central nonetheless—all the more so in that Governor Stevens's meetings with the Puget Sound people that "forced the series of treaties 'legally' ceding land from Idaho to the Pacific... were held in January, at the time of the year natives devoted to their religious ceremonies" (J. Miller 1999, 42). These included potlatch ceremonies, which might or might not have reference to the dead; they also had much to do with what Jay Miller has called the "shamanic odyssey" to the land of the dead. Miller notes that "the dead remain more significant in the lives of Lushootseed people than anything else except the spirits. For people living in close and caring communities, the bonds of the flesh, like those of the spirit, continued far beyond the grave" (1999, 36).⁵⁵ Indeed, "most spirits... visited their human partner in the winter months. During these long rainy winters, people gathered to welcome back their spirits by singing and dancing" (31). This sense of the relation between the living and the dead may go a long way toward explaining the conclusion of Sealth's speech.

The whites' relation to the dead, Sealth says, is very different from his People's. "Your dead," he says, "cease to love you and the homes of their nativity, as soon as they pass the portals of the tomb. They wander far off beyond the stars, are soon forgotten and never return. Our dead never forget the beautiful world that gave them being. They still love its winding rivers, its great mountains and its sequestered vales, and they ever yearn in tenderest affection over the lonely hearted living and often return to visit and comfort them" (qtd. in Furtwangler 15).⁵⁶ These complex relations between the dead and the living, Sealth insists, must continue but their continuance, as he expresses it, will not be sufficient to secure the People's survivance, neither as Indians nor even, it may be, as some facsimile of white people. "The Indian's night promises to be dark," Sealth is represented as saying. "A few more moons, a few more winters and not one of all the mighty hosts that once filled this broad land...will remain to weep over the tombs of a people once as powerful and as hopeful as your own" (16). In this manner he works toward his grand but grim conclusion. I will quote him at some length:

> And when the last red man shall have perished from the earth and his memory among white men shall have become a myth, these shores shall swarm with the invisible dead of my tribe, and when your children's children shall think themselves alone in the field, the store, the shop, upon the highway or in the silence of the woods they will not be alone. In all the earth there is no place dedicated to solitude. At night, when the streets of your cities and villages shall be silent, and you think them deserted, they will throng with the returning hosts that once filled and still love this beautiful land. The white man will never be alone. Let him be just and deal kindly with my people, for the dead are not altogether powerless. (17)

The warning here is not strictly rhetorical. The dead might kill the living so that they would be less lonely in the land of the dead. Also dangerous to the living was the power of the dead to cause illness by stealing a person's soul or some portion of it. A cure could be achieved by what Jay Miller (1988, 1999), as noted above, has called the "shamanic odyssey," in which shamans in the rainy winter months prepared for and undertook a trip to the land of the dead to bring back the missing soul and restore it to the person from whom it had been taken, thus curing his or her illness. Sealth would have been quite certain that the whites did not have the capacity to undertake such cures, so that the power of the dead could indeed be very great among them and very dangerous to them. (But he also would, of course, have been aware of Catholic views of these matters.) Sealth's farewell does *not* envision or enable the continued life of his People except as a nation of powerful Indian ghosts (or ghostly simulacra of white people). It is thus an example of Native elegiac expression very different from most examples we have considered thus far.

Although Sealth may at some time have "progressively" believed that his People could survive by becoming like the whites, although he may have spoken to that effect and drawn "hoorays" from many at Mukilteo, his speech as published by Dr. Smith—even if Dr. Smith's own pessimism played some part in this—strongly articulates Sealth's sense that there was *nothing* he and his People could do to ensure their continuance and survivance as tribal nations. His farewell address makes clear that apart from their power to visit their homelands after death and engage in detrimental relations to the living, his People will *not* live.

Two Farewells by Cochise

> This is the country of the Chiricahua Apaches. This is the country where the Chiricahua Apaches belong.... The men with steel came and tried to take it from us and we defeated them. Now the Americans—and none is more treacherous than the Americans and none more arrogant.
> Cochise, as recalled by Tom Jeffords, late 1860s (Arnold 322)

Cochise was a Chiricahua Apache leader of the Chokonen band, born about 1810.[57] At the end of the Mexican War in 1848, the Chiricahuas and their frequent raids on the sheep, cattle, and horses of settlers in Arizona and New Mexico territories became the responsibility of the United States. As Americans increasingly invaded the Southwest, a series of "wars" broke out around 1860 between the Apaches and the various governments protecting the whites; these continued through the period of the Civil War (during which time troops were withdrawn from the Southwest) and after, until the capture of the Chiricahua leader Geronimo in 1886.

In June 1871, Colonel George Crook, a Civil War veteran and an experienced Indian fighter, was given command of the U.S. Army in Arizona. Employing a number of Native scouts—a radical notion at the time—Crook tracked Cochise, and, in September that year, urged him to engage in negotiations at Canada Alamosa with General Gordon Granger, commander of the district of New Mexico. Cochise reluctantly agreed. But when he learned that Granger proposed sending him and his People to Fort Tularosa, New Mexico, he broke off all talks.

In response, President Ulysses S. Grant ordered another Civil War veteran and experienced Indian fighter, General O. O. Howard, to treat with the Apaches. Howard enlisted the aid of Thomas Jeffords (or Jefferds), a former captain of the California volunteer cavalry, who had earlier established friendly relations with Cochise. With Jeffords's help, Howard arranged another meeting between Cochise's Apaches and Granger in March 1872, also at Canada Alamosa (Turrill 17; Sweeney xx). But this meeting as well failed to produce its intended result when Cochise once more rejected the offer of a reservation for his People at Tularosa (and perhaps as well an offer for a reservation at Canada Alamosa). It was only later, in October that year, when Jeffords led General Howard to meet with Cochise alone, that an agreement was worked out by which Cochise and his People would live on a reservation along Apache Pass, in southeastern Arizona, with Jeffords serving as government Indian agent.

According to his twentieth-century biographer, Edwin Sweeney, Cochise is supposed to have made his farewell speech to the Americans sometime during the negotiations, which ended on March 20, 1872. "Two...eyewitnesses," Sweeney writes, "recorded fascinating descriptions of the aging chief" (338), and both published versions of the speech. The "eyewitnesses" were "assistant [army] surgeon Henry Stuart Turrill...and Dr. Anderson Nelson Ellis" (338). Others have also assumed that Turrill and Ellis each recorded a single speech made by Cochise, although that speech is usually said to have been delivered earlier, in September 1871.[58] But the two speeches are completely different (see the appendix), and the differences are far too great to attribute to the vagaries of either recollection or translation.

Turrill listed General Gordon Granger, General J. Irwin Gregg, Lieutenant-Colonel J. P. Willard, and himself, each with "a mounted orderly fully armed" (17), as making up the entire military party at the March 1872 parley. He did not mention the presence of an army doctor named Ellis. Ellis himself does not specify the year in which he heard Cochise speak, although he clearly specifies September as the month when the encounter with Cochise took place (390). Ellis's "Recollections of an Interview with Cochise" differs from Turrill's account not only in the speech Ellis attributes to Cochise but in several other regards as well. Where Turrill, for example, recalls Granger going on at excessive length,[59] Ellis reports that Granger spoke "in a few plain, blunt words peculiar to the soldier" (391). According to Ellis, the Indians then withdrew for "about one hour" (391), after which time, Cochise delivered his speech. I am fairly certain that the speech Ellis heard was delivered in September 1871 and that it was in March 1872 that Turrill heard Cochise speak. Turrill, however, was the first to make public a speech by Cochise, in a talk he gave called "A

Vanished Race of Aboriginal Founders," delivered on February 14, 1907, to the New York Society of the Founders and Patriots of America, and published that same year. Ellis's account appeared later, in 1913, in his "Recollections of an Interview with Cochise." The two speeches are entirely different (see the appendix).

Early in his 1907 talk, Turrill says that he "had picked up a sort of polyglot language, consisting of English, Spanish, Apache and Navajo words, with quite a bit of 'sign talk' that rendered communication with the Indians easy." He boasts that "for a long time [his] name among these Indians was 'Big Soldier Man that Talks Apache" (6). Describing the conference between Cochise and the soldiers, he again notes his ability to "speak Apache," remarking that Jeffords, more friendly to Cochise than to Turrill (Turrill had observed Jeffords in what he took to be some illegal trading with the Indians),[60] warned "Cochise to look out, as I could understand him" (18).

Once General Granger had finished his address,[61] Turrill says that Cochise commenced in "meager, somewhat guttural" Apache, "but as he warmed to his subject he slid into the more graceful Spanish, of which he was a master, and with the expressive 'sign talk' he made an address that affected me as but one other orator ever has, and that was Wendell Phillips in one of his early abolition speeches" (19). Turrill then offers Cochise's words as direct quotation, acknowledging, however, that the speech is only "*as I remember it* after a lapse of thirty-five years[!]," a speech, he writes, that went "*about as follows*" (19; my emphasis). We will, of course, examine Turrill's version of Cochise's speech. But I suspect the reader will have already found much to remark on in Turrill's introductory remarks.

This is to say that Turrill cannot reconcile two competing views of Cochise and the Apaches. The first derives from his sense of Apache "primitiveness." For example, he discusses the peopling of Apache country, initially by the Aztecs, who left "little islands of semi-civilization" (8). They were followed, he says, by "an entirely *primitive* man, a thorough and complete *savage*, the Apache, inventing nothing, copying little from their more intelligent neighbors" (8; my emphasis). If this was the case, then it should come as no surprise that Turrill says Cochise's Apache was "meager, somewhat [?] guttural," and distinct from the language of those who came later, the Spanish, speakers of a "more graceful" language. (Cochise, as I will soon note, however, probably did not deliver any of his speech in Spanish.)

But Turrill has a second opinion of the Apache. He refers to a mission to the Chiricahua, when, "alone with more than a hundred of the wildest Indians of the frontier," he noted of his "wild entertainers": "Never in all my service have I received such constant care for my personal safety" (6)—a thoroughly "civilized" care, one would think. Cochise is also in Turrill's estimation "the only Indian chief that I ever knew that could enforce instant obedience to a given command" (21). In retrospect, Turrill judges Cochise "the greatest Indian [he had] ever met," quite a compliment in that he had made the acquaintance of a number of eminent Native leaders, among them Chief Joseph, Young Man Afraid of His Horses, Gall, Red Cloud, and Satanta (18). Turrill speaks of Cochise's own family as Native nobility, strong men, all of whom, Cochise in particular, commanded the greatest respect. Thus when Turrill hears Cochise deliver "the finest bit of Indian oratory that [he] ever listened to" (19), he encounters an impossible amalgam of meager, crude, and primitive language coming from the lips of a noble and articulate leader.

It is perhaps worth mentioning that this ambivalence or, indeed, schizophrenia in thought about Indians was typical of some of the most renowned Indian fighters of the nineteenth century—Crook, Howard, and Nelson Miles, among others—and it has been typical of some historians of the American West at least up to the 1960s. Crook and Howard, for example, like Turrill, in their reports and later autobiographies, spoke abundantly of the fine and decent and humane and "civilized" aspects of life they had encountered among several different tribal nations. But they nonetheless continued to regard Native peoples as savages who clearly had to be dominated if not destroyed, and they show no ambivalence whatever about their missions.

As Turrill had done earlier, Ellis prepares his readers for Cochise's speech with a number of generalizations about the Apaches and their neighbors that will also strike the contemporary reader as troubling. For example, Ellis seeks to explain his estimate that southwestern peoples are "the most cruel and bloodthirsty tribes" (388) by means of a crude geographical determinism. These peoples are "cruel and bloodthirsty," he writes, as a consequence of the "cruelty, the aridity, the barrenness" of the southwestern landscape. These qualities of the landscape, Ellis writes, must "impress themselves on the brain and leave their shadow on the soul" (388).[62] Ellis then cites what he calls Cochise's "touching and eloquent address" (392) without considering how it can be that cruelty and bloodthirstiness coexist so readily with highly articulate sentiment.[63] Nor does he offer any explanation whatsoever as to how he came by the words he offers as direct quotation. (Turrill had readily admitted that his was an attempt to reconstruct Cochise's remarks after more than thirty-five years—although he, too, put Cochise's words in quotation marks.)

Ellis states that "the talking was done in Spanish" (391). Turrill had said that Cochise began in Apache and only later switched to Spanish. These were, as I've said, different occasions, but I think the memories of both men may be mistaken. Joseph Alton Sladen, long an aide to General Howard and with him at the October 1872 meeting in which Cochise accepted the Apache Pass reservation, noted in his journals that on that occasion Cochise spoke exclusively in Apache. A Chokonen known as El Cautivo (he had been captured by Mexicans as a boy) translated from Cochise's Apache to Spanish—with Cochise, whose understanding of Spanish was said to be good, occasionally suggesting an alteration. One of the American soldiers who understood Spanish provided an English translation. El Cautivo had served as an adviser to and interpreter for Cochise since 1857 (Sweeney 93–94 n. 122; 158–59), and I would guess that the procedure followed in this last (1872) encounter would have replicated procedures followed earlier—in the meeting with Granger in September 1871 at which Ellis was present, and the meeting in March 1872 attended by Turrill. Ellis notes that while some of the Apaches agreed to go to Tularosa, "Cochise drew off his chosen warriors and went back to his old mountain home in Arizona" (392). He concludes by mistakenly giving September 1872 (the correct date is October 1872) as the date when General Howard "prevailed upon [Cochise] to make peace again, giving him his old haunts [Apache Pass] for a reservation" (392).[64]

In the speech Turrill recalls, Cochise begins by saying: "This for a very long time has been the home of my people; they came from darkness, few in numbers and feeble" (19). Such an opening is consistent with many records of Indian oratory in which white recorders noted the tendency of Native speakers to commence with a history of their people rather than immediately "getting to the point." Geronimo, another renowned Chiricahua leader, opens his autobiography as follows: "In the beginning the world was covered with darkness. There was no sun, no day. The perpetual night had no moon or stars" (3). Turrill has Cochise continue with an account of the coming of his People to their homes, and the attacks on them by the Spanish, the Mexicans, and, most recently, the Americans. He mentions the fact that American "soldiers did [him] a very great wrong," referring to the Bascom affair of 1861.[65]

Turrill represents Cochise as unsentimentally stating: "I have come to you, not from any love for you or for your great father in Washington, or from any regard for his or your wishes, but as a conquered chief, to try to save alive the few people that still remain to me" (20). The acknowledgment of defeat and the determination to protect the People are constants in surrender and farewell oratory and two of the few elements of this oratory that ring true to my ears. Cochise, like Black Hawk and other defeated chiefs, may well have spoken to this effect under these straitened circumstances.[66]

The speech Ellis ascribes to Cochise is far briefer than that reported by Turrill. According to Ellis Cochise begins with the observation that he has gone from heated—"my blood was on fire"—to cool, "having drunk of these waters and washed myself in them and they have cooled me" (391). The phrasing has a biblical quality, although in the Old Testament it is victorious kings who drink and are cooled,[67] and Cochise appears here as a conquered leader—or, according to Ellis, "but a poor man" (391). Cochise then notes that "when God made the world he gave one part to the white man and another to the Apache." This may be more or less accurate, as Chiricahua mythology, while not attributing creation to Ussen or God, does say that "Child of the Water [an important culture hero] creates the white man at the same time as the Indian. In the division of the goods of the earth, Child of the Water chooses for the Indian (the Chiricahua) and Killer of Enemies [another culture hero] for the white man" (Opler 198).

There follows some apparent wonderment on the part of Cochise as to why the whites are so interested in him, since he is "no longer chief of all the Apaches"—he never was that, but he still holds a position of authority among the Chiricahuas—and "but a poor man." This is followed by a brief exercise in comparative ethnography, in which Cochise distinguishes between the ways of the whites and those of the Apaches, who "were born like the animals, in the dry grass, not on beds like you." Because of this, Cochise continues, the Apaches "do as the animals, go about at night and rob and steal" (Ellis 391). It is extremely unlikely that Cochise would have spoken of animals as robbing and stealing, and equally unlikely that he would have described Apache raiding as robbing and stealing.

In his introduction to *An Apache Life-Way*, subtitled *The Economic, Social, and Religious Institutions of the Chiricahua Indians*, Morris Opler makes the important point that in his organization of the materials for his monograph, "raid and warfare are subsumed under *the maintenance of the household*...because, at the period described [roughly, from late in Cochise's life until Geronimo's 1886 surrender], the Chiricahuas considered the raid a legitimate *industry* and trained faithfully for its proper fulfillment" (x; my emphasis). Opler later notes that "for men, raiding approaches hunting in economic significance" (332), and "raid and warfare are viewed as *industrial* pursuits" (333; my emphasis). Add to this the fact that among Cochise's People "theft is uncommon enough so that anyone who is guilty of it is viewed as an aberrant" (459) or a witch, and the robbing and stealing comment Ellis attributes to Cochise is, as I have said, extremely suspect.

Cochise next says: "I came in here because God told me to do it. He said it was good to be at peace—so I came. I was going around the world with the clouds, and the air, when God spoke to my thought and told me to come in here and be at peace with all" (Ellis 392). Cochise may indeed have prayed and received instruction to make peace. But because raiding for largely economic purposes, warfare to attain revenge, and the training of young men for both, as noted (Opler 72), were important cultural practices, peace as a general good seems an unlikely notion for an Apache of that time. Nor is this the first time Cochise has negotiated with the Americans. Necessity rather than God would seem to have moved him on all occasions.

Ellis has Cochise go on to reminisce about the days when he was "young [and] walked all over this country, east and west, and saw no other people than the Apaches." If he said anything like this, it would have to mean that when he was young he encountered no whites, for he surely would have seen Navajos, Walapais, Yumas, Papagos, possibly some Pueblo people, and most certainly a considerable number of Mexicans. In time, he says, others came, and now, "the Apaches wait to die...[and] carry their lives on their fingernails." This extraordinary image is repeated as Cochise affirms that the Apaches "want to die and so carry their lives on their fingernails." "They roam over the hills and plains and want the heavens to fall on them" (392).

I don't know what the original that Ellis has rendered as "carry[ing]...lives on their fingernails" might have been, but I doubt that Cochise would have spoken of an Apache longing for death. Chiricahua people exhibited the "ghost phobia" that we have noted among the Paiutes (as well as most southwestern tribal peoples). They buried the dead quickly, destroyed their possessions, burned their houses, and moved to a location distant from the place where death had occurred. Although suicides were known among the Apache (see, e.g., Opler 409), they were rare and generally disapproved of. "The topic of death," Opler affirms, "is sedulously avoided" (471). Hence my skepticism that Cochise actually told these uncomprehending Americans that the Apaches "want to die," or to have "the heavens fall on them."

Ellis has Cochise move toward a conclusion with statements very like those Logan is said to have made: "I have no father nor mother; I am alone in the world." "No one cares for Cochise," Ellis has him say, using a third person we have seen in both Black Hawk's and Logan's "farewell." Cochise then apparently shifts back to first person, explaining that loneliness "is why I do not care to live" (Ellis 392). This, too, is unlikely. Whatever Logan's family situation might have been at the time of his communication—the details are uncertain—Cochise did have two sons, a wife, and other relations; he was not alone. Ellis nonetheless has Cochise continue morbidly wishing "the rocks to fall on [him] and cover [him] up" (392). Ellis also has Cochise addressing "Americans and Mexicans" (392), although there were probably no Mexicans present, nor would any Mexicans have a say as to which reservation Cochise's People might occupy. Cochise rejects Tularosa and says he wants "to live in these mountains" (392). That can't be accurate because "*these* mountains"—the mountains where Cochise met with General Granger in 1871 and 1872—are the mountains at Canada Alamosa, New Mexico Territory. What Cochise wanted and was eventually granted for his People's reservation was Apache Pass, in Arizona, between *those* mountains, the Chiricahua Mountains to the east and the Dragoon Mountains to the west.[68] Ellis concludes by noting that some time later General Howard did indeed prevail on Cochise to make peace, although, as I've said, he mistakenly gives the date as September, rather than October, 1872.

There are bits and pieces of both speeches that probably did derive from things Cochise actually said; that much it is possible to estimate on the basis of cultural and historical facts. But, as we will see as well in considering the more famous speech of Chief Joseph, there is very little of traditional elegiac expression in what Ellis and Turrill have given us.

The Surrender of Chief Joseph

> Their history since 1855, and particularly in the war of 1877, tells how they were repaid for their loyalty to the white brother.... Their habitat through traditional and mythic times included the same valleys which we took from them by right of might.
>
> Edward S. Curtis (1976 [1911], 8: 15)

The Nez Perce or Nimipu—the People—are Sahaptian speakers whose traditional homelands were in the southeast of what is now Washington State, the southwest of present-day Idaho, and northeastern Oregon. They first enter U.S. history in 1805 when the exhausted and ill members of Lewis and Clark's party came down from the Rockies to the banks of the Clearwater River where they were fed and healed by Nez Perce people who could easily have destroyed them had they so chosen. In 1855, Isaac Stevens, governor of Washington Territory, negotiated treaties not only with the Puget Sound peoples but with bands of the Nez Perce as well. Tuekakas, known as Old Joseph, was one of the signers.[69] In 1858, gold was discovered on Nez Perce lands, and in 1863 the government urged the Nez Perce to sign a much more restrictive treaty. Although Old Joseph had signed the 1855 treaty, he refused to sign this one; leaders of other Nez Perce bands, however, did.

When Old Joseph died in 1871, his son, Hinmatowyalahtquit (Thunder Traveling High),[70] known as Young Joseph or Chief Joseph, became the leader of his father's band of nontreaty Nez Perce (see fig. 8). It was not long before Joseph found white settlers moving onto his People's Wallowa Valley homelands. The Indians strongly objected to this invasion, and, in 1873, a Bureau of Indian Affairs investigation agreed that the treaty of 1863 did not bind Joseph and his band—who had not signed it—thus rendering the settlements illegal. President Grant signed an executive order prohibiting further settlement, but, in a pattern familiar in American history, the whites refused to leave; more came, and in 1875 Grant "formally rescinded the executive order and once again officially opened the Wallowa region to white settlement" (McCoy 108).

In May 1877, the government sent General O. O. Howard, known to the Nez Perce as "Arm-Cut" or "Armless" (Aoki 1979, 115),[71] to meet with Joseph to order him and his band onto a small reservation at Fort Lapwai in what is now Idaho by June 15. Recognizing that military resistance could not succeed, Joseph reluctantly agreed to take his People to Lapwai. But on June 12 or 13, as preparations for the move were under way, three young men of Chief White Bird's band, partly in revenge for family members murdered by whites, killed five settlers and wounded another.[72] Nonetheless, Joseph took his band to Whitebird Canyon so that they might collect their stock for the trip to the reservation that he still intended to make. Howard, however, on hearing of the outbreak—for which he mistakenly blamed Joseph[73]—ordered two troops of the First Cavalry, civilian volunteers, and a number of the treaty Nez Perce, under the command of Captains David Perry and Joel Trimble to march from Fort Lapwai to force the Indians onto the reservation. When the soldiers reached Whitebird Canyon they attacked, and what came to be called the "Nez Perce War" was under way. Because the soldiers' first attack did not go well, Howard himself soon rode into action, and it was not long before the "war" began also to be called the "Retreat" or the "Flight of the Nez Perce" as Joseph first led his People to join the Crows in Montana, and then attempted to seek refuge in Canada, "Grandmother's Land," or "Old Woman's Country," ruled by Queen Victoria, where Sitting Bull and his People had earlier settled.

After several unsuccessful battles against the Indians, Howard ordered General Nelson Miles to march west from Fort Keogh to reinforce his own command. Miles attacked Joseph's band at Snake Creek on the northern end of the Bear Paw Mountains on the last day of September 1877, ran off the Indians' horses, and besieged the camp. On October 5, Joseph "surrendered" to Howard and to Miles. It was at that time that Joseph is said to have delivered an elegiac farewell speech that was widely reproduced in his own lifetime (Joseph died in 1904), and that has continued to be printed and cited to the present.[74] Before examining the speech, let me first return to the words I have enclosed in quotation marks above—which I will, for the most part, omit from this point forward—war, retreat, flight, and surrender.

In an essay published in 1964, Merle B. Wells observes that "those who interpret the Nez Perce War in terms of a United States Army campaign have all too frequently presented a military picture which distorts Indian

Figure 8. Chief Joseph, Nez Perce, before 1877. National Archives and Records Administration.

operations during that conflict" (35). Wells notes Joseph's reluctant but determined decision to move onto the reservation before he was attacked by the forces Howard sent to Whitebird Canyon, and he makes clear that Joseph later concluded hostilities with exactly the same goal in mind, to settle his People at Lapwai. In regard to the so-called retreat or flight over the Lolo Trail, Wells explains that rather than retreating or fleeing, the

Indians were engaged more nearly in "an exodus in which [they]...were bringing along their women and children" (36). The biblical reference is misleading, but Wells's point is that the movement of the Indians essentially "resembled a traditional hunting expedition to the buffalo country" (36).[75] When it became clear to these Nez Perce people "that they would not be permitted to settle down peacefully with the Crows...they headed north, hoping to cross the Canadian border." In doing this, Wells writes, "they were not engaged in a military campaign, nor were they retreating; they were simply leaving a hostile area" (36).[76] Wells notes that when Joseph and Howard reached the agreement to end the fighting (which we will consider just below), "those Indians who wanted to settle in Canada continued on their way" while those "who wished to live in the United States turned back with Joseph" (36).[77]

The agreement to end the fighting, Wells explains, was in no way a surrender, nor could General Miles—Howard allowed Miles to accept the official "surrender"—"have succeeded in explaining the white man's notion of a military surrender" to the Nez Perce even had he wished to do so. "In any event, Joseph had no army to surrender and no authority to make other Nez Perce warriors come to any agreement or terms" (Wells 37). Indeed, he had on several prior occasions failed to persuade the tribal council—consistently the decision-making body for these Nimipu bands—to cease fighting. By October 5, 1877, however, with the leaders Looking Glass, Toohoolhoolzote, and Joseph's younger brother Ollokot having been killed, Joseph's view at last prevailed. Yellow Wolf, a warrior who was with Joseph's band, says in his account of these events published a great many years later in 1940, that when Captain John and Old George,[78] two treaty Indians serving Miles and Howard, appeared with a white flag, saying: "'Those generals said tell you: 'We will have no more fighting.... We will have no more war!'" (Yellow Wolf 223–24) final negotiations for the termination of hostilities proceeded quickly. As Alvin Josephy has explained, that the generals could be seen as calling for an end to the fighting was "a significant point to the Indians." They could now accept Joseph's repeated recommendations to end hostilities *not* as a defeat, but simply as "agreeing with Miles and Howard to end the fighting" (Josephy 1965, 628).

Yellow Wolf did not mention Joseph delivering a speech as he presented his rifle to Miles.[79] Only two men ever did report actually having heard such a speech—some 150 words long in English, with different versions giving slightly different word counts—and only one man ever claimed to have written it down on the spot. Joseph himself later said that he spoke only a single sentence to Miles—we have versions of that sentence ranging from eleven to fifteen English words—and there are some eyewitness accounts to corroborate this brief communication.

Work by George Venn, expanding on earlier work by Mark H. Brown and Haruo Aoki, makes it quite certain that there was no longer speech by Joseph at the "surrender," and that the various texts are the work of General Howard's adjutant and aide-de-camp, Lieutenant Charles Erskine Scott Wood. In Wood's fullest account of how he obtained the text of the speech[80]—an account that appeared in 1936, almost sixty years after the event itself!—he states that he was present as Joseph handed his rifle to Miles, "standing very close to Howard, with a pencil and paper pad which I always carried at such times, ready for any dictation that might be given" (qtd. in Fee 329). With the interpreter Arthur ("Ad") Chapman translating, Wood says: "Joseph again addressed himself to General Howard" (qtd. in Fee 329–30) and delivered the speech, a version of which I give in the appendix. Wood's account is corroborated by Howard himself, who, in his official report to the secretary of war for 1876–77, wrote that the "*reply* of Joseph was taken verbatim on the spot by Lieutenant Wood, Twenty-first Infantry, my acting aide-de-camp and acting adjutant general, and it is the only report that was ever made of Joseph's *reply*" (630–31; my emphasis), What Howard calls Joseph's "reply" appears in his report, as we will note further, exactly as Wood had reported it.[81] Wood's 1936 account, however, was by no means the last time he would attribute a speech to Joseph; neither was Howard's *Report* the first to publish such a speech.

The first publication of the surrender speech ascribed to Joseph was in the *Bismarck* [Dakota Territory] *Tri-Weekly Tribune* for October 26, 1877, in an article titled "Joseph's Speech in Full." The *Tribune* reported that its text was provided by "one of the officers of the steamer Silver City, arriving today" (qtd. in Aoki 1989, 17). That officer was not named. Haruo Aoki (1989), on the basis of a conjecture by Merle Wells, speculated it was probably Lieutenant Wood himself. George Venn, however, points out that Wood and General Howard had passed through Bismarck four days earlier, and that Thomas Sutherland, a reporter from the Portland, Oregon, *Standard,* who had followed the campaign, "is the likely courier here" ("Brief Chronology" n.p. [hereafter cited as BC]), passing along a copy of the speech given him by Wood.[82] Sutherland's "leaking" of the speech, Venn writes, was "remembered...fifty eight years later" by John Rea, a *Bismarck* reporter. But Rea recalled it as a "reply" or a *message* sent by Joseph to Howard before the actual "surrender," "not a face-to-face oration" (Venn, BC)

The text next appeared, also without attribution, "in a story signed by Sutherland" (Venn, BC) in the Chicago paper *The Inter-Ocean* for November 9, 1877. Venn writes that the account as presented here "seems to be the earliest [description of a] face-to-face delivery by Joseph directly to General Howard, a context not used again by Wood until his 1893 version" (BC) in an article for the *Century Magazine*. Wood is identified as the source of the speech for the first time on November 16 in the *New York Times,* in an article titled "General Howard and Chief Joseph: Speech of the Indian Chief in Surrendering to Gen. Miles." Venn speculates that Wood had given this version "to the Washington press while he [was in Washington] lobbying for Howard" (BC), and that the story had been sent out on the wire, from which it was picked up by the *Times*. Inasmuch as Wood was "lobbying" to establish the fact that Howard had been importantly involved in the "surrender," he would have been pleased by the *Times*'s linkage of Joseph and Howard, although less pleased by the *Times*'s reminder that the surrender had indeed been to Miles (although the speech is obviously addressed to Howard, not Miles).

Wood was next identified as the source of the speech in Sutherland's paper, the Portland *Daily Standard* for December 4, 1877 (Venn, BC). Howard's *Annual Report to the Secretary of War, 1876–77* appeared on December 26, 1877, and it would have been the third source—and a particularly authoritative one[83]—to identify Wood as the man who had "taken" down Joseph's words to Howard, leaving unclear whether those words were a speech by Joseph or a message sent by Joseph through Captain John. Colonel Mark Brown was probably the first researcher to examine the original pencil draft of Howard's report, and in a 1967 publication he noted that it is "in the handwriting of two persons, apparently Howard and Wood" (407). But Joseph's speech did not appear in the draft in the place it would later appear in the published version. Instead, Brown found the words "Here insert Joseph's reply to the demand for surrender" written in the margins (407). Brown states that "Joseph's reply" was indeed inserted at some point and that it is "in Wood's handwriting" (407). But he also says that "Joseph's reply does *not* appear in this draft" (407; my emphasis)—again, that there are only the instructions to insert it. Venn's work makes clear that Brown is mistaken in the former assertion—although both Wood "and General Howard collaborated on the writing and revising of this official document" (BC)—but correct in the latter. This is to say that Wood had simply marked "the place for the printer to add the text" (Venn, BC)—which he later did. Thus, the speech does *not* appear in the pencil draft of the *Report* in anyone's *handwriting*.

Jerome Greene noted that "Captain John was identified by Lieutenant Wood as the speaker [of the message sent by Joseph] in *Harper's Weekly*, November 17, 1877" (484 n. 105). Wood repeated this version—message/reply, no speech—in his "Chief Joseph, the Nez Perce," which appeared in the *Century Magazine* in 1884. There he describes the presence in Joseph's camp of the two treaty Indians we encountered earlier, Old George and Captain John. Wood writes that "Joseph asked [the two] if he would be allowed to return to Idaho. He was told that he would, unless higher authority ordered otherwise" (Wood 1884, 141). Without any transition, the next paragraph begins: "Then old 'Captain John' brought this reply (and his lips quivered and his eyes filled with tears as he delivered the words of his chief)" (141).[84] The text Wood gives here is very close to the earlier texts he had provided, but, to repeat, now Joseph's words clearly do not come from a *speech* he delivered to Howard, but rather from a *reply* or a *message* sent to Howard via Captain John.[85]

Wood continued to provide a number of different texts for the Joseph speech or message over the years; Venn counts no fewer than nineteen versions between 1877 and 1939! The last published in Wood's lifetime appeared as an appendix to Chester Fee's work cited above.[86] Wood acknowledged that this final text was no more than a reconstruction from distant memory; for a more accurate accounting, he directed the reader to an article he "wrote for a Chicago newspaper," and also an "article [he] later wrote for the *Century Magazine*" (qtd. in Fee 331). Venn points out that this only further confuses matters, because, among other things, "there's no comparable speech in his Chicago newspaper article" (BC), and because there are two *Century* articles: the one Wood wrote in 1884, calling the speech a *message;* and the other, as I noted, published in 1893, in which

Wood returned to the face-to-face version he would in the future seek to sustain, of an actual *speech*.

At this point in time there seems no doubt that all of the texts of the longer speech derive from Lieutenant Wood; the words are his.[87] But are they based on anything Joseph said to Howard on October 5, 1877, or sent to Howard earlier? The answer would seem to be no—although Aoki concluded: "It is not likely but it is *possible* that something like the long text was given as a message by Joseph" (1989, 21; my emphasis).[88] But even if the words did not come earlier from Joseph, could it be that some of them came from him later, so that although the text is Wood's, some of the content is Joseph's? It is not possible to say. Venn believes that Wood did indeed get a number of the details of the speech from two interviews he conducted with Joseph, the first taking place "immediately after the 'surrender,' when Howard turned Joseph over to Wood as a POW ... in a private tent with Chapman [the translator] present," and the second taking place "some days later" (personal communication, July 6, 2010). But we don't know what Joseph said or how Chapman rendered his words.

Chapman, the translator, was an interesting fellow. Married to a Umatilla woman, he "spoke Nez Perce" (Aoki 1979, 98) and had served as a scout and interpreter for General Howard.[89] In the 1960s, when Aoki interviewed Mrs. Agnes Moses, who, as I've noted, was nine years old in 1877, she remembered Chapman as "'just a white man'"—that is to say, someone "without a shred of authority" (Aoki 1979, 112). Nonetheless, it was Mrs. Moses's view that Chapman was himself specifically responsible for the Chief Joseph "War" because it began as a consequence of his having had three Indians hanged (Aoki 1979, 98). Edward Curtis gives a different account of the matter, but one that also blames Chapman for bringing on the war. Calling Chapman "a hot-headed settler leading [Captain Perry's] volunteers" (8: 26), Curtis cites the Nez Perce warrior Three Eagles, who recounts that early on, Joseph and his brother Ollokot (Curtis spells this Alokut) saw a treaty Nez Perce whom they knew, Jonah Hayes, begin to ride toward them. Surmising that his intention was to see if some peaceful arrangement might be worked out, they sent two of their men toward him. But Chapman fired at the two. Three Eagles stated that "if Chapman had not fired, Jonah Hayes would have come and talked with Joseph, *and the whole war would have been avoided*" (qtd. in E. Curtis 8: 26n; my emphasis).

Speaking in her own language—Chief Joseph's language—Mrs. Moses, Aoki wrote, "characterizes Chapman most succinctly in one word, pexu uye 'thief'" (1979, 112). Ruth Bordin, the editor of L. V. McWhorter's *Hear Me, My Chiefs*,[90] remarks of Chapman that "to the Nez Perces [*sic*] he was known as a coward and a bad man who had given them nothing but trouble, and was not thought of as a friend" (496). Yellow Wolf, in contrast, recalled that Chapman had lived with his "uncle, Old Yellow Wolf...in the same house, just as brothers" (55). While it is fairly certain that Chapman understood and spoke the Nez Perce language—just how well is impossible to say—many Nimipu would have had doubts about the trustworthiness of any interpretation he offered. Because there do not seem to be any surviving notes or records of translations Chapman made either of a message from Joseph (unlikely but possible) or of interviews between Wood and Joseph, there is no way to judge the accuracy of anything he might have reported.

There are also no notes for Chapman's translation of the interview Joseph later gave in Washington, D.C., that was published in the *North American Review* in 1879 under the title "An Indian's View of Indian Affairs," in which Joseph confirmed that he had indeed spoken a single sentence to Miles. Of the article as a whole, Bordin wrote that it "was the opinion of Mr. McWhorter that [it] was in all probability highly edited" (McWhorter 502–3), and that "in the Nez Perce tradition of oral history, Joseph would not have spoken as the article reads" (503). But Chapman himself had made exactly this point in a letter to Howard in which he stated that the published article was "nothing more like [Joseph's] statement than day is like dark!" (qtd. in Venn 2005, 61). This is because the text had indeed "been extensively revised by A[lbert] B[enjamin] Meacham and others" (61). But did Joseph actually deliver the single sentence communication to which he testified in that publication?

The earliest version of the communication appeared in the *Chicago Times* on the same date as the longer speech appeared in the Bismarck paper: October 26, 1877. It comes again from C. E. S. Wood, and it has Joseph saying: "From where the sun stands, forever and ever, I will never fight again" (qtd. in Aoki 1989, 18). The second text, apparently authorized by Joseph himself, appeared, as I have said, in his *North American Review* article of 1879. It reads: "From where the sun now stands I will fight no more" (qtd. in Aoki 1989, 18; qtd. in Moquin and Van Doren 249). The next two texts of the brief speech are given in two memoirs by General Miles, his *Personal Recollections,* published in 1896, and *Serving the Republic,* published in 1911 (Aoki 1989, 18). In the former, Miles writes: "As Joseph was about to hand his rifle to me he raised his eyes toward the sun which then stood at about ten o'clock,[91] and said, 'From where the sun now stands, I fight no more against the white man'" (1896, 275). In Miles's later memoir Joseph's words are nearly the same: "From where the sun now stands, I will fight no more against the white man" (1911, 175). The final text of this brief address "appears in an unpublished letter dated January 31, 1936, from Wood to Lucullus Virgil McWhorter" (Aoki 1989, 18). In it, Wood told McWhorter that Joseph's words were "From where the sun now stands Joseph will fight no more forever" (qtd. in Aoki 1989, 18). It is, as I have said, possible that Joseph did speak some version of these few words to General Miles[92]— Aoki (1989) mentions eyewitnesses other than Miles who claimed to have heard Joseph speak briefly, as he himself had (apparently) affirmed—and that Chapman had translated these words in 1877 and again in 1879. Even so, there is not much one can say about them as elegiac expression.

What of the longer speech? Although it was Wood's creation, he almost surely based some of it on interviews conducted with Joseph, as I have noted. Mrs. Wilson thought the speech worth back-translating into Nimipu; she used Haines's 1955 English text (Aoki 1979 123; this comes from the 1939 letter to Lyman). She begins with an equivalent of "Tell Howard I know...his heart" (qtd. in Aoki 1979, 123), and continues with Joseph remarking the loss of his peers Looking Glass and Ta-hool-hool-shute (various spellings), as well as the one who led the young men. Nez Perce people traditionally avoided speaking the names of the dead,[93] so it is unlikely that Joseph would have named Looking Glass and Ta-hool-hool-shute. If he referred to them, he would have said something like what he is reported to have said of his brother Ollokot; he would *not,* that is, have named them but instead referred to them in terms of their roles, just as he refers to Ollokot as "he who leads the young men" (more accurately, "who *led* the young men").

Mrs. Wilson translates Joseph's deep concern for the desperate state of his People. She also translates the well-known address "Hear me, my chiefs," although that must come entirely from Wood. No message Joseph might have sent would have been heard by other chiefs, nor would any of the few surviving chiefs have been present later when Joseph spoke to Wood.[94] The words "From where the sun now stands I will fight no more forever" with which the farewell concludes may well repeat what Joseph himself reported having said to Miles as he tendered him his rifle.

Mrs. Wilson might well have been attracted to the speech because it had won wide renown and, regardless of the specifics of its production, was a text of which the Nez Perce could be proud (cf. Slickpoo 193). Just as Jefferson wanted Logan's message to be a speech, so, too, did Lieutenant Wood ultimately want Joseph's message—if indeed there was one—to be a speech. The soldier and the poet in Woods, as Venn has argued (2005), were at odds, and by the time the "Nez Perce War" ended, it seems clear that Wood had fully identified with his poetic side. In his biography of his father, Erskine Wood quotes lines his father had written some fifty years after his service in the Indian wars—"Though in my youth, I, stupid, fought, / wearing the livery of the State" (105)—as an introduction to the fact that his father developed a friendship with Joseph and worked to have his People returned to the Northwest from Indian Territory. Noble redmen make noble speeches, and noble speeches from Jefferson's time to our own testify to the "genius" and nobility of the speaker—especially when he "tragically" yields and bids the world farewell.

So much for Lieutenant Wood. But there is almost nothing to say about Chief Joseph's "farewell" as an example of Native American elegiac oratory. Perhaps some of the details did come from Joseph; nonetheless, the speech as we have it in all its versions sheds no light on Nimipu response to grief and loss.

Logan, Black Hawk, Cochise, Sealth, Joseph: all "chiefs" who said farewell in celebrated (Logan, Sealth, Joseph) or at least frequently quoted (Black Hawk and Cochise) speeches. Logan almost surely communicated with General John Gibson at the conclusion of Lord Dunmore's War in 1774, but it is not possible today to determine the differences between what he may have told Gibson to take as a *message* to Dunmore and the *speech* Thomas Jefferson lauded as comparable to those of the classical orators. For Jefferson and his audience, this was, in David Murray's phrase, "the renunciation of power by a nobility" (36) whose day had passed.

The earliest text of Black Hawk's farewell speech appears two years after he is said to have delivered it, published in a wide-ranging history of Native Americans by Samuel Drake in 1834. Drake, as we have seen, contextualizes it ambiguously and does not provide a source. He seems to suggest that Black Hawk delivered the speech on his surrender to General Street in late summer of 1832, although the very thorough transcript of that occasion does *not* record a speech by Black Hawk. Black Hawk's broad concern for the People's welfare expressed in the speech printed by Drake is nonetheless consistent with traditional Native American elegiac expression, as is his enunciation of a warrior's pride in having fought for the People. But there is no way to know whether these words actually came from Black Hawk, or, if they did, when or where he spoke them.

The two very different farewell speeches attributed to Cochise are based on addresses he almost surely gave on two separate occasions in his own language, each with—very likely—an adequate translation into Spanish that would have readily been rendered into English. But the men who published these speeches did so a great many years after they claimed to have heard them, nor were they very specific about how they arrived at the texts they offered. I have tried to show that each of these speeches contains thoughts and sentiments we may reasonably attribute to Cochise, as well as others that are very unlikely to have come from him.

After much reflection, it seemed to me reasonable to conclude that the lengthy speech Dr. Henry Smith attributed to Sealth and published in 1887—also a great many years after Sealth is said to have spoken—had a great deal in it that probably came from Sealth himself, speaking on two separate occasions. Sealth's speech differs from the vast majority of Native elegiac expression in that it does not offer means by which the People might live. Much of what he said, however, accurately represents the way in which the People had lived, and, perhaps as Black Hawk intended in his autobiography, the symbolic act of telling these things in some detail might yet be a way to keep those lifeways alive.

Chief Joseph's brief farewell "speech" is also possibly a *message* Joseph sent to General O. O. Howard, agreeing to end hostilities between his nontreaty band and the U.S. Army, including a single sentence Joseph may have spoken to Howard at the time of his actual "surrender" to General Nelson Miles on October 5, 1877. Far more likely, however, is that both speeches are entirely the creation of Lieutenant C. E. S. Wood. It is he who provides us with these noble words of a noble Indian to mark the tragic passing of his People. If Joseph did say anything that expressed a traditional Nimipu sense of the events that had transpired, it has not come across in the speech Wood has given us.

Because all of the speeches considered above have appeared in garbled, confused, and erroneous versions, with the circumstances and dates of their presumed delivery and publication regularly mistaken—I spare the reader what I could easily provide, lengthy notes documenting these many errors—I offer an appendix containing the "best," that is to say, the most accurate texts we have, along with a summary of the contexts of their production.

3

AUTHORS AND WRITERS

Black Hawk's *Life*

> I stood upon the ashes of my home, where my own wigwam had sent up its fires to the Great Spirit; where I summoned the spirits of the braves who had fallen in their vain attempt to protect their homes from the grasping invaders. And, as I snuffed up the smell of their blood from the earth, I swore eternal hatred—the hatred of the avenger.
> Tecumseh in 1812, after the Battle of Tippecanoe (Armstrong 53)

> The Indians are remarkable for the reverence they entertain for the sepulchres of their kindred.
> Washington Irving, "Traits of Indian Character" (1996b [1814], 243)

In the previous chapter I examined the August 1832 surrender speech attributed to Black Hawk by Samuel Drake in which Black Hawk apparently acknowledged that his "plans" to "save" his nation were "stopped": "He can do no more. He is near his end. His sun is setting, and he will rise no more. Farewell to Black-hawk" (Drake 155). But that moment of defeat was not at all the "end" of Black Hawk. After his imprisonment, his meeting with President Andrew Jackson, his trip through the East, and then, following further confinement, his return to his exiled people, Black Hawk worked with the government interpreter for the Sacs and Fox, Antoine LeClaire, to produce a life history that was edited by a young newspaperman named John Barton Patterson and published in Cincinnati in 1833. Black Hawk thus contributed to the production of the first Indian autobiography, which I earlier (1985) defined as a genre consisting of original, bicultural, composite composition: a text produced by an Indian subject named in the title in collaboration with a translator and an editor who is ultimately responsible for the published English text. Black Hawk was not, of course, a Native American *writer*, but he may nonetheless be placed among the earliest Native American *authors*, as his autobiography appeared just four years after the first full-fledged autobiography by an Indian,[1] *A Son of the Forest* (1829) by the Reverend William Apess, a Pequot. (We will examine elegiac work by Apess below.)

About two-thirds of the way through his story, Black Hawk tells of a highly charged encounter with Major General Edmund Gaines of the U.S. Army. Exasperated as a result of Black Hawk's unwillingness to depart the village he understands the Sauks to have sold, Gaines, "apparently angry, rose and said:—'Who is *Black Hawk*? Who is *Black Hawk*?'" Black Hawk responds: "'I am a *Sac!* My forefather was a SAC! And all the nations call me a SAC'" (2008, 65).[2]

This is a classic Native American mode of self-identification, what I have elsewhere called the "synecdochic" mode, in which one's identity is foremost a matter of the larger whole or collectivity to which one belongs.[3] Jace Weaver has referred to this form of identity as an "I-am-we" construction of the self (43); it is very different from the modern, Western self with its egoistic sense of unique and bounded individuality. I argue first that the story Black Hawk sought to tell in his autobiography is the story of what it means to be a Sauk—that is, it is a national rather than a personal story, expressing a "communitist" (Weaver 303) rather than an individualist identity.[4] My further argument is that Black Hawk tells his story—his People's story—so that the People might live; its elegiac aspects—what might appear to be grief for the loss of times that are gone—are consistent with traditional Native American elegiac expression: that is to say, they tell of what is lost as a form of narrative symbolic action functioning in the interest of its recovery. This is the sort of "melancholic mourning" (Ramazani xi) I have remarked earlier that will not quite release the past so that it may be included in any possible future.

What it means to live as a Sauk is to work the land and hunt its animals, to perform the appointed feasts and ceremonies, to make war on traditional enemies like the Osages and Cherokees, to conduct relations with traditional friends like the Potawatomis, to bury and to honor the dead properly, and to narrate the old stories and legends. Black Hawk's most sustained account of what the title page of the *Life* calls the "manners and customs" of the Sauk appears roughly in the middle of the book, occupying some six pages in J. Gerald Kennedy's edition. Here Black Hawk recounts the powerful myths of the coming of corn, beans, and tobacco to the Sauk and tells of the Great Swan spirit of Rock Island. He details the seasonal practices of the planting and harvesting of corn, of ball games involving no less than three hundred to five hundred people on a side, and of the Sauk lead mines worked by older people. He mentions what he calls "a great *medicine feast*" and then a "*crane* dance," in which the women join after they have planted corn (47). There is also what he calls "our *national* dance" (48).

Because the Sauk had by this time been enmeshed in a global capitalist economy for some 150 years, Black Hawk also mentions negotiations with white traders before his People, in the later fall, go out to hunt for skins. "Near the close of winter," Black Hawk recounts, the "young men...start on the beaver hunt; others to hunt raccoons and muskrats—and the remainder of our people go to the sugar camps to make sugar" (51). In the middle of these rich descriptions, Black Hawk suddenly says: "But I am digressing from my story" (46). I suspect these words may more nearly be Patterson's than Black Hawk's, and indicative of Patterson's predominant interest in the history of Sauk-white relations. Black Hawk will go on to tell us much about those relations, but not before he continues with what is centrally his story, the story of what it means to be a Sauk.[5]

To be a Sauk for Black Hawk is also to possess with honor and pass on to the next generation the medicine bundle that is the "soul," and the heart of Sauk national identity. Indeed, stories about receiving and passing down the medicine bundle structure Black Hawk's story, for he opens by narrating an account of the first historical passing of the great medicine bundle, and he closes—despite a number of odd interpolations—by relating his attempt to retrieve it after his defeat. I believe that Black Hawk did indeed retrieve it, and that near the end of his life he would have continued the story of what it means to be a Sauk by passing the medicine bundle on to his son, that the People might live. This is a matter to which I will return.

The story with which Black Hawk begins references "the *tradition* given me by my father, Pye-sa" (9; my emphasis), a Sauk oral history that relates the origin of the Sauks in the area of present-day Montreal, in the time of his great-grandfather, Na-na-ma-kee or Thunder. Na-na-ma-kee, inspired by the Great Spirit, blackened his face and fasted with the expectation that "he should see a *white man* who would be to him as a father" (9). Just as Na-na-ma-kee had been ceremonially dreaming of this meeting, so, too had the white man "been dreaming for four years" (9); so, too, was it that the white man "remained four days" (11) with the Indians. Four is the pattern number of the Sauks, as it is of many Native nations; thus in his preparatory dreaming and in the length of his stay, the white father is said to have behaved just as Sauk historiography would expect him to behave.

Upon Na-na-ma-kee's return to his nation, his father, Muk-a-ta-quet, prepares a dog feast. When this is completed, he confers his powers on Na-na-ma-kee and presents him with "the great medicine bag." He tells him that it "is the soul of our nation—it has never been disgraced—and I will expect you to keep it unsullied" (11)—words Black Hawk will echo. Only a little later, Black Hawk speaks of having "made a *dog feast,* preparatory to leaving my camp with a large party." Before "my braves commenced feasting," he says, "I took my *medicine bags* and addressed them [his braves] in the following language": we then get a set speech, in which he rehearses the lineage of the medicine bags, passed from Muk-a-ta-quet, "the father of the Sac nation," to "the great war chief of our nation, Na-na-ma-kee" (80). All of his followers would know that Black Hawk himself "fell heir to the great *medicine bag* of his forefathers" upon his father's death from wounds suffered in battle with the Cherokees. When this ceremonial feast has been completed, Black Hawk leads his warriors west, toward the sunset, "following my great medicine bags" (15).

After the dog feast to celebrate the passing of the medicine bag from Muk-a-ta-quet to Na-na-ma-kee, Black Hawk tells us of some "dissension," "in consequence of so much power being given to Na-na-ma-kee," on account of his youth (11). To allay such concerns, Na-na-ma-kee demonstrates some of the weather control powers often possessed by shamans and prophets: he brings on a thunderstorm, and lightning from the storm strikes a tree and sets it aflame. Black Hawk himself may have witnessed demonstrations of this sort by the Shawnee prophet, Tenskwatawa, and the Potawatomi shaman, Main Poc. I consider them and some other contemporary men of power briefly here to fill out the religious context of Black Hawk's world.

Tenskwatawa, the twin or younger brother of the great Tecumseh, was known in his youth as Lalawethika, the Rattle or Noise-Maker (Edmunds 1985, 28), perhaps as a consequence of his affinity for alcohol. Early in 1805, Lalawethika dreamed an encounter with the Master of Life, after which he took the name Tenskwatawa, the Open Door, to proclaim his intention to lead his People through to a happier existence. Another prophet known to Black Hawk was the Potawatomi Main Poc, "the most significant" prophet among the Sauks according to Patrick Jung (25). Known among his People as "Wenebeset (Crafty One)" (Edmunds 1978, 166), Main Poc, whose name R. David Edmunds translates as "Crippled Hand" (1985, 260) or "Withered Hand" (1978, 166), was born "without a thumb or fingers on his left hand" (1983, 65). In the 1790s, he "led large war parties" that included "Sacs and Foxes against the Osages," and his warriors "cut a large swath of destruction against American settlements in southern Illinois" (1985, 261). Determined to resist the invasions of the Americans, he allied his People with Tenskwatawa and his brother, Tecumseh, to fight them on several occasions before and during the War of 1812. Main Poc's particular power was that of "*wabeno* or fire handler" (1983, 65), and among the fire handler's powers was the ability to "bring about changes in the weather" (1985, 259).[6]

It's also possible that Black Hawk was aware of or had contact with the Creek prophet, Hillis Hadjo (*hilis,* "medicine"; *hadsho,* "crazy"), also known as Josiah Francis or Francis the Prophet (ca. 1770–1819). Hadjo had been taught by another prophet named Seekaboo, a follower of Tecumseh and Tenskwatawa, who may have been a Shawnee or perhaps a Creek himself (Edmunds 1983; Cave 141). Hadjo was, like Black Hawk, a strong supporter of the British in the War of 1812, even traveling to England after the Treaty of Ghent (1814) to try to secure their further help. Tecumseh's mother—and perhaps (surely if they were twins) Tenskwatawa's as well—was Creek. It also seems likely that Black Hawk knew the Kickapoo prophet, Kenekuk, who had been inspired by Tenskwatawa. When his People ceded their lands in 1819—something like half of Illinois!—Kenekuk urged that they not remove, but remain, abstaining from alcohol, and worshipping with prayer sticks innovated by Kenekuk himself (see Forsyth 2: 280ff.; Cave 224–43). He did not actively support the Black Hawk War, but he did offer "refuge to some of Black Hawk's people" (Cave 236). For a time, some of the Potawatomis of Michigan (Black Hawk was allied with Potawatomis nearer to his People) also accepted Kenekuk's teaching. When Kenekuk's Kickapoo band was removed to Kansas, he went with them as chief. Active in these years as well was the Ottawa prophet, Maya-Ga-Wy, also called Le Magouis (or Magovis) and known as The Trout. Initially noted around Mackinac, Michigan, he later moved to the area of present-day Peoria, Illinois. A long speech of his, echoing the doctrines of earlier prophets like his fellow Ottawa Pontiac and the Delaware prophet, Neolin, appeared in *Fraser's Magazine* for April 1836.

Black Hawk knew some of these Algonquian (and at least one Muscogean) religious resisters to the Americans east of the Mississippi from early in the nineteenth century onward, and he may have heard of others. In any case, it seems clear that he was attracted to and impressed by these men with powers greater than any he could claim. Gregory Dowd's discussion of this period, for example, includes the Seneca Handsome Lake, of whom he writes: "Handsome Lake's first set of visions and teachings conforms to the pattern of northwestern [the old Northwest] prophecy, so well...as to suggest an unstudied depth of common understanding, and thus, of communication, among the different peoples" (124).[7]

We know that Black Hawk was much influenced by the "Winnebago prophet," Wabokieshiek, whose predictions of British and Potawatomi aid for Black Hawk's cause were badly mistaken. What particular powers he may have had are not clear. As Anthony F. C. Wallace wrote, "Little is known of his teachings except that he seems to have preached a return to moral purity among the Indians, and to have had various apocalyptic visions" (1982, 281). His encouragement of Black Hawk's resistance put him in disrepute in Black Hawk's time, and our own time has not restored his reputation.

After his travels through the east, Black Hawk, upon returning to his People, spoke of two pressing concerns. First, that upon his death he might be buried in the graveyard where his relatives lay, and, second, that for the time remaining to him, he might continue to possess the medicine bag of his forefathers. To attend to the first matter, Black Hawk pays a visit to a white trader, of whom he asks "permission to be buried in the graveyard at our village, among my old friends and warriors." Upon obtaining such permission, he pronounces himself "satisfied" (68).

Next he must reclaim his medicine bag. It was just before the final campaign of the war that Black Hawk, knowing that he must soon surrender, had entrusted the bag to one of the chiefs of the Winnebago. He had told him that the medicine bag was "the soul of the Sac nation—that it had never been dishonored in any battle—[and that] it is dearer than life" (86). The Winnebago chief "said he would keep it, and take care of it, and if [Black Hawk] was suffered to live, he would send it to [him]" (86). Apparently with Black Hawk's approval, the Winnebago chief gave the medicine bag for safekeeping to the Indian agent, General J. M. Street. It is to Street that Black Hawk appeals for the medicine bag, telling him that he "was anxious to get it, that I might hand it down to my nation unsullied" (94). Black Hawk says nothing further about this, and I assume that Street did indeed return the medicine bag to him. I further assume that Black Hawk, before his death in 1838, passed the medicine bag to his son, Nasheaskuk or Whirling Thunder. Passing the medicine bundle on to the next generation, as I've said, is an important part of what it means to be a Sauk.

I would also speculate that Black Hawk very likely did say he intended to hand it down "to my *nation*" (94; my emphasis). Although the possessor of a medicine bundle would usually pass it on to a son or another relative, this is not strictly a family affair. Rather, caring for, honoring, and passing on the medicine bag to the next generation is important for the ongoing vitality of the People, of the Sauk Nation.[8] M. R. Harrington, for example, transcribed a story told by a man named Mecabekwa of the coming of the first medicine bundle to the Sauks. Mecabekwa concluded that story with the observation that the progressive Sauk chief Keokuk's medicine bundle "has never been taken care of as it should have been, since he died. We [the Sac tribe] are now suffering from the effects of this neglect" (1914, 155).[9] What Black Hawk asserted to General Gaines years ago remains true to the end: he is first and foremost a Sauk, one of the People, whose collective, national life he works to sustain both by proper care of the medicine bundles and by telling the stories—by telling *this* story.

When Patterson includes an extended account by Black Hawk of the traditional life of his People, he has him say of it, "But I am digressing from my story" (46)—that is to say, the story of Sauk-white relations. Patterson also has Black Hawk mourning traditional Sauk lifeways in a language apparently resigned to its demise. Reflecting on his rich descriptions of tribal life, he exclaims: "But these are the times that were!" (51); earlier he had said: "Now we are as miserable as the howling, hungry wolf in the prairie" (46). These words—especially in relation to the surrender speech he was said to have delivered—might well be taken as an instance of what W. David Shaw, in a study of Western elegiac expression, called "apocalyptic" elegy, "a lament not just for a dead person, but for the passing of a world" (155). But in the same way as several recent critics have judged the *Life*'s final words of "friendship" and "peace" to come from Patterson rather than from Black Hawk himself,[10] and just as I have taken the categorization of Black Hawk's recollections of the traditional and ceremonial life of his People as a "digression" also to come from Patterson, so, too, do I suspect that the lament for irrecoverable "times that were" is also more likely Patterson's than Black Hawk's.

Or if it did indeed come from Black Hawk,[11] we nonetheless can read it in the framework of Native American elegiac expression. From this perspective, as we have seen in other instances, such as the Ghost Dance songs, the elegiac lament for "the times that were" does not presume that those times are gone for good. Loss of persons and of lifeways threatens the community; one cannot help but deeply grieve. But the life of the People must continue. Traditional Native American elegiac expression offers an active and dynamic consolation that is directed toward the People's recuperation and restoration. The processes we have seen at work in the Iroquois Condolence Rites, in the Tlingit *koo.'eex'* or potlatch, and in many of the Ghost Dance songs of the 1890s are also at work, I am claiming, in Black Hawk's *Life*.

Just as some of the Ghost Dance songs invoked the memory not only of individuals who had passed away but also of traditional practices of various tribal peoples—making camp, gambling, eating certain foods—so, too, does Black Hawk invoke the dances, feasts, traditions, legends, and seasonal activities of his People. Jeffrey Anderson's observation, quoted in chapter 1, that traditional Arapaho rituals concentrated on suffering or "life-negating" conditions in order to "release or discard them for lighter, life-generating movement" (453), may have bearing on Black Hawk's concentration on Sauk lifeways as "times that were." So, too, might Black Hawk's grief that now "we are as miserable as the hungry, howling wolf in the prairie" (46) also work ritually to transvalue present sorrow into "a condition that could be discarded." His lament for his People's lifeways is, again, no digression, nor is it strictly mourning, but, potentially, a symbolic act of recovery.

While there is every likelihood, as his interpreter Antoine LeClaire wrote in his introductory note to the *Life,* that Black Hawk told his story so "that the people of the United States...might know the *causes* that had impelled him to act as he had done, and the *principles* by which he was governed" (n.p.), it is surely time to recognize that Black Hawk also told his story for the Sauk People. If men like Antoine LeClaire could turn Black Hawk's Sauk into English, then others might also turn his English into Sauk, and in times to come, Sauk people might read Black Hawk's words both in English and in Sauk. In this sense, like many a later Indian autobiographer, he leaves his story "for those who come after."[12]

For Black Hawk to speak intensely of the traditional life of the Sauks is an action akin to passing the medicine bundle down to his *nation.* He narrates his life as a Sauk not only to remember it but to re-member it, to make it whole once more in language, in the interest of what Gerald Vizenor has called the continuance and survivance of his People.[13] Black Hawk tells his story as a Sauk for the Sauk, in Jace Weaver's phrase once more, so the People might live. Articulating what Weaver has called "communitist" values, Black Hawk's *Life* "participate[s] in the grief and sense of exile felt by Native communities and the pained individuals in them" (Weaver xiii), and seeks to heal and restore them by narrative means so that they may move beyond defeat and loss. In the manner of Native American elegiac expression generally, to tell of these things is not finally to mourn and consign them to the past, but rather to keep them alive, so the People might live.

Black Elk Speaks

> I am just telling you this, Mr. Neihardt. You know how I felt and what I really wanted to do is for us to make that tree bloom. On this tree we shall prosper. Therefore my children and yours are relative-like and therefore we

shall go back into the hoop and here we'll cooperate and stand as one.... Our families will multiply and prosper after we get this tree to blooming.

Black Elk in *The Sixth Grandfather* (DeMallie 1985, 294)

It was in August 1930 that John G. Neihardt, a poet and Christian visionary from Nebraska, researching material for his projected epic poem, *The Song of the Messiah*[14] (1935), first met a Lakota man in his sixties named Black Elk, in Manderson, South Dakota. All reports of the meeting indicate that the two men were strongly impressed with one another. Neihardt returned the following year, and, with Black Elk's son Ben serving as translator (Black Elk spoke little English), and with Neihardt's daughter Enid serving as stenographic transcriber, Neihardt elicited the material from Black Elk that he would shape into the book called *Black Elk Speaks,* published in 1932. It is the best-known of all Indian autobiographies.[15]

Black Elk Speaks is the life story of a man who, like Black Hawk before him, was a warrior, but unlike Black Hawk, was also a healer and a holy man. In the book, Black Elk recalls having a vision as early as the age of five; a second powerful and detailed vision when he was nine would shape his entire life. He mentioned this vision to no one until his eighteenth year, when he began to hear the Thunder Beings from whom the vision had come urging him to "Make haste" (159). Then, Black Elk says, the "crows in the day and the coyotes at night" called to him: "It is time! It is time!" (159–60). To discover what it is that he is supposed to do, he consults a man named Black Road, who instructs him to "do what the bay horse in your vision wanted you to do. You must do your duty and perform this vision for your people on earth. You must have the horse dance first for the people to see" (161).

Enlisting the help of "Bear Sings...[who] was very old and wise" (162), Black Elk oversees the performance of the extended ceremony that is the Horse Dance. At its conclusion, Black Elk reports Black Road's prayer: "To all of you I offer this pipe that my people may live" (175). Of himself, Black Elk says: "After the horse dance was over I felt very happy, for I could see that my people all were happier" (175). His vision was so the People might live; so, too, will the narration of his life story attempt to sustain the ongoing life of the People.

In the winter of 1881, the year he had had the Horse Dance performed, Black Elk again had visions and heard a voice saying: "Make haste your people need you" (186). Once more he consults with "some very old men who were good and wise." This time, he is instructed by them to "perform the dog vision...to help the people." Because "the people were discouraged and sad," he is to do this "with heyokas, who are sacred fools, doing everything wrong or backwards to make the people laugh" (187). Neihardt includes more detail about the killing and the ceremonial use of dogs in *Black Elk Speaks* than Patterson did in the *Life* of Black Hawk, although not as much detail as Black Elk actually provided.[16] We do learn that during the ceremony the heyokas chase Black Elk and a companion named One Side, "trying to get a piece of the [dog] meat," while "the people rushed to the pot, trying to get a piece of the sacred flesh," because "*ever so little of it would be good for them*" (193; my emphasis).

Later, in his twentieth year,[17] Black Elk has the bison ceremony performed: "This ceremony was not a long one," he says, "but it had great meaning because it made a picture of the relation between the people and the bison, and the power was in the meaning" (206). He also "performed the elk ceremony, as a duty to that part of [his] great vision" (208). As Julian Rice has noted, Black Elk now is invested not only with the black powers of the western Thunder Beings, "making [him] preeminently effective at renewing life in situations of conflict or illness,"[18] but also with the red powers of the East, the powers of *tatanka,* the buffalo bull, "defender and generator of the nation's life" (Rice 13).

All this time, the invading whites increasingly disturb and constrain Black Elk's Oglala People. In the hope that he might "learn some secret of the Wasichu that would help [his] people somehow" (Black Elk 214–15),[19] Black Elk joined Buffalo Bill's Wild West show and toured Europe (see fig. 9). Upon his return home in 1889, he began to hear of the Paiute messiah, Wovoka. Black Elk's "younger brother and sister had died before [he] came home" (234), and soon his father dies as well. This is a time of drought and hunger for Black Elk's People, and, moreover, by now, "all the traditional public rituals of the Lakota religion...were prohibited by the government" (DeMallie 1985, 260). "Our people," says Black Elk, "were pitiful and in despair" (Black Elk 231). Initially skeptical of the idea that dancing and singing could "make the Wasichus disappear and bring back all the bison" (232), Black Elk hears from Good Thunder and Yellow Breast, then from Kicking Bear and Short Bull (we met them earlier), all of whom had traveled west to meet Wovoka, "that...it was all true" (235). It then occurs to him that

Figure 9. Black Elk and Elk in dance costume, 1880. National Anthropological Archives, Smithsonian Institution. INV 506100.

"maybe this sacred man [Wovoka] had had the same vision" as he himself had had; that "maybe [he] was not meant to do this [i.e., restore the People] [him]self" (234). Finally, although the notion that the dead would live again, an aspect of the Ghost Dance almost surely influenced by Christianity, "was not," Black Elk firmly states, "like [his] great vision" (236), he eventually does participate because, as he says, "so much of my vision seemed to be in it" (237). Yet looking back, Black Elk judges his participation in the Ghost Dance to have been an error. He regrets following "the lesser visions that had come to [him] while dancing on Wounded Knee Creek" (249–50), and believes he should have depended instead strictly on his own great vision. In 1904, long after the massacre at Wounded Knee (1890), Black Elk was baptized a Catholic and spent more than thirty years of his life as a Catholic catechist; this, too, he did so that the People might live.[20]

For many years, *Black Elk Speaks* was read as an "apocalyptic" elegy (Shaw 155) for the traditional life of the Lakota People,[21] and it's easy to see why. Very early in his story, Black Elk comments that his vision was "given to a man too weak to use it; of a holy tree that should have flourished in a people's heart...and now is withered; and of a people's dream that died in bloody snow" (2) at Wounded Knee Creek. Later, he laments that his "vision was for the nation; but I have done nothing with it" (180). In the book's final chapter, called "The End of the Dream," Black Elk concludes his story, again with reference to the events at Wounded Knee, with the further admission that "I did not know then how much was ended.... A people's dream died there...."[22] And I, to whom so great a vision was given in my youth,—you see me now a pitiful old man who has done nothing, for the nation's hoop is broken and scattered" (270). In the final words of his narrative, "There is no center any longer, and the sacred tree is dead" (270). This would certainly seem to confirm the exile of the people, the end of a world and a way of life!

In 1972, however, Sally McCluskey wrote that Neihardt had told her: "The beginning and ending are *mine*, they are what [Black Elk] *would have said if he had been able*" (qtd. in Holloway 20–21; my emphasis). This seems extraordinary, if indeed casual, hubris on Neihardt's part![23] Surely one could reasonably conclude that if Black Elk did *not* say these things at the beginning and end of his story, it wasn't because he was unable to say them, but because he did not mean to say them. *The Sixth Grandfather,* the transcripts of the interviews between Neihardt and Black Elk, ably edited by Raymond DeMallie, confirm that neither the opening nor the closing statements of failure that Neihardt ascribed to Black Elk derive from anything Black Elk actually said. There simply are no such definitive statements of failure by Black Elk at the points where Neihardt placed them.

Thus, for example, we find that the final chapter of the transcript is *not* called, as it is in *Black Elk Speaks,* "The End of the Dream," but rather "Teaching Flaming Rainbow," the name Black Elk gave to Neihardt. To further this teaching, Black Elk expressed a desire to Neihardt to visit Harney Peak, the center of his world, where he wished to call again on the six grandfathers of his great vision. Black Elk tells Neihardt: "You know how I felt and what I really wanted to do *is* for us to make that tree bloom. On this tree we *shall* prosper.... You remember I saw many happy faces behind those six grandfathers and maybe it will be that Mr. Neihardt['s] and my family will be happy faces. Our families will multiply and prosper *after we get this tree to blooming*" (DeMallie 1985, 294; my emphasis). I'm not sure how much to make of the present tense of the verb—"what I wanted...*is* for us [still] to make that tree bloom"—or the future tense—"we *shall* prosper"—because the verb tenses in English may or may not reflect what Black Elk actually said in Lakota. But there is surely a sense of active, purposive hope in Black Elk's projection of the happiness that will attend his and Neihardt's family "after we get this tree to blooming." I've used part of this quotation as the epigraph to this section of the chapter; it does not at all sound like despair to me.[24]

Once at Harney Peak, Black Elk prays to the six grandfathers, recalling that "at this very place, the center of the earth, you have promised to set the tree that was to bloom." He indeed goes on to say, "But I have fallen away thus causing the tree never to bloom again," adding immediately, however, "but there may be a root that is still alive, and give this root strength and moisture" (DeMallie 1985, 295). Black Elk states clearly: "In sending up my voice I prayed that you may set the tree to bloom again so that my people will see many happy days" (295). Neihardt notes that Black Elk had "told his son, Ben, that if he still had power with the spirits that it would rain a little sprinkle." "It did rain out of a perfectly bright sky," Neihardt attests, "and then it cleared up immediately afterward" (DeMallie 1985, 296). The transcript ends with Black Elk's words: "Grandfathers, behold this pipe. In [*sic*] behalf of my children and also my nephew's [Neihardt's] children, I offer this pipe, *that we may see many happy days*" (296; my emphasis).

Remarking that Neihardt had indeed once "thought of ending the book" with the elegiac words he had ascribed to Black Elk in his last chapter, "The End of the Dream," Brian Holloway sees Neihardt's addition of a "Postscript" recording the trip to Harney Peak as evidence that he also did not want to emphasize "the end of the Lakota journey" (Holloway 168). So far as this is true, I think it is because, as Julian Rice has remarked, Neihardt saw Lakota beliefs as "precursors of Christian salvation" (Rice 49). Neihardt's was "a vision entirely Western in conception and metaphor" (61).

But unlike Christianity, which is focused on salvation, "Lakota religion enhances life on earth through ritual disciplines...the primary spiritual concern is always creation rather than salvation" (Rice 65). Ritual and verbal expression are thus "directed toward physical and spiritual continuance on the earth" (xi). Rice quotes Clyde Holler's assessment that "the narrative was *spoken as a healing ritual,* to revive the Lakota consciousness" (qtd. in Rice 23; my emphasis). As with traditional Native American expression generally, it is the practical, social power of a discursive act that is paramount, and Black Elk's narrative is entirely consistent with his religion. Like Black Hawk before him, Black Elk seeks to heal and restore his People by telling his story in an act of "melancholic mourning," and *Black Elk Speaks* is a major example of Native American elegy, working so that the People might live.

William Apess's *Eulogy on King Philip*

On January 8, 1836, the Reverend William Apess, a Pequot, delivered an address at the Odeon in Boston called *Eulogy on King Philip*. Metacom or Metacomet, the Wampanoag sachem based at Mount Hope, Rhode Island, and known as Philip, had died 160 years earlier, in 1676, at the end of what had been called "King Philip's War." Apess later presented a shorter version of the *Eulogy* on January 26, 1836, publishing the longer version the same year, and the shorter version the following year, in 1837. These were the last works he would publish before his death in 1839.

Philip Gould has called Puritanism "a protean metaphor for the early republic" (8); it served, he writes, as "an arena in which early nationals negotiated the contemporary meanings of republican virtue" (9). At least since 1814 and the initial publication of Washington Irving's "Philip of Pokanoket,"[25] Philip had become a central figure in these negotiations—negotiations that became particularly acute with the election of Andrew Jackson as president in 1828. Jackson had made clear his intention to "remove" the Cherokees of Georgia and other southeastern Indian nations to lands west of the Mississippi, something the great majority of American artists and intellectuals based in the East opposed as unjust. But if Jackson's proposed actions against the Indians were currently unjust, was it the case that the Puritans' actions against Philip and his People earlier had also been unjust?

In an 1835 address eulogizing the Puritans who had died fighting Philip, Edward Everett attempted to make "the fine distinction of exonerating the conduct of seventeenth-century New England Puritans while criticizing contemporary Indian policy" (Lepore 207).[26] "Unless we deny altogether," Everett had said, "the rightfulness of settling the continent,—unless we maintain that it was from the origin unjust and wrong to introduce the civilized race into America...I am not sure that any different result [than the destruction of Philip and his People] could have taken place" (1835, 10–11). In a lengthy footnote preceding the words I have just quoted,[27] Everett sought to establish the "fine distinction" between the "rightfulness," however regrettable, of the Puritans' actions and the wrongfulness of Jackson's proposed actions. "It can be scarcely necessary to state," Everett's footnote reads, "that considerations of this kind have no applicability to the questions recently agitated in the United States relative to the rights acquired by Indian tribes under solemn compacts voluntarily entered into by the United States, at the instance and for the benefit of an individual State, and for considerations deemed advantageous at the time, both to the individual State and the general government" (10). This puts the matter rather obliquely, although Everett's audience would probably have understood that the "questions recently agitated" were those surrounding congressional passage of the Indian Removal Act of 1830, which granted President Jackson the authority to negotiate treaties with the eastern Indians for their removal west of the Mississippi.[28] His audience would also have known that the "individual State" referred to was the state of Georgia, and the "solemn compacts" were treaties signed by the United States and the Cherokee Nation, in particular, the treaty of Hopewell of 1785. But the actions of the Puritans, Everett asserted, "have no applicability to the questions recently agitated." However unfortunate those actions were for Philip and his People, they were nonetheless right and necessary "for settling the continent."

William Apess will have none of this.[29] In his view, the Puritans were the true savages in King Philip's War in the seventeenth century, and their American descendants would again be the true savages should they force the Cherokees west of the Mississippi in the nineteenth century. Indeed, as I have argued elsewhere, Apess's *Eulogy on King Philip* is in substantial measure a direct response to Everett's "Address" (the text from which I have just quoted).[30] In addition to his subject matter—again, nothing less than the meaning of King Philip's War for Jacksonian America—Apess also takes his form from Everett. Everett had delivered an elegiac eulogy for the "Flower of Essex"; Apess counters with an elegiac eulogy for Philip, whom he will call "the greatest man that ever lived upon the American shores" (1992a, 290).

But Apess does not strictly mourn Philip; this is because, as he had insisted on the first page of his text, Philip is not dead but "yet lives in [the] hearts of his descendants" (1992a, 277).[31] Indeed, on the second page of his published text, Apess affirmed Philip's ongoing life by rhetorically asking: "Who *is* Philip?" (278; my emphasis). Washington Irving, John Augustus Stone, James Eastburn, and Robert Sands, among others, might mourn the tragic loss of Philip, as they also mourned a loss that had not yet occurred, the tragic passing of the Indians around them,[32] but Apess will not. As Eric Wolfe has cogently put the matter, "Apess resists the Euroamerican desire to mourn the Indian and redefines his relation with Philip as melancholia." Wolfe continues: "In the framework within which I am working here, melancholia is a more politically active stance than mourning, insisting upon the significance of past losses and upon the connections between past and present" (3). He cites David Eng and David Kazanjian, who write that "while mourning abandons lost objects by laying their histories to rest, melancholia's continued and open relationship to the past finally allows us to gain new perspectives on and new understandings of lost objects" (Eng and Kazanjian 2003a, 4; qtd. in Wolfe 18–19).[33]

Consistent with traditional Native American elegiac performance, Apess delivers his eulogy so the People might live—Cherokee people, all Indian people, and as well, all people of color. He eulogizes Philip and demonizes the Puritans, whose direct political descendants are the Jacksonians, subversively rewriting American history from the seventeenth century to the present, and substituting for the dominant *comic* narrative of American ascent and its complementary *tragic* narrative of Native decline, an *ironic* narrative in which neither the "happy" ending (for the Americans) nor the "sad" ending (for the Indians) is just or necessary. Rather, these outcomes are only the bitter consequence of might making right.

Apess is adamant in his insistence that this cruel and brutal story began with the Puritans, and although it is not possible to go back in time and rescue Philip and his People, it is entirely possible to re-member Philip,[34] not to mourn him but "to reconceive the unresolved grief in melancholic mourning as a foundation for an affirmative theory of endless mourning" (Clewell 56), one that can help us "to establish an intimate, indeed ethical relation between past and future" (65). Such an "ethical relation between past and future" would better enable the rendering of justice to the Cherokees in Apess's America, to Indian people more broadly, and, as I have said, to all people of color in the United States.[35] Refusing to mourn King Philip and efficiently put him to rest, Apess's *Eulogy* forcefully demonstrates, as Maureen Konkle summarized it, "how one gets from the Puritans to New Echota" (133), from the Puritans' Massachusetts Bay Colony to the town where the 1835 treaty was signed acquiescing to the removal of the eastern Cherokees. Apess engages in melancholic mourning for King Philip so that the People might live. His *Eulogy on King Philip* is the first written Native American elegy. Although Apess's own immersion in his People's traditional culture was not very deep, his *Eulogy* is consistent with the functions of ritual and ceremonial mourning.

The Elegiac Poetry of Jane Johnston Schoolcraft, John Rollin Ridge, and Others

> Now elate—with pleasure smiling,
> Kindness mutual—time beguiling.
> But how transient! Oh how soon,
> Every bliss is turn'd to gloom!
>   Jane Johnston Schoolcraft, "The Contrast,
>   a Splenetic Effusion, March, 1823" (116)

A contemporary of both Black Hawk and William Apess, Jane Johnston Schoolcraft (1800–1842) or Bamewawagezhikaquay, "Woman of the sound the stars make rushing through the sky," herself once only a "footnote" to her eminent husband, Henry Rowe Schoolcraft, is the first Native American writer who clearly thought of her writing in literary terms. That is to say that although the Mohegan minister Samson Occom had written a short account of his life and published some sermons and hymns in the eighteenth century, and the Pequot minister William Apess in the first third of the nineteenth century, as we have seen, had published accounts of his life, the lives of other Christian Indians, and a variety of historical and polemical texts, it is unlikely that either of them saw their writing as *literature*. Schoolcraft, however, wrote poems and short fiction. Few of these were published in her lifetime, and those that were appeared only in the works of her husband, Henry. It is only recently that a comprehensive scholarly edition of Schoolcraft's writing has appeared, ably edited by Robert Dale Parker (2007). The page references given below are to Parker's volume.

After the death of her son William Henry Schoolcraft at age two years and eight months in 1827, Schoolcraft wrote four elegiac poems to mourn and remember him.[36] The first of these is called "Elegy: On the death of my son William Henry, at St. Mary's." It consists of nine stanzas of rhymed trimeters, and its work of mourning uses a conventional Christian perspective to console a mother's grief. The penultimate stanza of the poem reads:

> To know thou art blest
>   Half assuages the smart,
>   That sorrow inflicts
>   On a fond mother's heart. (133)

An elegiac "Sonnet" on the same subject develops much the same perspective:

> Oh, Cherub Babe! thy mother mourns thy loss,
>   Tho' thou hast op'd thine eyes in endless day;
>   And nought, on earth, can chase away my grief
>   But Faith—pleading the merits of the Cross,
>   And Him, whose promise gives a sure relief. (134)

A third elegy, "To my ever beloved and lamented Son William Henry" ends each of its eleven, three-line tetrameter stanzas with either "Sweet Willy" or "My Willy." Thus, as Parker notes, it follows "the form of Ann Taylor's... once famous 'My Mother' (1804) where the refrain is 'My mother' rather than 'My Willy'" (136). Schoolcraft consoles herself in conventionally Christian fashion with the words

> But soon my spirit will be free,
> And I, my lovely Son shall see,
> For God, I know, did this decree!
> My Willy. (136)

"A hundred moons and more"—as Parker reckons, "over eight years and four months after" (139) the child's death—Schoolcraft wrote "Sweet Willy," yet another elegy for her son. Here, she attempts to assuage her grief using the metaphor of sowing and reaping, particularly as found in Psalms 125 and 127:

> And often comes the memory
> Of my darling little boy,
> For he was sown in bitter tears,
> And shall be reaped in joy. (139)

It may well be that while these poems appear successfully to mourn the child through the adoption of a Christian perspective, the mother-author still clings—poignantly—in melancholic fashion to the memory of her son, for whose loss not even these elegies entirely provide consolation.

Schoolcraft also published a poem called "Elegy on the death of my aunt Mrs [*sic*] Kearny of Kilgobbin Glebe Dublin, Ireland." I quote its last three lines:

> Her aims looked ever up to heaven
> That heaven, that all her ardour shared,
> And hope now tells—is her reward. (160)

The identity of their author requires us to see all of these poems as Native American elegies, but little or nothing of Schoolcraft's Ojibwe heritage has made its way into her laments for her lost son or her tribute to her aunt. (This is not the case, it should be said, with some of Schoolcraft's writings on a variety of other subjects.)

Although he, too, like Schoolcraft, died young, at the age of barely forty, Chees-quat-a-law-ny, Yellow Bird, or John Rollin Ridge (1827–67), a member of a distinguished Cherokee family,[37] was as well a literary writer. Author of the first Native American novel, *The Life and Adventures of Joaquin Murieta, the Celebrated California Bandit* (1854), Ridge's posthumous volume, *Poems* (1868), was also the first volume of poetry to be published by a Native American. Ridge was as well a journalist and an accomplished essayist.

I know of only three elegiac poems by Ridge. "The Forgiven Dead," from *Poems,* memorializes one who "wandered," as "truth she forsook for gold"—although she "could not bear to sin and live." The speaker forgives her in the final line of the poem, acknowledging that, after all, "Her soul was virgin unto me" (Parker 2011, 94). The other two elegies by Ridge have Native American subject matter, although neither of them appeared in *Poems*. The first, dated "Osage July 18, 1847," signed "Yellow Bird," and untitled, was not published until 1941, when it appeared in the Arkansas *Gazette*. The University of Virginia's reproduction of the 1868 *Poems* includes the first of the two other elegies among several "Fugitive Poems," where it is given the title "[Far in a Lonely Wood]," the first words of the poem. It appears as "The Indian's Grave" in Robert Dale Parker's *Changing Is Not Vanishing* with slightly different line breaks (2011, 70–72), although otherwise the two texts are exactly alike. The second of Ridge's other two Native elegies (1848) has a title, and a long one at that: "The man twenty feet high, having the features of the Indian race, said to have been recently discovered in a cave somewhere in the Rocky Mountains" (Parker 2011, 79–81). I will look briefly at each of these.

After a Wordsworthian opening, "Far in a lonely wood I wandered once," the speaker of "The Indian's Grave" describes coming on "A mound of moss-grown earth." Reflecting, he concludes that "This must be the grave of one / Who ranked among the warriors of the / Wilderness," a dejected remnant of "a noble race" that "Had roamed these forest wilds among," until at last, "save but a few, they all had fled." The speaker perorates, "Sleep on, dark warrior," and vows not to disturb his resting place. Now, "All is changed. Then *sleep* thou on! Perchance that peace, denied / In life, within the lonely grave is found" (Parker 2011, 70–72). In this instance, changing *is* vanishing;[38] there is no continuance or survivance to be imagined here for the Indian dead, only quiet rest.

"The man twenty feet high...," despite his difference in size (so I presume) from the warrior in his Indian grave, has much in common with him. This giant, too, was "A solitary remnant" of "His tribe departed from the earth," "His language and his nation dead." For this particular warrior of long ago, Ridge imagines four stanzas of love with "Perhaps a queenly one and proud": "How lovely she, and he how brave—/ The Eden of the West was there." This giant and his People lived much too long ago to be defeated by the Euramericans. Rather, they were overcome when "In countless numbers rising strong—/ The banded nations of the West" attacked and "wasted" them. Then, "marked, a bleeding fugitive, / Retired far back this last lone man" (Parker 2011, 81).

Parker's anthology also makes available poems by Native American poets from the seventeenth century until 1930,[39] most of whom were less well-known in their time than Schoolcraft and Ridge.[40] So far as their poems address death and loss, they do so, like the elegiac poems of Schoolcraft and Ridge, from the conventional perspectives of the dominant society. That is to say that although they often *disagree* with the dominant society—in other words, all condemn wrongs against the Natives and oppose the removal of tribes from their homelands, whether before or after Jackson's presidency—their disagreement is a matter of ethics and politics, not epistemology. In adopting the written poetic *forms* of the Western tradition, they adopt its *modes of reasoning* and to some extent its Christian *perspective* as an apparently necessary consequence. But as later work, some of which I will examine (e.g., Linda Hogan, Gerald Vizenor, and Lance Henson, among others), and some of which I will not (e.g., Ray Young Bear), this is *not* an absolutely necessary consequence of writing.

Consider the manner in which Joshua Ross (Cherokee), David Brown (Cherokee), DeWitt Clinton Duncan (Cherokee), and Alexander Posey (Muscogee; but unlike these others, Posey was a prolific and even celebrated writer in his time and ours) memorialize Sequoyah's life and legacy. Ross has Sequoyah

> ...to the deep wood fly
> In solitude alone to die;
> No well loved hand or sister dear
> To wipe away the last sad tear. (Parker 2011, 133)

DeWitt Clinton Duncan remembers Sequoyah and concludes that

> No low-built grave for thee shall e'er be found
> Beneath the sky: 'tis needless to inhume
>   A Sun gone out—the universe its tomb. (Parker 2011, 211)

There is no sense that that "Sun" will rise again, or that its light will reappear.

David Brown writes of Sequoyah: "Stand thou didst on Pisgah's height / And gazed into the future's deep." Like Moses before him, however, he did not bring his People into the Promised Land: "But day was ne'er unclasped from night, / E'er thy spirit silently fell asleep" (Parker 2011, 140). Nor does Alex Posey's "Ode to Sequoyah" imagine Sequoyah's invention of a way to write the Cherokee language as sufficing to guarantee the People's ongoing life; rather, like so many of these poems, it wishes him only quiet rest:

> By cloud-capped summit in the boundless west,
>   Or mighty river rolling to the sea,
> Where'er thy footsteps led thee on that quest,
>   Unknown, rest thee, illustrious Cherokee! (Parker 2011, 169)

The "removal" of Sequoyah's Cherokee People, and their suffering on the "Trail of Tears," as well as the exile of other Native peoples, were commemorated in several "apocalyptic" (Shaw) elegies mourning the loss of homelands and lives. Israel Folsom, a Choctaw, was a member of one of the "five civilized tribes" to suffer removal. He borrows from a well-known line by Alexander Pope—"Lo! The poor Indian, whose untutor'd mind / Sees God in clouds or hears him in the wind"—for the title of his "Lo! The Poor Indian's Hope."[41] The first of Folsom's five four-line stanzas concludes: "Native land farewell." His third stanza asks: "Why do our brothers bid us go / From our native home?" for "Here our fathers' graves are laid,—/ Must we leave them all?" The reader will recognize here a familiar subject in Native elegy, concern for the burial places of the dead, a concern we have seen expressed, for example, in Black Hawk's *Life* and in Sealth's speech.[42] Insofar as the answer to the question, "Must we leave?" is clear, Folsom's final stanza poses yet another question:

> Whiteman, tell us, God on high
> So pure and bright in yonder sky,—
> Will not then His searching eye
>   See the Indians' wrong? (Parker 2011, 67)

A poem thought to have been written by the prominent Cherokee minister and leader Jesse Bushyhead, who led one of the contingents of his People on the Trail of Tears, is called "The Indian's Farewell." "Adieu ye scenes of early sports," it begins, while its sixth and seventh stanzas continue:

> Adieu the land that gave me birth,
>   Thou God that rules the sky,
> Protect that little spot of earth
>   In which our fathers lie.
>
> Tread lightly on the sleeping dead,
>   Proud millions that intrude,
> Lest, on your ashes be the tread
>   Of millions still more rude.

The poem concludes: "Dear native land, adieu" (Parker 2011, 69).

William Walker Jr., a polyglot graduate of Kenyon College, the Wyandots' principal chief in 1835–36, and a staunch opponent of his People's removal from Ohio, marked the year of Wyandot exile (1843) with "The Wyandot's Farewell."[43] The poem shares many traits with the other removal poems we have considered. "Farewell, ye tall oaks," Walker begins, opening his second stanza with "Adieu, ye dear scenes which bound me like chains." "Dear scenes of my childhood, in memory blest," he continues, "I must bid you farewell for the far distant West." He concludes: "Far away from the pale-face, oh, there let me go" (Parker 2011, 66). But even this small consolation was, of course, soon not to be.

Ruth Margaret Muskrat (Bronson), a Cherokee who majored in English at Mount Holyoke College (Parker 2011, 32) and went on to be an important educator and activist, was also a poet. Two of her poems from the early 1920s elegize, first, the entirety of Native losses to the whites and, more specifically, Cherokee exile.[44] "Sentenced (A Dirge)" opens, with reference to the invading whites: "They have come, they have

132   Chapter 3

come"; its second stanza begins: "We must die, we must die." Here is its final stanza:

> They have won, they have won,
> Thru fraud and thru warfare they have won,
> Our birthright for pottage the white man has won,
> And the red man must perish alone. (Parker 2011, 322)

The off-rhymes "won" and "alone" reinforce the sense that the People will not live (although Muskrat's public work was very important in seeing to it that the People would indeed live). Muskrat's "The Trail of Tears" insists that that terrible event is present still in the minds of Cherokee people in the twentieth century. Here is the final stanza:

> From the homes their fathers made,
> From the graves the tall trees shade
> For the sake of greed and gold,
> The Cherokees were forced to go
> To a land they did not know;
> And Father Time or wisdom old
> Cannot erase, through endless years,
> The memory of the trail of tears. (Parker 2011, 328)

Other Native poets wrote elegies for noted resistance fighters like King Philip, whom James E. Waters/Wild Pigeon (Montaukett and Mattinnecock) denominates "The Patrick Henry of his Times" (Parker 2011, 298). Hen-toh/Bertrand Walker (Wyandot) calls Pontiac a "Patriot" whose battle "to thwart the tide of / Progress and the whiteman's civilization" was nonetheless in "vain" (Parker 2011, 260). William J. Kershaw (Menominee) composes a monologue for Chief Joseph titled "Joseph Fights No More," in which he has the defeated Joseph say: "To a stranger we yield the homes of our sires / And our vanished hopes like a dream that is o'er." His People will not live, and his only hope for their homeland is the following: "We ask Thee, Great Spirit, to keep her and bless her, / And make her forever the home of the free" (Parker 2011, 295).

There are as well a number of Indian "laments." Particularly stark and poignant is DeWitt Clinton Duncan's "The Dead Nation," which he calls "An Elegy at the tomb of the Cherokee Nation, / by one of her own sons."

This begins: "Alas! poor luckless nation, thou art dead / at last!" (Parker 2011, 202).[45] Olivia Ward Bush-Banks (Montaukett), in "On the Long Island Indian," concludes:

> Just as time with all its changes
>   Sinks beneath Oblivion's Wave,
> So today a mighty people
>   Sleep within the silent grave. (Parker 2011, 217)

In much the same way, Alfred C. Gillis (Winnemem Wintu), in "Where Sleep the Wintoon Dead," notes the place "Where a thousand Wintoon warriors lie," while only "soft winds whisper through the pines, / In dirges o'er their mountain tomb" (Parker 2011, 339). The Yuma poet Arsenius Chaleco, in his "The Indian Requiem," acknowledges the imminent demise of his People—adding, however, his warning that the conquering whites may also one day face their end:

> They waste us—ah, like April snow
> In the warm noon, we shrink away,
> And fast they follow as we go
> Towards the setting day.
>
> But I behold a fearful sign
> To which the white man's eyes are blind,
> Their race may vanish hence like mine
> And leave no trace behind. (Parker 2011, 341)

These poems mourn a past that is gone forever, with few or no indications of its possible continuance. Only solitude, sleep, and rest in a natural setting can be envisioned—with an occasional warning to the white man.

4

Elegy in the "Native American Renaissance" and After

Prose Elegy in Momaday, Hogan, and Vizenor

> Practical social power, not aesthetic originality or genius, is the category of understanding in Native art, [so that] for a Native community the beauty of expressive oral culture is synonymous with its practical social power.
>
> Eric Cheyfitz (2006b, 68–69)

N. Scott Momaday's *The Way to Rainy Mountain* appeared in 1969, the same year that his novel *House Made of Dawn* (1968) won the Pulitzer Prize for Fiction.[1] In part an autobiography, *The Way to Rainy Mountain* has also been called a "prose poem," an "epic," and the record of a "pilgrimage." It is in some measure all of those things, although these descriptive terms are not strictly consistent with one another.[2] Here, I want to consider *The Way to Rainy Mountain* as what it so clearly is—an elegy for Momaday's grandmother Aho and also for the traditional culture of the Kiowa People.[3] In linking his grandmother's death to the "end" of Kiowa traditional culture, Momaday adopts the "communitist" perspective of much traditional Native elegy. Does his elegiac performance also work so that the People might live?

The book opens with a poem called "Headwaters":

> Noon in the intermountain plain:
> There is scant telling of the marsh—
> A log, hollow and weather-stained,
> An insect at the mouth, and moss—
> Yet waters rise against the roots,
> Stand brimming to the stalks. What moves?
> What moves on this archaic force
> Was wild and welling at the source.

It is noon, not morning, to be sure, but this is a poem about an "archaic force...welling at the *source*" (n.p.; my emphasis), perhaps Momaday's imagined version of both the birth of the Kiowa People—the hollow log, as we will soon learn (1969, 17), is the passage through which the People emerged into this world—as well as their movement into the "intermountain plain" from the headwaters of the Yellowstone in what is now Montana, initiating what Momaday will later call their "golden age" (114).[4] The poem is followed by a prologue whose first paragraph announces a "journey [that] *began* one day long ago," and whose second paragraph affirms an apparent truth to which, however, not all cultures strictly subscribe: "'You know, everything had to *begin*'" (1; my emphasis),

Just as the book opened with a poem and a prologue, it ends with an epilogue and a concluding poem, "Rainy Mountain Cemetery":

> Most is your name the name of this dark stone.
> Deranged in death, the mind to be inheres
> Forever in the nominal unknown,
> The wake of nothing audible he hears
> Who listens here and now to hear your name.
> The early sun, red as a hunter's moon,
> Runs in the plain. The mountain burns and shines;
> And silence is the long approach of noon
> Upon the shadow that your name defines—
> And death this cold, black density of stone. (89)

Matthias Schubnell sometime ago noted that this "not only suggests the *end* of Kiowa culture but also reflects Momaday's reaction to his ancestors' graves" (147; my emphasis). It is not clear who is addressed and whose name is "Most...the name of this dark stone." The listener wishes to hear "your name" but hears, at noon, only "silence" "Upon the shadow that your name defines." I had for long assumed that "this dark stone" was the tombstone of Momaday's grandmother. But Momaday has stated that his grandmother lies "in an unmarked grave" (qtd. in Schubnell 142–43) in Rainy Mountain cemetery, so perhaps the stone is that marking the grave of his grandfather, Mammedaty, or that of Kau-au-inty, Mammedaty's grandmother (1969, 80). In any case, what the "listener" experiences in both the first and the last lines of the poem is "death"—both the death of the speaker's ancestors and the death of Kiowa culture—in the material form of "this cold, black density of stone."[5] The speaker expresses no grief at these losses, nor will Momaday throughout the book express grief at the loss of persons or lifeways. It will be necessary to speculate why this might be.

For Momaday, cultures, like individual persons, begin, flourish, decline, and end; his is, as we will see further, an evolutionary perspective. The migration of the Kiowas onto the Southern Plains began in the seventeenth century and evolved to the high point of what Momaday calls a "golden age," one, as noted, that dates "from about 1740...until about 1875" (1969, 114). I will return to that latter date, which must be close to the date of Momaday's grandmother's birth if, as he writes, "when she was born the Kiowas were living that last great moment of their history" (6). Momaday specifies the date of her birth somewhat more precisely—although somewhat differently—a bit later when he writes: "She was about seven when the last Kiowa Sun Dance was held in 1887 on the Washita River above Rainy Mountain Creek" (11) (fig. 10).[6] Although Momaday does not give the date of her death, it is possible to learn that his grandmother Aho died in the spring of 1965 (Roemer 157) and that Momaday "returned to Rainy Mountain in July" (Momaday 1969, 5) of that year.

His journey to his grandmother's grave in the shadow of Rainy Mountain in Oklahoma is presented as a parallel to the journey the Kiowas had made onto the Southern Plains. Of this Momaday writes: "They had conceived a good idea of themselves, they had dared to imagine and determine who they were" (1969, 2). "From the beginning," Momaday asserts, "the

Elegy in the "Native American Renaissance" and After 137

Figure 10. Anonymous Kiowa drawing of people bringing in the center pole for the Sun Dance ceremony, 1875–1878. Ms 98-45, National Anthropological Archives, Smithsonian Institution. MS 98-54.

migration of the Kiowas was an expression of the human spirit" (3), and, although the time of Kiowa greatness "is *gone forever*... the *human spirit* endures" (2; my emphasis). The "way to Rainy Mountain"—and also *The Way to Rainy Mountain*—is "preeminently the history of an idea, man's idea of himself, and it has old and essential being in language" (2). Again, there is no grief expressed for these losses—that which is "gone forever"—nor are they mourned. This is so because Momaday believes that "imagined ideas," and an "essential being" that inheres in or can be communicated in literary language—importantly, the language of *The Way to Rainy Mountain*— "endure." So far as this is so, there is no loss to mourn, no cause for grief.

"The journey herein recalled," Momaday writes (he could well have said "journeys"), "continues to be made each time the miracle"—that is, "the history of an idea, man's idea of himself"—"comes to mind" (2). As Momaday put the matter in a much-celebrated talk he gave in 1970, "We are what we imagine. Our very existence consists in our imagination of ourselves" (1975, 103); and *The Way to Rainy Mountain* provides "language" in which his grandmother and Kiowa high culture can "endure" in their "essential being" in the "human spirit," most particularly in the "imagination."[7] Imagined ideas, "spirit," and essential being in language, unlike individuals and cultures, have no end in Momaday's Platonic, romantic-modernist view of things. And it is *there* and in *that way only* that the People might live.

Let me illustrate the point just made by a close look at a passage of *The Way to Rainy Mountain* that has not, so far as I know, been singled out for critical attention. The passage occurs in chapter 6 of the first section of the book, called "The Setting Out." There Momaday writes:

> In the autumn of 1874, the Kiowas were driven southward toward the Staked Plains. Columns of troops were converging on them from all sides, and they were bone-weary and afraid. They camped on Elk Creek, and the next day it began to rain. It rained hard all that day, and the Kiowas waited on horseback for the weather to clear. Then, as evening came on, the earth was suddenly crawling with spiders, great black tarantulas, swarming on the flood. (1969, 33)

Why tell of a rainy autumn day in 1874? In general, Momaday is not much interested in historical dates. As I've noted, he had written in his introduction that his grandmother Aho had been born *around* the time when "the Kiowas were living that last great moment of their history" (6; my emphasis), and also that "she was *about* seven when the last Kiowa Sun Dance was held in 1887" (11; my emphasis). He dated that "last great moment" only in the epilogue, where he wrote that Kiowa culture "would persist for a while in decline until *about 1875,* but then it would be gone" (114; my emphasis). In the lengthy paragraph early on, noting his grandmother's birth and the "last great moment" of Kiowa history, Momaday had written that it was a time when the Kiowas had been "driven onto the Staked Plains in the cold rains of autumn" (6). "In Palo Duro Canyon," he said, "they abandoned their crucial stores to pillage...," and, finally, "in order to save themselves, they surrendered to the soldiers at Fort Sill" (6).[8] Once we complete the book, as just noted, we will know that this was "about 1875" (114).

The rainy day referred to in this passage must have been in the same period as or close to the time Momaday had mentioned earlier; in both passages he uses the same verb—"driven"—to describe the reason the Kiowas find themselves on the Staked Plains. Here, the Kiowas see "columns of troops...converging on them from all sides." This tells us—or, rather, it does *not* actually tell us—that Momaday is recounting an incident of the Red River War of 1874–75 involving the Kiowas, the Comanches, and the Southern Cheyennes. Almost surely present on that autumn day were Guipago (Lone Wolf) (see fig. 11) and the important shaman Maman-ti, known as the Owl Prophet.[9] Other of the Kiowas' most renowned leaders, among them Satanta (Set-t'ainte or White Bear) (see fig. 12), Man-yi-ten (Woman's Heart), and Pa-tadal (Poor Buffalo), might also have been present. This particular autumn day may have been just before September 28, 1874, when the Kiowas suffered a decisive defeat at the hands of Lieutenant Ranald Mackenzie at Palo Duro Canyon. Mackenzie captured some 1,400 of the Indians' horses and had more than 1,000 of them shot.[10]

Or, since Momaday tells us that these Kiowas were camped on Elk Creek, Dona'i P'o, or Pecan River on the north fork of the Red River (Mooney 1979, 201), perhaps this was later that autumn, perhaps October 21, 1874, when the Battle of Elk Creek took place. It was then that Major George Schofield surprised and overran a large Comanche camp, although a number of Kiowas were there as well. By early 1875, a great many of the Kiowas had indeed been forced onto the Fort Sill Reservation in Indian Territory, although the degree to which, after that date, Kiowa culture, as Momaday wrote, "would be gone" (114) remains an open question. I'll return to that use of the future conditional just below.

It is possible that after finishing *The Way to Rainy Mountain* the reader of the passage I have quoted, looking back upon it, might comprehend (more or less) what happened once the troops did, finally, converge on the Kiowas. But Momaday discourages this sort of comprehension. Rather, he turns the reader's attention toward the rains that came, and then to the "great black tarantulas, swarming on the flood." The sociohistorical facts of Kiowa experience—"the mean and ordinary agonies of human history," as Momaday wrote on the first page of *The Way to Rainy Mountain*, in a phrase that has continued to trouble me in the forty-some years I have known it—are dismissed in favor of the aesthetically interesting detail of the great spiders on the flood, an image that may "endure" in the

Figure 11. Lone Wolf, Guipago, 1868–1874. National Archives and Records Administration.

"imagination." Momaday will not say here that Kiowa culture *was* gone, only that it "would be gone." There is nothing to mourn in his account.

William Clements has suggested that the tradition in which Momaday's writing belongs "is not primarily that of Western belles lettres; instead it

Elegy in the "Native American Renaissance" and After 141

Figure 12. White Bear, Sa-tan-ta, 1869–1874. National Archives and Records Administration.

is that of Kiowa oral literature" (1985, 71). So far as that is true, let us consider what Momaday said of oral literature in that 1970 address. In oral literature, he said, "we are concerned... not so much with an accurate representation of actuality, but with the realization of the imaginative experience" (1975, 103). Oral literatures, Momaday said, "*evolve* into that *mature* condition of expression which *we* call 'literature,'" and it is "literature" that "is...the end-product of an *evolutionary* process"; the "so-called 'oral tradition' is primarily *a stage* within that process" (105; my emphasis).[11] I think this is quite spectacularly mistaken. As Karl Kroeber has written, American Indian oral poetry is not immature, nor is it in any way "primitive." "Primitive," Kroeber writes, "is exactly what it is not. It cannot accurately be described as an early or partially developed form of literature of which our own exemplifies advanced or perfected accomplishment"— Momaday's stated view. Rather, Kroeber insists, "Indian poetry is radically different from ours" (1983, 323).[12]

But Momaday's work, as Clements further notes, "occupies a unique position" in relation to the oral tradition in that it serves as "the *monument* which preserves the *unchanging* values of a cultural heritage that exists holistically only in the past, but *endures* in the *imagination*" (1985, 71; my emphasis); Clements continues: "The culture of the Kiowa, though ceasing to evolve [*sic*] since 1890, *endures* in the *imaginations* of Momaday and all his readers" (71; my emphasis). Again, Momaday's work serves "as a *monument* to what has gone before *so that this heritage may continue to inspire*" (75; my emphasis). Insofar as these comments are accurate, whatever relation *The Way to Rainy Mountain* may have to the oral tradition, it is not difficult to place it in the tradition of Western belles lettres after all.

Momaday's elegy for his grandmother and for Kiowa culture fits quite nicely in the tradition Peter Sacks has identified as the elegy from Spenser to Yeats. Sacks notes that "few elegies or acts of mourning succeed without seeming to place the dead, and death itself, at some cleared distance from the living" (19). This Momaday does with what appears to be little emotional effort. As Tammy Clewell summarizes an important aspect of Sacks's argument, the typical Western elegist over this long period "overcomes grief by deriving solace from a substitute for the lost object" (48); indeed, "the elegy itself emerges as a consoling substitute for the lost one" (48–49). "The elegy consoles," Clewell writes, "because the poet has accepted *his* surviving and masterful use of language as an adequate compensation for the loss" (48–49; my emphasis). *The Way to Rainy Mountain,* like the elegy from Spenser to Yeats, quite clearly "redirects emotional ties from the [lost] other to a literary object [think spiders] that in some sense replaces and transcends the one"—or ones—"it mourns" (Clewell 49) to the achieved art of the elegy itself (think *The Way to Rainy Mountain*). As

Clewell notes further, "That the traditional elegy transforms the lost other into the writer's own aesthetic gain raises certain political and ethical suspicions, at least from a contemporary perspective" (50). In similar fashion, *The Way to Rainy Mountain* might also be seen to raise "political and ethical suspicions, at least from a contemporary perspective," although I think the matter is more complex than this, both for the traditional Western elegy and for *The Way to Rainy Mountain*.[13]

I would guess that any analogy between his work and the work of social scientists would probably not please Momaday—I have already made one such analogy—but it is nonetheless the case that *The Way to Rainy Mountain*, in its "monumentalizing" use of the oral tradition in writing, engages in the production of a "salvage literature" parallel to the work of turn-of-the-twentieth-century "salvage anthropology."[14] Unable to envision any sociohistorical present (or future) for the "vanished" culture of his ancestors, Momaday, like the salvage anthropologists, preserves it by a sort of museum-ification, aesthetically monumentalizing it as an object for rapt but distanced attention. To cite Clements once more, "The specific tribal tradition from which Momaday operates...is one which has ceased to exist as a total way of life, at least as he seems to perceive the situation. His folk historical sense refers back to a memory culture preserved by an oral heritage in which his own work takes its place" (1985, 70).[15] The loss of the "specific tribal tradition" may not be so great a loss after all, as Clements has quoted Momaday to the effect that "the loss [of Kiowa culture] is less important to me than the spirit which informs the remembrance" (qtd. in Clements 71). It is that "spirit" to which he again and again gives expression in language, although on at least one occasion he has described his effort as an attempt to sustain and carry along "what was done a long time ago; there's no end to it that I can see" (qtd. in Clements 75). "No end," that is to say, so long as it continues to exist in the imagination, which Momaday values above all else.

But much of Kiowa culture still lives. The language is endangered but still spoken by perhaps a thousand Kiowa people. Momaday himself is a member of the Gourd Dance Society and has participated in the Black Leggings Society dances (Schubnell 32; Kodaseet 150). Members of the Kaigwu clan are still keepers of the Tai-Me bundle, and there are Kiowa storytellers, drum groups, and bead workers. In the words of the title of Robert Dale Parker's collection of Native periodical poetry, "Changing Is

Not Vanishing," nor is change inevitably decline. One could guess none of this from *The Way to Rainy Mountain,* which testifies to Momaday's belief that the cultural materiality and historical richness of Kiowa lifeways are gone along with his grandmother Aho. Yet, as I have noted, we are not to mourn, for these losses are merely among "the mean and ordinary agonies of human history" (Momaday 1969, 1).[16] Nor are they losses, for they "endure" in Momaday's monumental heritage language, which perpetuates their essential being in the informed "literary imagination." For Momaday, Kiowa culture and tradition will not continue "except," as Clements notes, "in the literary expressions which he is preserving" (1985, 75). Only in those may the People live.

> In those days we were still a tribe. Each of us had one part of the work of living.... All of us together formed something like a single organism.
> Linda Hogan, *Solar Storms* (262)

Linda Hogan's novel *Solar Storms,* published in 1995, tells the story of five generations of Native women. It is narrated by Angela Jensen—usually called Angel—upon her return, at the age of seventeen, to the place where she was born, the fictional town of "Adam's Rib on Tinselman's Ferry" (21). This is the land of Cree people, "the north country, the place where water was broken apart by land, land split open by water" (21), the boundary waters of Minnesota, between Canada and the United States. Angel takes up residence with a Chickasaw woman named Bush. Bush had been married to Harold, Angel's grandfather, who had left her for a woman named Loretta Wing. Harold and Loretta's daughter, Hannah Wing, Angel's mother, is, as I will note further, a very troubled person. It was Bush who cared for Hannah just after she gave birth to Angel, and it was Bush who cared for Angel when Hannah ran off. In time, however, the county authorities took Angel from Bush,[17] returning her briefly to her mother, before having to place her in a number of foster homes, from all of which she fled.[18] A journey yet farther north, and, importantly, a return home, undertaken by Angel with her grandmother Bush, her great-grandmother Agnes, and her great-great-grandmother Dora Rouge, structure the novel in which Angel comes to terms with her traumatic past, is "healed," and reintegrated into a traditional but thoroughly modern Native community.

The novel begins with a "Prologue" in the form of a monologue delivered by Angel's great-grandmother Agnes. Agnes tells of a ceremony performed by Bush years earlier to mourn her loss of Angel. Of course Angel had not died; now reunited with Bush, it is Angel who provides a frame for Agnes's monologue. She opens the novel with these words: "Sometimes now I hear the voice of my great-grandmother Agnes. It floats toward me like a soft breeze through an open window" (11). Then, for eight pages, Agnes describes in her own voice the "mourning feast" Bush had given years ago to assuage her grief at losing Angel. This "Prologue" to *Solar Storms* is an extraordinary example of elegiac expression in contemporary Native American prose.

Agnes tells us that Bush's feast was to "honor" Angel (13), and it was also for "the people," the Cree People among whom she—a Chickasaw woman—had lived for many years so that she and they too might live despite their loss. But there is an aspect of Bush's condolence ceremony that may perhaps make it different from other such traditional rites,[19] for, as Agnes explains, the honoring feast also serves as the culmination to a "battle with what amounted to human evil. Bush didn't win, but she didn't lose either. It was a tie, a fragile balance that could tip at any time. That was the reason she cooked the mourning feast" (13). A large part of "what amounted to human evil" has to do with Angel's mother, Hannah Wing, although the "evil" associated with Hannah is not easily comprehended, nor is it even entirely human. (Specifically human evil of an entirely recognizable sort is represented by the Canadian government's James Bay Hydroelectric Project, which Angel and the other women eventually work to halt.)[20]

As she earlier had described Bush's preparations for the mourning/honoring ceremony, Agnes also told of a dream she'd had of Hannah. "In the dream," Agnes says, "I saw your [Angel's] mother beneath the ice in the center of the lake. I was afraid of her. We all were. What was wrong with her we couldn't name.... Whatever your mother was in that dream, whatever she is now, it wasn't human. It wasn't animal or fish. It was nothing I could recognize" (12). To make sense of her harrowing dream-vision, perhaps to link it to a name, Agnes says: "Old stories I'd heard from some of the Cree began to play across my mind, stories about the frozen heart of evil that was hunger, envy, and greed, how it had tricked people into death or illness or made them go insane" (12–13). "In those stories," Agnes continues, "the only thing that could save a soul was to find a way to thaw the person's heart." She knows, however, that for Hannah, "there was no thawing for her heart" (13). What Agnes is suggesting—although she does not actually give it a name—is that Hannah Wing is to be not *understood,* but rather *thought about in relation to* the rich and frightening body of lore found among northern Algonquian people concerning the creature known as the Windigo.[21]

Just as the Windigo is associated with cold, winter, and ice, so, too, as Agnes makes clear, is Hannah. The Windigo is also said to give off a strange odor and to be associated with famine. Hannah, we are told, exudes the sweet, almond-like scent of cyanide, an unintentional legacy from her unfortunate ancestors, who, starving, were reduced to eating cyanide-poisoned caribou left by whites to rid the area of wolves. Himself starving, the Windigo often resorts to cannibalism, something also associated with Hannah, who, we learn later in the book, had several times severely bitten her daughter's face (So Angel: "It's true, my mother was a cannibal, a cold thing that hated life" [247]). She has also scarred her with wires and flame, acts that have no specific precedent in the behaviors associated with the Windigo. The reader will meet Hannah later in the book, and Hogan further elaborates the kinds of frightening things she can do as well as the possible ways—none of them fully adequate as explanation—to think about *why* she behaves as she does. But Agnes does not speak of these things further in the prologue, returning to the more traditional aspects of Bush's mourning ceremony.

Thus, "the last thing Bush did to prepare her feast in honor of you," Agnes tell us, "was to open the jar of swamp tea...[which] smelled like healing" (13). Agnes sees the People arriving for the ceremony and says: "Look at that.... They look beautiful" (14). Then, Bush "untied her hair. It was long and thick" (14). To get the People to come to what Agnes here calls Bush's banquet, "she'd told them this was her tradition, that it was the only thing that could help her get over her grief from losing you" (15). Although Agnes may well have known that Chickasaws a hundred years earlier, like a great many Native nations, concluded mourning ceremonies with a feast (Cushman 410), she remarks that probably "there wasn't one among us who didn't suspect that she'd invented this ceremony, at least in part" (15). But, she continues, "*mourning was our common ground* and that's why they came, not just for her, but out of loyalty for the act of grief" (15;

my emphasis)—or out of some recollection of the way in which grieving had always been a matter of "common ground," a communal matter.

"That night," Agnes continues, "in front of everyone, Bush cut her long hair. The way we used to do long ago to show we had grief or had lost someone dear" (16). Then Bush proceeds with a traditional giveaway in which "she gave each diner present some part of her world. It was only your things she parted with unwillingly" (17). During this time, "some of the people cried. Not only for her, but for all the children lost to us, taken away" (17)—exiled to the boarding schools or foster homes, lost to alcoholism, and suicide. When the People finally leave Bush's house, "each person carried away a part of her. She said it was her tradition.... She'd gone to the old ways, the way we used to live" (17). The "most important thing," the people carried away, Agnes says, "was Bush's sorrow" (17–18). She adds: "Some of us have since wanted to give it back to her, but once we felt it we knew it was too large for a single person" (18).

Giveaways were common among Native nations responding to a loss, and a sense that grief must be shared communally is found everywhere, as are the preparation and consumption of a large meal for the mourners. Bush's ceremony is also influenced by Christianity if Agnes is accurate in her sense that "the food taken into our bodies...was the holy sacrament of you we ate that day," the only "way open between us after the county sent you back to Hannah" (16). Angel eventually returns to her Cree community, which, though much threatened, will survive and continue. Near the end of the novel, Angel notes: "Even now the voice of Agnes floats toward me" (350). Then she turns to Bush and affirms: "Something wonderful lives inside me." To the reader she concludes: "Something beautiful lives inside *us*. You will see. Just believe it. You will see" (351; my emphasis).

I turn now to several prose texts by Gerald Vizenor. Vizenor, an Anishinaabe (Chippewa) poet, essayist, critic, and novelist, has published several different versions of what I will call an elegy for a red squirrel. With each return to and revision of the story, Vizenor moves from an account that treats the death of the red squirrel as an event that helped him define himself individually and vocationally as a writer to one in which his identity and vocation specifically contribute to the continuance and survivance of the People. In the final, most complex and developed elegy on the squirrel's death in the novel called *Dead Voices* (1992),[22] he mourns so that the

People might live, because, as the final words of the book assert, "We must go on" (144).

In "1956: In a Low Voice without Words," the penultimate section of an autobiographical essay called "I Know What You Mean, Erdupps-MacChurbbs" (1976), Vizenor recounts the story of how, as a young man, he had hunted a large red squirrel in the woods of Minnesota. His first shot shattered the squirrel's shoulder bone, a second shot "tore the flesh and fur away from the top of his skull," a third "tore his lower jaw away," and a fourth and final shot "shattered his forehead" (107). As this animal "who wanted to live more than anything" dies (107), Vizenor asks his forgiveness, weeps, and sings "a slow death song in a low voice without words until it was dark" (108).

This moving story is central to Vizenor's "Crows Written on the Poplars" (1987), a text he calls "a mixedblood autobiographical causerie and a narrative on the slow death of a common red squirrel" (101). "The first and third person personas," he writes, "are me" (101). The first pages of "Crows" alternate, in more or less standard autobiographical fashion, important events in the author's life—the terrible fact of his father's murder when the author was less than two years old (102), time spent in Japan (103–4), and studies in creative writing at New York University (104–5)—with references to the shooting of the red squirrel. Vizenor quotes passages from his earlier account and offers commentary on them. After a second quotation from the 1976 text, Vizenor, speaking of himself in the third person, writes that "the slow death of the squirrel burned in his memories; he sold his rifles and never hunted animals. Instead he told stories about squirrels and compassionate tricksters" (105–6). As a consequence of the squirrel's death, Vizenor gives up animal hunting and takes up in narrative the mythic figure of the trickster, who will become a-centrically central to his future work. Refusing "to accept the world as a hunter," Vizenor became, instead, a writer, a "word hunter" (106).

But his elegiac reflections on the death of the red squirrel have not yet been tied to the survivance of the People. Toward the end of "Crows," Vizenor quotes George Steiner, who wrote: "We speak first to ourselves, then to those nearest to us in kinship and locale" (qtd. in Vizenor 1987, 108). What Vizenor will increasingly find, however, as he returns twice more to the death of the red squirrel, is that there can be no such sequencing for the tribal person who can *only* speak fully to or of himself by speaking to or of

Elegy in the "Native American Renaissance" and After 149

those "nearest to us in kinship" or nation, by speaking in the first-person plural.[23]

He returned to the story of the red squirrel in his book-length autobiographical volume, *Interior Landscapes* (1990), where the story appears in a chapter called "October 1957: Death Song to a Red Rodent." Not only the date of the squirrel's death has changed. The first three paragraphs of this version add reflections developed by Vizenor in the years since "Erdupps MacChurbbs," but what is most curious about this account is the way it distances Vizenor from the red squirrel—he calls the animal a "rodent," writes short, terse sentences, interrupts the narrative with quotations, and suggests that the squirrel "*dared*" him to the hunt (1990, 168; my emphasis)—while it also draws him so close to the animal as to necessitate a shift in pronominal reference from "I" to "we." In "Crows," Vizenor had referred to himself, as I have noted, with both first- and third-person pronouns. In *Interior Landscapes* he alternates between first-person singular and first-person plural pronouns, the first-person plural extending to include both human and animal persons. This extension will become central in *Dead Voices*.

In *Interior Landscapes,* the narrator tells us that the hunter's first shot passed through the squirrel's "shoulder and shattered the bone. His right front leg and paw dangled from torn flesh. He dropped to the ground and tried to climb the tree again, and again. I understood his instinct to escape" (168). The speaker continues: "In a dream *we* reached up with *our* right paw, shattered and blood soaked, but it was not there to hold *us*" (168; my emphasis); thus the wounded squirrel "fell down again." In spite of the apparent identity of hunter and squirrel specified by "we" and "our," a radical separation between hunter and hunted is also noted: the squirrel "watched me with his dark eyes," says the narrator, and "I watched him." One last time the squirrel tries to escape, and the narrator speculates that what the animal most particularly sought to escape was "the *city* in *me*" (168; my emphasis), the urban identity Vizenor had earlier acknowledged for himself in "Erdupps MacChurbbs." "I pretended to be a tribal hunter," the narrator states here, "but my survival identities were urban...my time in the cities did not depend upon the hunt." "I owe so much to that red squirrel," the narrator says, and here, too, he sings "a death song in a low voice without words until dark" (170). The chapter concludes: "I sold my rifle and never hunted to kill animals or birds again. The violent death of a wild animal caused by my weapon was a separation from the natural world not a reunion. I would defend squirrels and comfort them in death; that would be the natural human response. I would not shoot an animal again unless my life depended on the hunt" (170).

Although Vizenor the hunter-turned-writer had several times identified himself as both an urban *and* a tribal person, his novel *Dead Voices* (1992) acutely raises the question of whether it is actually possible for tribal persons to survive *as* tribal persons in the cities. The novel's answer to this question in part involves the hunting of the red squirrel. As expanded and elaborated in *Dead Voices,* the elegy for the squirrel now becomes an elegy for the oral tradition and the tribes in the traditional manner of providing consolation and renewal, that the People might live. The urban hunter who, in 1956 or 1957, shot a squirrel in the woods will finally be forgiven for that act in the city (ca. 1992); his forgiveness comes about when he shows compassion for a squirrel crushed by a car. Elegies for the squirrels here affirm the author's achievement of an identity as a tribal writer with a specific commitment to preserving the oral tradition in writing, once more, that the People might live.

The narrator of the first and last chapters of *Dead Voices* is Laundry, a Native American college professor (a bit like Vizenor himself at the time).[24] Laundry has been given that name by a tribal woman named Bagese who believes that he smells like laundry soap. It will be Bagese who narrates the episode concerning the squirrel in *Dead Voices.* Bagese has invented a game she calls *wanaki,* whose rules involve a set of seven cards with images of animals, insects, or birds.[25] Each day she draws a card, identifies with the image on it, and then narrates stories in the first-person plural; she narrates, that is, from the plural but unified perspective of both herself and the natural creature on the card.[26]

In a chapter titled "Squirrels, *June 1979,*"[27] Bagese, having drawn the wanaki squirrel card, begins: "*We* are squirrels out on a thin branch, and *we* run at dawn with the leaves" (1992, 59; my emphasis). She also says that the "birches told their stories" (62), so that, strictly speaking, it is "the birch"—rather than Bagese herself—who tells of a "tribal hunter" who "pretended to be the animal he hunted for food" (63). Bagese then takes over the narration as the tribal hunter "listened to the stories of the birch" and also "pretended he was part of the birch" (63). The account that follows repeats material from Vizenor's earlier accounts of the hunting of the squirrel, but, again, with differences.

For one thing, the squirrel whose experience Bagese-as-squirrel narrates has acquired a proper name, Ducks, and a change of gender: Ducks is pronominally referred to as "she." For another, the depiction of her pain and her struggle to live has been much expanded. Although the hunter had previously taken four shots to dispatch the squirrel, Bagese now says: "That miserable hunter shot her five times" (63). She then goes on to describe a "first coup de grace" (63), a "second coup de grace," a "third coup de grace," and a "fourth coup de grace" (64).[28]

Bagese notes that "the hunter pleaded to the squirrel, pleaded to be forgiven" (66), and that he takes the very last blink of her eye "as her forgiveness." She then notes what Vizenor himself had earlier noted, that finally the hunter "cried, and...sang a slow death song without words until it was dark" (67). But according to the birch, "the hunter was *not* forgiven then.... He sold his rifle and never thought about hunting again, but he was not forgiven until later when he acted to save a squirrel in the city" (68; my emphasis). On that occasion, the hunter carried a red squirrel "about the same size as the one he shot" crushed by a car "to the boulevard," where "he stretched out beside the squirrel, touched his [*sic*] head and paws, and sang a death song.... The hunter was forgiven at last in the city" (68).

Whether it is Bagese or the birches who tell these stories of the hunter and the hunted, as orally transmitted "natural" stories, they are contrasted to the stories of the unfortunate "wordies," academics, or more generally people who write, and who, as Bagese sees it, have entirely "lost their stories" (63). So, too, would Laundry's/Vizenor's stories in print—presumably the ones he has earlier told about hunting the squirrel, but perhaps other stories as well—be "dead voices" (67). This last matter is an important question raised in the novel, for Bagese strongly believes that the oral tradition can*not* be preserved in writing, and, indeed, at one point Laundry had promised Bagese that he would *not* transcribe and publish the stories she had told him. But some time after he has been forgiven in the city, toward the novel's conclusion, he announces that he has, after all, decided to publish her stories.

Although she did not believe in the power of written words, Bagese firmly believes that the cities must become the sanctuaries for tribal people, because, as she puts it, "the tribes are dead" (134). This presents a desperate problem, because it is her sense that "there is nothing to be done with our *voices* in the cities" (134; my emphasis), although, as she also believes, it is only through the voiced story that the People might live. Bagese many times asserts: "We must go on." This synecdochic use of the first-person plural also appears at the end of the novel, as Laundry quotes Bagese and himself concludes: "We must go on" (136). "We must go on" is a revision of the last words of Samuel Beckett's novel *The Unnamable*—"I can't go on. I'll go on"—which Vizenor had placed as one of the epigraphs to *Dead Voices*. The shift from "I" to "we" on the part of Bagese and Laundry is, as I've tried to show, indicative of a commitment to the continuance and survivance of the People. We learn that Laundry "waited a few more years and then decided that the stories [Bagese had] told [him] *must* be published" (143; my emphasis). These stories in print will *not* be dead voices; rather, they will sustain the People: "We must go on" (144).

The commitment in *Dead Voices* to the continuance and survivance of the People—"We must go on"—is partly achieved by the revision of the elegy for the red squirrel Vizenor had shot some thirty-five years earlier. He produces in the novel an account of its death that is consistent with traditional, oral elegiac expression.[29] His earliest elegies on the death of the red squirrel, as I have noted, led to his decision to become not a hunter but a word hunter; here, his (not quite) final elegiac reflection, mediated by a tribal woman named Bagese and a birch, leads him to become a writer in the oral tradition committed to the continuance and survivance of the People.

Elegiac Poetry

> Sing her the prayer
>   of home dissolving.
> Sing her the seal
>   for her pouch of names.
> Sing her the way
>   to a home on the moon.
> Sing her dark disappearance
>   from the soft flesh of earth.
>   Wendy Rose, "Genealogical Research" (2002, 13)

I have found interesting examples of elegiac expression in the work of many contemporary Native American poets who have published in the last sixty years or so, including Sherman Alexie, Jim Barnes, Kimberley Blaeser, Lee Francis, Diane Glancy, Joy Harjo, Lance Henson, Maurice Kenny,

Adrian Louis, Simon Ortiz, Carter Revard, and Ralph Salisbury, among many others—more than I have space to consider. Many of their poems commemorate, mourn, and console not only individuals but the People in some of the ways I have sought to describe in oral performance and in some written work as well. Engaging in various forms of melancholic mourning, they tell the stories, recite the names, and re-member those who have died, so that the People might live. Although a fair number of elegiac poems by contemporary Native writers work in this manner, by no means is it the case that all do. That is to say that there are many poems, as we will see further, that commemorate and mourn in rather different fashion.

Although this section considers a wide range of Native poets, it does not, as I noted in the introduction, attempt anything like a full-fledged survey of the material, nor does it offer—to use a phrase I employed in another context (2002)—a systematic "theorized history" of elegiac expression in contemporary Native poetry. Readers will note in particular the absence of Louise Erdrich (I did not find elegiac expression in the work I examined), as they will also note the absence of other fine contemporary Native poets. (An excellent overview of contemporary Native American poetry may be found in Blaeser 2006.)

Let us begin by considering how "Columbus Day" (1983) by the Cherokee artist, activist, and poet Jimmie Durham attempts to re-member the stories and restore the names. I quote the poem in its entirety:

> In school I was taught the names
> Columbus, Cortez, and Pizarro and
> A dozen other filthy murderers.
> A bloodline all the way to General Miles,
> Daniel Boone and General Eisenhower.
>
> No one mentioned the names
> Of even a few of the victims.
> But don't you remember Chaske, whose spine
> Was crushed so quickly by Mr. Pizarro's boot?
> What words did he cry into the dust?
>
> What was the familiar name
> Of that young girl who danced so gracefully
> That everyone in the village sang with her—

Before Cortez' sword hacked off her arms
As she protested the burning of her sweetheart?

That young man's name was Many Deeds,
And he had been a leader of a band of fighters
Called the Redstick Hummingbirds, who slowed
The march of Cortez' army with only a few
Spears and stones which now lay still
In the mountains and remember.

Greenrock Woman was the name
Of that old lady who walked right up
And spat in Columbus' face. We
Must remember that, and remember
Laughing Otter the Taino who tried to stop
Columbus and who was taken away as a slave.
We never saw him again.

In school I learned of heroic discoveries
Made by liars and crooks. The courage
Of millions of sweet and true people
Was not commemorated.

Let us then declare a holiday
For ourselves, and make a parade that begins
With Columbus' victims and continues
Even to our grandchildren who will be named
In their honor.

Because isn't it true that even the summer
Grass here in this land whispers those names,
And every creek has accepted the responsibility
Of singing those names? And nothing can stop
The wind from howling those names around
The corners of the school.

Why else would the birds sing
So much sweeter here than in other lands? (10–11)

The reader will hardly need my help in recognizing the poem's commitment to reciting and recuperating the names of the many who died as a consequence of Columbus's invasion.[30] These names—like the names of the fifty chiefs of the Iroquois confederacy—will not die, for our grandchildren, and we may hope their grandchildren as well, will bear them proudly. So, too, will those names be whispered by the grass and howled by the wind "around / The corners of the school," where they may sound above the names of the "filthy murderers," so the People might live. "Why else would the birds sing / So much sweeter here than in other lands?"

Simon Ortiz's *From Sand Creek* (1981), recalling the massacre of Southern Cheyenne and Arapaho people by Colonel John Chivington and his Colorado Volunteers in 1864, opens in a manner that is similar to Durham's conclusion:

> This America
> has been a burden
> of steel and mad
> death,
> but, look now,
> there are flowers
> and new grass
> and a spring wind
> rising (n.p.)

Also commemorating this horrific event is an early poem by Lance Henson, "anniversary poem for the cheyennes who died at sand creek":

> when we have come this long way
> past cold grey fields
> past the stone markers etched with the
> names they left us
>
> we will speak for the first time to the season
> to the ponds
> touching the dead grass
> our voices the colour of watching (1976, 21)

Here, there is a somewhat more tentative commitment to the People's survivance—noting the "*names* they left us," speaking "for the *first* time to the season," touching, perhaps to revive it, "the dead grass," synesthetically speaking with "voices the colour of watching" (my emphasis). This commitment is stronger in *A Cheyenne Sketchbook* (1992), in which Henson reprinted this poem (15) and also published "wo he iv 11/29/90" (52), a note to which reads: "morning star, michael wayne henson's cheyenne name / born on the day and exact time of the sand creek massacre 1864." The latter, a poem to his son, concludes:

> for the first time this day
> i will speak your name
>
> waiting the night through
> for the morning
>
> star (52)

Henson had earlier remembered the Cheyenne leader Morning Star in "morning star / the passing of the northern Cheyenne" (1976, 56), a poem he included in a later collection (1985), where he added the note that Morning Star was the "cheyenne chief dull knife's sioux name" (23). The poem concludes with "the old women," "listening it is said to the laughter of children / in the cold / howling / wind" (1976, 56; 1985, 23). One may note similarities here to details I have cited in the poems by Durham and Ortiz. Very much a writer of and for his People, Henson frequently notes his Cheyenne tribal affiliation either in the title or dedication of his books.

Maurice Kenny's book, *Tekonwatonti/Molly Brant: Poems of War* (1992), also looks back at historical trauma to the People. Kenny, a Mohawk from New York State, re-members the story of Tekonwatonti, "She Who Is Outnumbered" or "Several Against One," known as Molly Brant (1735–95), also a Mohawk. "Molly," as Kenny notes, like many women and "particularly Native American women, [has been] shockingly ignored by the historians. In most books she remains a footnote, at best; an accessory to her husband, Sir William Johnson" (12). In a poem that comes late in the book, titled "Call Me...Woman," Kenny recreates New Amsterdam in 1652, where his unnamed speaker, in a manner not so different from Durham's speaker, details the atrocities her people have endured:

> My uncle hung from the elm in the square
> For taking a pig to roast above his fire.
> My cousin sewn into a leather bag—
> First beaten with rods, sodomized
> at the muzzle of Nicolaes Hildebrant's pistol—
> was tossed into the river. (174)

She concludes:

> My blood is everywhere. You can see it
> On the sun, taste it on the peach,
> hear it on the river, feel it on the cheek.
>
> *I have come a long way... call me woman.*
>
> My death cannot be denied, nor my *name* canceled.
>   (175; my emphasis in last line)

Nor will Jim Barnes in his "In Memory of a Day Nobody Remembers: 26 September 1874," about the day the Kiowas were defeated by federal troops at Palo Duro Canyon (the date more usually given is September 28, 1874), allow the names to be "canceled." In the first section of this chapter, I noted that N. Scott Momaday's allusion to that battle in *The Way to Rainy Mountain* did not provide the names of the Kiowa warriors. Barnes, however, "remembers" those names, even if "nobody" else does. He writes of Poor Buffalo, Maman-ti, and "white-tongued Tay-nay-angopte," Kicking Bird, who, "white-tongued," did not support Kiowa resistance at the Palo Duro Canyon.[31] "K'ya-been's bones lie buried in the bluff," writes Barnes, referring to the Kiowa sentry who discharged his rifle to alert the People of Mackenzie's attack. Barnes concludes with melancholic mourning that will not "get over" these losses, although I am not sure of the degree to which his "remembering" of this forgotten day actually envisions the continued life of the People. "Dance, ghosts, among the yellow leaves," he concludes, "before they turn to dust" (119).

The names of those who died violent deaths more recently are recalled in Joy Harjo's poem for the activist Anna Mae Pictou Aquash, killed during the occupation of Pine Ridge in 1972. Its full title conveys the poet's perspective: "FOR ANNA MAE PICTOU AQUASH, WHOSE SPIRIT IS PRESENT HERE AND IN THE DAPPLED STARS (*FOR WE REMEMBER THE STORY AND MUST TELL IT AGAIN SO WE MAY ALL LIVE*) (70; my emphasis). Harjo's "The Everlasting" is for another activist, the Menominee woman Ingrid Washinawatok, murdered by Columbian guerillas in 1999, as she worked with the U'wa Indians of Colombia to set up a school to teach their culture and language. Harjo begins with the trope often used after the Holocaust and the atomic bombs: "This is not poetry. Poetry cannot exist here / in the field where they killed her" (190).[32] The poem concludes:

> This is the story of the new world, revealed
> In the songline gleaming in the dark. It is thin, breakable.
>
> It can be broken into the smallest chips of bone and tears.
> *It can be put back together with sunrise and flint.* (191; my emphasis)

So, too, in Kimberly Blaeser's poem "Recite the Names of All the Suicided Indians," the speaker says:

> Obituaries
> read like tribal rolls ...
> Memorial wreathes
> cost more each year.
> Too many die
> from lack of the language.
> Too many too young
> too Indian or too little. (8–9)

But, the speaker continues,

> Go deaf if you must ...
> but keep singing your name
> your life
> keep singing
> your name
> your life.
> *Nagamon.*
> Sing. (9)

In the final stanza of the poem, the poet accepts that task:

> So let me
> chant
> for you
> each one
> the names
> of all

Elegy in the "Native American Renaissance" and After   159

> the suicided
> Indians. (9)

Again, the story must be told, the names "chanted," to console the People that they might live.

I'll offer just one more example of a contemporary Native poet working so that the "names" are not "canceled" or forgotten. Ralph Salisbury's poem "For a Shawnee Neighbor" commemorates his neighbor Puts Leaves Into Roots, who has "moved / for good, as all of us will / leaving a *name*" (1982, n.p.; my emphasis). In "These Sacred Names," Salisbury tells of the

> ...sacred names I chant against sleep,
> against death: Chief Guwisguwi (John Ross) Tsali (Charlie)
> Sequoia (George Guest, Guess, or Gist)
> Tagwadahi (Catawba-Killer) Itagunhi (John Ax)
> and Ayuwini (Swimmer).[33]
> In these the people (the Aniyunwiya) come
> back against bayonets, against extinction,
> rejoining kin. (1980, n.p.)

The names of these Cherokee dead are chanted here "against death… against extinction."[34]

In a book entitled *Lone Dog's Winter Count* (1991), Diane Glancy remembers Lone Dog, a Lakota man whose "winter count"—a year-by-year pictographic record of the most important events of his People's history—has been much studied and admired. In the prose poem called "Lone Dog," Glancy imagines him as both a recorder of events and also an active participant in them, warrior and artist at once. Lone Dog places the "stuffed skin of a kingfisher in his hair,"

> So he can ride swiftly into battle. It's a Power that came to him in fasting. His braids are wrapped in otter skin. He *draws* his flintlock & shield. His horse's tail tied up for battle & its ears notched. He *draws* himself riding across the plains again. *He starts once more into battle.* (42; my emphasis)

In Glancy's poem, Lone Dog acts in the present ("draws," "starts"), using his power to battle once more for the People.

The names of animals who have died must also be recalled and recited, as in Simon Ortiz's elegy "For Our Brothers: Blue Jay, Gold Finch, Flicker, Squirrel *Who perished lately in this most unnecessary war, saw them lying off the side of a state road in southwest Colorado.*" The poem concludes:

> I don't have to ask who killed you.
> I know, and I am angry and sorry
> and wonder what I shall do.
>
> This, for now, is as much as I can do,
> knowing your names, telling about you.
> Squirrel. Flicker. Gold Finch, Blue Jay.
> our brothers. (1992, 254)

Knowing the names, one recites them, remembering all of "our brothers."

Wendy Rose's "Retrieving Osceola's Head" is a final example of how the story of one of those many who succumbed to Euramerican violence is quite literally re-membered in the interest of the continuance and survivance of the People. Rose's poem begins with a quotation from a text published in the *Florida Historical Quarterly* for 1955 by the great-granddaughter of a Dr. Weedon, who, in the first quarter of the nineteenth century severed the head of the defeated Seminole leader Osceola, which he took with him to his home in Florida. Near the beginning of the poem, Rose writes:

> We speak to the perpetrator
> or risk becoming him...
> but we have learned
> to keep our heads...

She concludes:

> We became the whirlpool
> stealing all the books...
> We became
> all of the murders
> returning
> *We*
> *became whole again.* (1994, 107–8; my emphasis)

Elegy in the "Native American Renaissance" and After 161

This commitment to re-membering the past, the refusal simply to mourn-and-be-done in the interest of wholeness, may be found in a wide range of Native American expression in the elegiac mode, from the nineteenth century to the present—although, once more, as we will see just below, by no means in all.

Adrian Louis, for example, has written elegiac poems from what Jahan Ramazani, in a study of twentieth-century Western elegy, has called an "anti-elegiac" perspective (89), a perspective that produces "mock elegies" (90). In some of the Western elegies he considers, Ramazani finds "a deep nostalgia for meaningful social and poetic rites of mourning" (90). The phrase "meaningful social and poetic rites of mourning" of course describes quite well the practices of traditional elegiac expression. But I do not see a "deep nostalgia" for these rites in, for example, Louis's "Pabst Blue Ribbon at Wounded Knee." Placing himself at the scene of the Ghost Dance and of the Seventh Cavalry's massacre of Big Foot's band of Minneconjou Sioux in 1890, Louis's speaker says, "we sit in our cars drinking Pabst Blue Ribbon," and "slur our song of self-pity,"

> we are at no loss to understand
> the one mass grave that America gave
> to those eighty-four warriors
> and their sixty-two women and kids. (1989, 3)

And that is all; the dead, here, are not named, although they are numbered. Self-pity is rather different from "melancholic mourning." There is no consolation here for the People beyond what Pabst Blue Ribbon, ironically, can offer.

Louis's "White Clay, Nebraska" names the town two miles outside the Pine Ridge Reservation in South Dakota that is the nearest place Indian people can buy beer and liquor. Louis bitterly remembers:

> Two miles, five years, and eighteen deaths
> this blood road of wine has reddened us
> past the mocking song of our skin.
> Yes, here is where our children die
> on their way to getting born. (1989, 5)

To cite only one more bitter anti-elegy by Louis, consider his "Farewell to Synthesis." "Yes we are the children of Crazy Horse," he writes,

> Sandy, you remember her?
> Firm and dark with braided hair
> she went to school at Pine Ridge High?
> Well, on coke she choked her baby good-bye
> yes, she was a daughter of Crazy Horse.

The poem concludes:

> In the cockless eye of the white man's God
> we stand and mumble, needing drink
> and wasted to the point where we cannot think of
> Crazy Horse, or who he was. (1989, 6)

Louis himself quite obviously *does* think of Crazy Horse, and he surely knows "who he was." But the "we" in which he includes himself—Indian people—"cannot think of / Crazy Horse, or who he was." "Wasted" and "needing drink," one may wonder indeed whether the People will live.

Among other mock elegies, Louis also has also published the bitter "Elegy for One of Us," and, set on July 4, the longer poem "Elegy for the Forgotten Oldsmobile," (1989), along with the violent anti-elegies "Tears of One Hundred Years" and "At the Burial of a Ball-Player Who Died from Diabetes." These too provide little consolation.

A poem mourning one of the Indian heroic dead is Duane Niatum's "A Tribute to Chief Joseph," the Nez Perce chief who, as we have seen, in 1877 almost led his People to "the promised land in Canada." Niatum concludes with an image of Joseph "Holding rage in the palm of his fist" as "his people's future spirals to red forest dust." Joseph "leaves his bones on the track, / his soul in the whistle" (Dodge and McCullough 82), with little in the way of continuance or survivance imagined.[35]

Paula Gunn Allen's sharply titled volume, *Life Is a Fatal Disease* (1997), begins with the powerful "Elegy for My Son." This might well fit into the section of Sandra Gilbert's anthology of Western elegies called "'Sorrow's Springs': Grieving for the Death of Children." I'll quote Allen's brief poem in its entirety:

> I wanted to write 1968 for today's date—as though
> somewhere between then and
> then, some step taken could be untaken, or a word
> spoken be unsaid
> some little thing done
> not
> wouldn't lead into
> where with bewildered hands I sit
> holding your small body dead. (74)

The awkward, halting syntax—"done / not / wouldn't..."—and the negative terms express the pain and bewilderment of a mother whose hands hold the small body of the child who has died. Her grief is powerfully conveyed, and it is deeply personal not collective; nor does the speaker find consolation. (This may also have been the case, as I have said, for Jane Johnston Schoolcraft in her several elegies for her son. The Christian perspective of those elegies provides a framework for consolation, although the mother's grief still seems in some measure unassuaged.)

Skins: Drum Beats from City Streets, "Chicago Indian poetry...by Chicago Indian people" (5), is an edited volume published in 1994 with no editor's name attached to it. I think E. Donald Two Rivers is the editor, but even the introduction to the book is unsigned. All the poetry in this volume, the reader is told, was "primarily written for performance; it reaches the community as oral communication" (4), and most of the poets included have not, to my knowledge, pursued a print career. The book contains a number of elegies that mourn loss largely in conventional Western terms. I say this descriptively with no value judgment implied.

Alice Hatfield Azure offers an "elegy for my cowboy." Here are its last two stanzas:

> Oh, Love,
> More measures
> So surely I thought
> We'd have for this
> Wonderful waltz,
>   Song now so ended.
> Someday I pray
> A melody again

> Will lift us away
> At very first measure
> Line after line,
> Refrain ever flowing. (13)

In "grandfather," Jim Fenelon commemorates his grandfather "Vincent E. Fenelon, Sr. who now lives with the spirits" (23). He follows that poem with four more "GRANDFATHER" poems, the last of which concludes:

> WANBLIN G'LESKA
> Old yet untethered
> Spotted Eagle above,
> KOLA LECHE
> A Big Bull of a Man. (25)

Mary Little Field Lundgren, "who has never written poetry before" (50), in "1838" and "one tear for Tahlequah" commemorates the losses suffered on the Cherokee Trail of Tears. I quote the penultimate stanza of the latter:

> And when the final roll was taken
> thousands fell
> along the way
> Before they met in
> Tahlequah
> to begin a brand new day. (52)

She ends on rather a brighter note than did those many other chroniclers of "removal" whom I considered earlier.

I turn now to work by Native American poets that might be compared to the poems Ramazani has called "American family elegies" (chaps. 6–8), or, simply, in Gilbert's phrase, poems "mourning deaths in the family" (sec. 2, chap. 2). The degree to which these commemorate and console so that the People might live is an open question. Carter Revard's poem "*Wazhazhe Grandmother,*" for Josephine Strikeaxe Jump (*wazhazhe* means Osage), appears in a volume of poems and autobiographical writing called *Winning the Dust Bowl* (2001). "*Wazhazhe Grandmother*" remembers "the way Grandma was quiet," but also the way in which she spoke in Osage, and the time long ago when

> an Osage bride and her man came riding one
> special day
> and climbed down from the buggy in
> all their
> best finery
> to live in their first home. (2001, 111)

In that same volume, Revard tells of learning from his brother that "a tall catalpa which [they] had loved to climb" had been "felled by lightning" (106). Revard explains: "I had to write an elegy for it. And because our mother had died not so long ago before the tree was struck, and this was better than anything I had been able to write for her, I thought it would be right to give her this one, which probably was for her all along" (106). The poem, called "That Lightning's Hard to Climb," is "For Thelma Louise Camp." But the only identifiable mother in the poem is the "long-tailed mother" of some scissortails, as the poet remembers the "sunburst / tree in bloom," a "musical tree to sing from." What is clear is the fact that Revard's memorials to members of his family are explorations of his own identity, an identity that is and will always importantly be Osage.[36]

Much the same is true of many of Ralph Salisbury's poems in *Rainbows of Stone* (2000), which celebrate not only his Cherokee family but his "Caucasian" family as well. "I would give all of my love to my Indian people and all of my love to my white people," Salisbury writes. "I am not part Indian, part white, but wholly both" (preface, n.p.). Salisbury's verse works powerfully to heal and console both Indian and white people. One sees this, for example, in his "Among the Savages...," dedicated both to Father Christian Priber, S.J., who compiled a "Churakee Dictionary," and to "Sikwaya" (Sequoya), who became "our language's second lexicographer" (49). In the title poem of the volume, "A Rainbow of Stone," Salisbury imagines a time beyond "crime, monoxide, disease / and other city uncertainties," when

> the whole earth will be toe-to-toe
> rainbows, my own
> and Thunder's and your home
> again. (66)

The fourth and final section of the book is called "Death Songs" and includes a number of family elegies (among them, "To My Father's Mother," "For Mary Turner Salisbury," "A Violet in My Fist for My Mother's Mother," and "To My Mother's Father"). It concludes with "Death Song, My Own" a "self-elegy" (Shaw). The poem begins with the calm reflection that

> When I die, time will be still
> the same for all
> who loved me and
> for all. (134)

The poet's "climb / to the Great Spirit in the sky" is only "a final, faint erosion touching shore." He will be no more, but "time will be still / the same" (134): time will be *still,* silent, in respectful recognition that something *has* changed, that a poet has passed on, and yet it will be "still / the same" for all who loved him, and for all others as well.

The final poem of Jim Barnes's book of "memoirs and impressions," *On Native Ground,* titled "Lamentation and Farewell," might also be called a self-elegy. The poem begins: "A time / ago the time / to go seemed years away." It concludes: "Now *we* / leave with spent hearts, / flat wallets, a gambler's / wish, but *we* were oh so rich / so long" (279; my emphasis). "We" is Barnes's Choctaw People, other poets, everyone. An earlier poem, "Legacy of Bones," is a self-elegy as well—or, rather, an elegy for the capacity of poets in some measure to help all people live. "Our songs will grow dry in the wind / that passes through the mindless moon," Barnes writes. Then, with implied reference to W. H. Auden's "In Memory of W. B. Yeats," he both agrees with Auden's statement that "Poetry makes nothing happen,"[37] and dissents from it:

> For living language makes every-
> thing happen, or nothing, as it rides
> the tongue into desert places,
> solitude where heart still resides. (135)

"*Nyah* Songs," the second section of Lee Francis's *On the Good Red Interstate: Truck Stop Tellings and Other Poems,* contains a number of elegies for the *nyahs,* the women, who, family or not, Francis calls mother, *nyah*. "Nyah Agnes" begins: "Gran'ma didn't make fry bread"—a line that could well be the poem's title—and concludes:

> Gran'ma never made frybread
> Now she dances among the stars
> Her gossamer shawl still glitters
> And at night I hear her laughter. (33)

His commemoration of "Nyah Kay," a woman who seems to have appreciated the Laguna language, along with Spanish, Italian, German, and French, concludes:

> Miracle worker
> *Canta mi hija para la madre*
> give your gift of lyric sound
> *luce e vita*
> because *un bel di*
> *Nessun dorma! Keiner schlafe!*
> and you shall sing her song
> *Je vaincrai!* (41)

    Sherman Alexie's work often deals with death and loss. His first feature film, *Smoke Signals* (1998), directed by Chris Eyre, is deeply (and sentimentally) elegiac, representing a search for and final reconciliation with a dead father. His second film, *The Business of Fancy-Dancing* (2002), opens with images of a corpse covered with a star quilt while the soundtrack plays the Hebrew Kaddish for the dead. "Fire Storm," an early work from *First Indian on the Moon,* published in 1993 when Alexie was only twenty-seven, is an elegy in nine sections of poetry and prose for his sister Mary and her husband. The structure is that of a free-associative set of themes and variations.

    The first section, in verse, asserts that "Fires are everywhere," so that the speaker "won't be going home tonight." This is followed by the sort of generalizing gesture that occurs often and sometimes forcefully in Alexie's work, although it is gratuitous here: "Five hundred years / and nothing has changed" (1993, 23). The second section, in prose, explains how the fire that took his sister and her husband's lives came about. Creating what he calls "cruel images for flames," the speaker "gives them names like Custer and Columbus"; again, it seems a bit facile, here to assign these terrible deaths directly to the General and the Captain. The third section presents the words "The fire crowned the trees above my head," in several verse possibilities before the prose sentence I have quoted appears (23–24). Fires more generally and elsewhere are catalogued in the fifth and sixth sections, mostly in verse, while the seventh section, in short prose paragraphs—prose poems, perhaps—presents several visions of his sister Mary. Had these visions somehow been "real," perhaps she would not have had to die. Section 8 is a very short story in which the narrator, apparently Alexie himself (but see just below), recalls the time when his dad came to tell him of his sister's death. The narrator lives in the home of a woman and her lover, who, on this fateful day (as, doubtless, on other days), ask him to build them a fire in the fireplace that serves to heat the place, giving the narrator an opportunity to play ironically with the notion of fire making. Section 9, in verse, is not titled but rather is headed by the words "**fire sale:** a sale of merchandise damaged in a fire" (27). The section concludes: "Here I offer what I own: grief / like a burning bush that shouts forgiveness and never forgives" (28). Apart from the gratuitous references to a five-hundred-year history of colonization that I have noted from Columbus on to Custer and after, Alexie's prose and poetic fugue does not much involve the People. Rather—and powerfully—it is a meditation on the poet/speaker's attempt to come to terms with what is a very personal loss.

"Sittin' on the Dock of the Bay," also from *First Indian,* is not so much an elegy for Otis Redding as it is for "the three Indians who drowned" by the dock of Benjamin Lake during the speaker's lifetime, "one by accident, one on purpose / one because there was nothing else to do" (Alexie 1993, 94). The poem goes no further; these drowned Indians have no names and would seem to be remembered only in the speaker's flat mention. The ironically—and excessively—titled "The Game between the Jews and the Indians Is Tied Going into the Bottom of the Ninth Inning" remembers the slaughter of Indians and Jews. The Indian speaker wonders whether, when his Jewish lover touches his skin, she will "think / of Sand Creek, Wounded Knee?" When her skin is next to his, will he think, "Auschwitz, Buchenwald?" No, he says, in answer to these questions,

> but every once in a while
> we can remind each other

Elegy in the "Native American Renaissance" and After

> that we are both survivors and children
> and grandchildren of survivors. (80)

Sherman Alexie's "One Stick Song" from the book of that name (2000a) is a "family elegy" that functions powerfully to console the People that they might live. Although Alexie is Spokane-Coeur d'Alene, and the central metaphor of the poem refers to the stick game traditionally played by many northwestern and Canadian Native peoples, the poem works for the "return" of *all* Indian peoples. The speaker of the poem says that he is "near the end of the game / when I have only one stick to lose." At this critical moment, he determines to "sing a one-stick song / to bring back all the other sticks / to bring back all the other sticks." The "sticks" are the many lost members of the speaker's family. There is his uncle "and the vein that burst in his head"; his cousin "who jumped off the bridge"; his grandfather "killed by the sniper in Okinawa"; another uncle "crushed beneath the fallen tree"; his grandmother "and her lover called tuberculosis"; his aunt "who looked back and turned into a pillar of sugar," succumbing to diabetes; another cousin "who hitchhiked over the horizon." The litany continues, as the speaker "sings back" his "sister / asleep when her trailer burned," and another uncle, whose "lover" this time is "called cirrhosis." There is as well his grandmother "heavy with tumors," and a cousin "shot in the head by a forgetful man," a "drunk cousin." The speaker sings them back from both the cities and the lands of the Spokane.

And, as we have found in traditional Native American elegiac expression, here, too, the singing functions in the manner desired:

> and so now, near the end of the game
> when I have only one stick left to win with
>
> I will sing a one-stick song
> I will sing a one-stick song
>
> to celebrate all of my sticks
> returned to me
>
> returned to me
> returned to me
>
> returned to me
> returned to me. (Alexie 2000a, 40)

Although it seems to be powerfully *autobiographical,* the poem may not be that at all. Alexie has mocked those who take the "I" of any narrative or poem of his as actually referring to him or his own life (see "The Unauthorized Autobiography of Me" in the same book); this might be said of "Fire Storm," which does seem to refer to an actual event in the poet's life. But whether these texts recount the history of Alexie's "real" family or not, at least in "One Stick Song" the details chosen most certainly represent the actual history of a great many Native persons on the reservations: teen suicide, death by drink or diabetes or violence.

I'll bring these considerations to a close with brief quotations once more from Simon Ortiz and Wendy Rose. Ortiz's memorial to his parents, "Mama's and Daddy's Words," concludes:

> Sure it's hard,
> sure it's not easy
> working for the People and the land,
> to fight for the People and the land.
> That's the only way that they'll learn.
> That's the only way. (1992, 330)[38]

These lines themselves are "working for the People and the land." In "The Itch: First Notice," Rose writes:

> I am looking for my People.
> As I find the names
> I write them down ...
> and wonder
> if the green eyes on paper
> know they can climb the pen
> and pierce my veins. (2002, 7)[39]

Yet again the names of the People must be re-membered and recited, mourned but not released from memory, that the People might live.

Appendix

Best Texts of the Speeches Considered in Chapter 2

Logan's Speech

If Jefferson did indeed hear or "learn" of Logan's "speech" at Lord Dunmore's in 1774, either from General Gibson or from someone whose name he did not recall, then his version would be the earliest recorded, although not the earliest to appear in print. As noted above, by the time Jefferson published it in 1784, it had already appeared in William Bradford's *Pennsylvania Journal* for January 20, 1775, which used a text sent by James Madison. The two versions are substantially the same. Because the speech is very short, I give both versions. The version from the Williamsburg letter of February 4, 1775, which has often been said to have appeared in the *Virginia Gazette* of that date, is again slightly different from both of these but only slightly. See Sandefur for a brief accounting of the differences.

Madison's 1775 Text

> I appeal to any white man to [s]ay if ever he entered Logan's Cabin hungry and I gave him not meat, if ever he came cold or naked and I gave him not Cloathing. During the Course of the last long and bloody War, Logan remained Idle in his Tent an Advocate for Peace; Nay such was my love for the Whites, that those of my own Country pointed at me as they passed by and said Logan is the friend of White men: I had even thought to live with you but for the Injuries of one man: Col. Cresap, the last Spring in cold blood and unprovoked cut off all the Relations of Logan not sparing even my Women and Children. There runs not a drop of my blood in the Veins of any human Creature. This called on me for Revenge: I have sought it. I have killed many. I have fully glutted my Vengeance. For my Country I rejoice at the Beams of Peace: But do not harbor a thought that mine is the Joy of fear: Logan never felt fear: He will not turn his Heal [sic] to save his life. Who is there to mourn for Logan? Not one. (Qtd. in Hutchinson and Rachal 136)

Jefferson's 1784 Text

> I appeal to any white man to say, if ever he entered Logan's cabin hungry, and he gave him not meat; if ever he came cold and naked, and he clothed him not. During the course of the last long and bloody war Logan remained idle in his cabin, an advocate for peace. Such was my love for the whites, that my countrymen pointed as they passed, and said, "Logan is the friend of the white men." I had even thought to live with you, but for the injuries of one man. Colonel Cresap, the last spring, in cold blood, and unprovoked, murdered all the relations of Logan, not even sparing my women and children. There runs not a drop of my blood in the veins of any living creature. This called upon me for revenge. I have sought it: I have killed many: I have fully glutted my vengeance: for my country I rejoice at the beams of peace. But do not harbor a thought that mine is the joy of fear. Logan never felt fear. He will not turn on his heel to save his life. Who is there to mourn for Logan? Not one. (Qtd. in Sandefur 291)

Black Hawk's Speech

The only contemporary record of a speech Black Hawk is said to have made to General Joseph Street is a paraphrase in the Illinois *Galenian* of September 5, 1832. The article that includes that paraphrase first refers to events at the end of August, and then from September 4, when "Street arrived...on board the steam boat Winnebago, with about 100 Sac prisoners, guarded by an escort of troops, under the command of Lt. Jefferson Davis [!]." One of those prisoners is "the celebrated Black Hawk." Several paragraphs later, the article states that "Black Hawk, this morning [September 4, 1832] desired to speak to Gen. Street. The amount of what he said was—"; and then follows the paraphrase, from an unidentified source:

> That he [Black Hawk] was not the originator of the war. He was now going where he would meet Ki-o-kuk—and then he would tell the truth. He would tell all about this war, which had caused so much trouble. There were Chiefs and Braves of his nation who were the cause of the continuance of the war. He did not wish to hold any council with him [*sic*]. He only wanted to tell him [?] that when he got where Ke-o-kuk was, he would tell the whole of the origin of the difficulties, and those who continued it. He wanted to surrender long ago—but others refused. He wanted to surrender to the steam boat, (Warrior), and tried to do so till the second fire. He then ran, and went up the river, and never returned to the battle ground. His determination then was to escape if he could. He did not intend to surrender after that. But when the Winnebagoes came upon him, he gave up.—And he would tell all about the disturbances when he got to Rock Island. (*Galenian*, September 5, 1832)

The first actual text of a farewell speech attributed to Black Hawk appears in the third "enlarged" edition of Samuel Drake's *Biography and History of the Indians of North America from Its First Discovery,* published in 1834. Drake does not provide a source for the speech, and his comments about it, as I have noted, are complex and ambiguous. He recognizes that one might doubt the speech's authenticity, but he offers it as likely to have come from Black Hawk nonetheless. Some of what Drake gives is consistent with the *Galenian*'s paraphrase, although there is a good deal more than that paraphrase contains. Drake gives Black Hawk's speech as follows:

> You have taken me prisoner with all my warriors. I am much grieved, for I expected, if I did not defeat you, to hold out much longer, and give you more trouble before I surrendered. I tried hard to bring you into ambush, but your last general understands Indian fighting. The first one was not so

wise. When I saw that I could not beat you by Indian fighting, I determined to rush on you, and fight you face to face. I fought hard. But your guns were well aimed. The bullets flew like birds in the air, and whizzed by our ears like the wind through the trees in the winter. My warriors fell around me; it began to look dismal. I saw my evil day at hand. The sun rose dim on us in the morning, and at night it sunk in a dark cloud, and looked like a ball of fire. That was the last sun that shone on *Black-hawk*. His heart is dead, and no longer beats quick in his bosom.—He is now a prisoner to the white men; they will do with him as they wish. But he can stand torture and is not afraid of death. He is no coward. *Black-hawk* is an Indian.

He has done nothing for which an Indian ought to be ashamed. He has fought for his countrymen, the squaws and papooses, against white men, who came, year after year, to cheat them and take away their lands. You know the cause of our making war. It is known to all white men. They ought to be ashamed of it. The white men despise the Indians, and drive them from their homes. But the Indians are not deceitful. The white men speak bad of the Indian, and look at him spitefully. But the Indian does not tell lies; Indians do not steal.

An Indian who is as bad as the white men, could not live in our nation; he would be put to death, and eat up by the wolves. The white men are bad school masters, they carry false looks, and deal in false actions; they smile in the face of the poor Indian to cheat him; they shake them by the hand to gain their confidence, to make them drunk, to deceive them, and ruin our wives. We told them to let us alone, and keep away from us; but they followed on, and beset our paths, and they coiled themselves among us, like the snake. They poisoned us by their touch. We were not safe. We lived in danger. We were becoming like them, hypocrites and liars, adulterers, lazy drones, all talkers, and no workers.

We looked up to the Great Spirit. We went to our great father. We were encouraged. His great council gave us fair words and big promises; but we got no satisfaction. Things were growing worse. There were no deer in the forest. The opossum and beaver were fled; the springs were drying up, and our squaw and papooses without victuals to keep them from starving; we called a great council and built a large fire. The spirit of our fathers arose and spoke to us to avenge our wrongs or die. We all spoke before the council fire. It was warm and pleasant. We set up the war-whoop, and dug up the tomahawk; our knives were ready, and the heart of *Black-hawk* swelled high in his bosom, when he led his warriors in to battle. He is satisfied. He will go to the world of spirits contented. He has done his duty. His father will meet him there, and commend him.

Black-hawk is a true Indian, and disdains to cry like a woman. He feels for his wife, his children and friends. But he does not care for himself.—He cares for his nation and the Indians. They will suffer. He laments their fate. The white men do not scalp the head; but they do worse—they poison the heart; it is not pure with them.—His countrymen will not be scalped, but they will, in a few years, become like the white men, so that you can't trust them, and there must be, as in the white settlements, nearly as many officers as men, to take care of them and keep them in order.

Farewell, my nation! *Black-hawk* tried to save you, and avenge your wrongs. He drank the blood of some of the whites. He has been taken prisoner, and his plans are stopped. He can do no more. He is near his end. His sun is setting, and he will rise no more. Farewell to *Black-hawk*. (Qtd. in Drake 136–37)

Chief Sealth's Speech

Dr. Henry Smith wrote that he had heard Sealth's lengthy address at the time the newly arrived governor of Washington Territory, Isaac I. Stevens, introduced himself to the Puget Sound Indians and the white settlers of Seattle. I believe that would have been on January 12, 1854. Sealth was also present at the Point Elliott negotiations Stevens held with the Indians for the cession of lands just over a year later, on January 22, 1855. Dr. Smith almost surely was not then present. It's my contention that the speech Dr. Smith published in 1887 came substantially from the Chinook Jargon and English translations of a talk in Lushootseed that Sealth gave in Seattle, early in 1854, augmented with material from remarks Sealth made a year later at Point Elliott. These would likely have been reported in local newspapers at the time. My text comes from Albert Furtwangler, who based it on his examination of the original publication in the *Seattle Sunday Star* for October 29, 1887. Furtwangler notes that the material in square brackets derives from Frederick Grant's reprint of the speech just four years later, in 1891.

Dr. Smith's Text

Yond[er] sky that has wep[t tears] of compassion on our fathers for centuries untold, and which, to us, looks et[erna]l, may change. Today it is fair[, tom]orrow it may be [overca]st with [clou]ds. My [words are like the] stars that never set. What Seattle says, the great chief, Washington,... can rely upon, with as much certainty as our pale-face brothers can rely upon the return of the seasons.

The son of the white chief says his father sends us greetings of friendship and good will. This is kind, for we know he has little need of our friendship in return, because his people are many. They are like the grass that covers the vast prairies, while my people are few, and resemble the scattering trees of a stormswept plain.

The great, and I presume also good, white chief sends us word that he wants to buy our lands but is willing to allow us to reserve enough to live on comfortably. This indeed appears generous, for the red man no longer has rights that he need respect, and the offer may be wise also, for we are no longer in need of a great country.

THERE WAS A TIME

when our people covered the whole land, as the waves of a wind-ruffled sea cover its shell-paved floor. But that time has long since passed away with the greatness of tribes now almost forgotten. I will not mourn over our untimely decay, nor reproach my pale-face brothers for hastening it, for we, too, may have been somewhat to blame.

When our young men grow angry at some real or imaginary wrong, and disfigure their faces with black paint, their hearts, also, are disfigured and turn black, and then their cruelty is relentless and knows no bounds, and our old men are not able to restrain them.

But let us hope that hostilities between the red-man and his pale-face brothers may never return. We would have everything to lose and nothing to gain.

True it is, that revenge, with our young braves, is considered gain, even at the cost of their own li[v]es, but old men who stay at home [in] times of war, and old women, who have sons to lose, know better.

Our great father Washington, for I presume he is now our father, as well as yours, since George has moved his boundaries to the north; our great and good father, I say, sends us word by his son, who, no doubt, is a great chief among his people, that if we do as he desires, he will protect us. His brave armies will be to us a bristling wall of strength, and his great ships of war will fill our harbors so that our ancient enemies far to the northward, the Simsiams and Hydas, will no longer frighten our women and old men. Then he will be our father and we will be his children.

BUT CAN THIS EVER BE?

Your God loves your people and hates min[e]; he [folds his strong] arms [lovingly around the white man and] leads him as a father leads his infant son, but he has forsaken his red children; he makes your people wax strong every day, and soon they will fill the land; while my people are ebbing away like a fast-receding tide, that will never flow again. The white man's God cannot love his red children or he would protect them. They seem to be orphans and can look nowhere for help. How then can we become brothers? How can your father become our father and bring us prosperity and awaken in us dreams of returning greatness?

Your God seems to us to be partial. He came to the white man. We never saw Him; never even heard His voice; He gave the white man laws but He had no word for His red children whose teeming millions filled this vast continent as the stars fill the firmament. No, we are two distinct races and must ever remain so. There is little in common between us. The ashes of our ancestors are sacred and their final resting place is hallowed ground, while you wander away from the tombs of your fathers seemingly without regret.

Your religion was written on tables of stone by the iron finger of an angry God, lest you might forget it. The red man could never remember nor comprehend it.

Our religion is the traditions of our ancestors, the dreams of our old men, given them by the great Spirit, and the visions of our sachems, and is written in the hearts of our people.

Your dead cease to love you and the homes of their nativity as soon as they pass the portals of the tomb. They wander far off beyond the stars, are soon forgotten, and never return. Our dead never forget the beautiful world that gave them being. They still love its winding rivers, its great mountains and its sequestered vales, and they ever yearn in tenderest affection over the lonely hearted living and often return to visit and comfort them.

Day and night cannot dwell together. The red man has ever fled the approach of the white man, as the changing mists on the mountain side flee before the blazing morning sun.

However, your proposition seems a just one, and I think my folks will accept it and will retire to the reservation you offer for them, and we will dwell apart and in peace, for the words of the great white chief seem to be the voice of nature speaking to my people out of the thick darkness that is fast gathering around them like a dense fog floating inward from a midnight sea.

It matters but little where we pass the remainder of our days.
THEY ARE NOT MANY.

The Indian's night promises to be dark. No bright star hovers about the horizon. Sad-voiced winds moan in the distance. Some grim Nemesis of our race is on the red man's trail, and wherever he goes he will still hear the sure approaching footsteps of the fell destroyer and prepare to meet his doom, as does the wounded doe that hears the approaching footsteps of the hunter.

A few more moons, a few more winters, and not one of all the mighty hosts that once filled this broad land or that now roam in fragmentary bands through these vast solitudes will remain to weep over the tombs of a people once as powerful and hopeful as your own.

But why should we repine? Why should [I murmur at the] fate of my people? Tribes are made up of individuals and are no better than [th]ey. Men come and go like the waves of the sea. A tear, a tamawanus, a dirge, and they are gone from our longing eyes forever. Even the white man, whose God walked and talked with him, as friend to friend, is not exempt from the common destiny. We *may* be brothers after [all.] We shall see.

We will ponder your proposition, and when we have decided we will tell you. But should we accept it, I here and now make this the first condition: That we will not be denied the privilege, without molestation, of visiting at will the graves of our ancestors and friends. Every part of this country is sacred to my people. Every hill-side, every valley, every plain and grove has been hallowed by some fond memory or some sad experience of my tribe.

EVEN THE ROCKS
that seem to lie dumb as they swelter in the sun along the silent seashore in solemn grandeur thrill with memories of past events connected with the fate of my people, and the very dust under your feet responds more lovingly to our footsteps than to yours, because it is the ashes of our ancestors, and our bare feet are conscious of the sympathetic touch, for the soil is rich with the life of our kindred.

The sable braves, and fond mothers, and glad-hearted maidens, and the little children who lived and rejoiced here, and whose very names are now forgotten, still love these solitudes, and their deep fastnesses at eventide grow shadowy with the presence of dusky spirits. And when the last red man shall have perished from the earth and his memory among white men shall have become a myth, these shores shall swarm with the invisible dead of my tribe, and when your children's children shall think themselves alone in the field, the store, the shop, upon the highway or in the silence of the woods they will not be alone. In all the earth there is no place dedicated to solitude. At night, when the streets of your cities and villages shall be silent, and you think them deserted, they will throng with the returning hosts that once filled and still love this beautiful land. The white man will never be alone. Let him be just and deal kindly with my people, for the dead are not altogether powerless. (Qtd. in Furtwangler 12–17)

Cochise's Speeches

Although they have often been taken to be different versions of the same speech, there are actually two substantially different speeches that have been attributed to Cochise. The first was published by Dr. Henry Stuart Turrill in 1907, and the second by Dr. Anderson Nelson Ellis in the *Kansas State Historical Society Collections* for 1913–14. Ellis heard Cochise speak in September 1871 during negotiations with General Gordon Granger. Turrill heard Cochise speak in March 1872 during negotiations with General O. O. Howard.

Ellis's Version

> The sun has been very hot on my head and made me as in a fire; my blood was on fire, but now I have come into this valley and drunk of these waters and washed myself in them and they have cooled me. Now that I am cool I have come with my hands open to you to live in peace with you. I speak straight and do not wish to deceive or be deceived. I want a good, strong and lasting peace. When God made the world he gave one part to the white man and another to the Apache. Why was it? Why did they come together? Now that I am to speak, the sun, the moon, the earth, the air, the waters, the birds and beasts, even the children unborn shall rejoice at my words. The white people have looked for me long. I am here! What do they want? They have looked for me long; why am I worth so much? If I am worth so much why not mark when I set my foot and look when I spit? The coyotes go about at night to rob and kill; I can not see them; I am not God. I am no longer chief of all the Apaches. I am no longer rich; I am but a poor man. The world was not always this way. I can not command the animals; if I would they would not obey me. God made us not as you; we were born like the animals, in the dry grass, not on beds like you. This is why we do as the animals, go about of a night and rob and steal. If I had such things as you have, I would not do as I do, for then I would not need to do so. There are Indians who go about killing and robbing. I do not command them. If I did, they would not do so. My warriors have been killed in Sonora. I came in here because God told me to do so. He said it was good to be at peace—so I came! I was going around the world with the clouds, and the air, when God spoke to my thought and told me to come in here and be at peace with all. He said the world was for us all; how was it? When I was young I walked all

over this country, east and west, and saw no other people than the Apaches. After many summers I walked again and found another race of people had come to take it. How is it? Why is it that the Apaches wait to die—that they carry their lives on their finger nails? They roam over the hills and plains and want the heavens to fall on them. The Apaches were once a great nation; they are now but few, and because of this they want to die and so carry their lives on their finger nails. Many have been killed in battle.... You must speak straight so that your words may go as sunlight to our hearts. *Tell me, if the Virgin Mary has walked throughout all the land, why has she never entered the wigwam of the Apache? Why have we never seen or heard her?*...

I have no father nor mother; I am alone in the world. No one cares for Cochise; that is why I do not care to live, and wish the rocks to fall on me and cover me up. If I had a father and a mother like you, I would be with them and they with me. When I was going around the world, all were asking for Cochise. Now he is here—you see him and hear him—are you glad? If so, say so. Speak, Americans and Mexicans, I do not wish to hide anything from you nor have you hide anything from me; I will not lie to you; do not lie to me. I want to live in these mountains; I do not want to go to Tularosa. That is a long ways off. The flies on those mountains eat out the eyes of the horses. The bad spirits live there. I have drunk of these waters and they have cooled me; I do not want to leave here. (Qtd. in Ellis 391–92)

Turrill's Version

This for a very long time has been the home of my people; they came from the darkness, few in numbers and feeble. The country was held by a much stronger and more numerous people, and from their stone houses we were quickly driven. We were a hunting people, living on the animals that we could kill. We came to these mountains about us; no one lived here, and so we took them for our home and country. Here we grew from the first feeble band to be a great people, and covered the whole country as the clouds cover the mountains. Many people came to our country. First, the Spanish, with their horses and their iron shirts, their long knives and guns, great wonders to my simple people. We fought some, but they never tried to drive us from our homes in these mountains. After many years the Spanish soldiers were driven away and the Mexican ruled the land. With these little wars came, but we were now a strong people and we did not fear them. At last in my youth came the white man, your people. Under the counsels of my grandfather who had for a very long time been the head of the Apaches, they were received with friendship. Soon their numbers increased and many passed through my country to the great waters of the setting sun. Your soldiers came and their strong houses were all through my country. I received favors from your people and did all that I could in return and we lived at peace. At last your soldiers did me a very great wrong, and I and my whole people went to war with them. At first we were successful and your soldiers were driven away and your people killed and we again possessed our land. Soon many soldiers came from the north and from the west, and my people were driven to the mountain hiding places; but these did not protect us, and soon my people were flying from one mountain to another, driven by the soldiers, even as the wind is now driving the clouds. I have fought long and as best I could against you. I have destroyed many of your people, but where I have destroyed one white man many have come in his place; but where an Indian has been killed, there has been none to come in his place, so that the great people that welcomed you with acts of kindness to this land are now but a feeble band that fly before your soldiers as the deer before the hunter, and must all perish if this war continues. I have come to you, not from any love for you or for your great father in Washington, or from any regard for his or your wishes, but as a conquered chief, to try to save alive the few people that still remain to me. I am the last of my family, a family that for very many years have been the leaders of this people, and on me depends their future, whether they shall utterly vanish from the land or that a small remnant remain for a few years to see the sun rise over these mountains, their home. I here pledge my word, a word that has never been broken, that if your great father will set aside a part of my own country, where I and my little band can live, we will remain at peace with your people forever. If from his abundance he will give food for my women and children, whose protectors his soldiers have killed, with blankets to cover their nakedness, I will receive them with gratitude. If not, I will do my best to feed and clothe them, in peace with the white man. I have spoken. (Qtd. in Turrill 19–21)

Chief Joseph's Speech

All the variants of the longer speech attributed to Joseph come from C. E. S. Wood. Wood's many revisions—most have to do with the spelling of Indian names and with punctuation, but there are also some changes in wording—have been catalogued by George Venn (2001), who kindly sent them along to me on July 7, 2010. I give, as noted above, the earliest text, the one first published after Wood's time with Joseph immediately following his "surrender." It comes from the *Bismarck* [Dakota Territory] *Tri-Weekly Tribune* for October 26, 1877, as reprinted by Haruo Aoki.

> Tell General Howard I know his heart. What he told me before I have in my heart. I am tired of fighting. Our Chiefs are killed. Looking Glass is dead. Ta-hool-hool-shoot is dead. The old men are all dead. It is the young men who say yes or no. He who leads the young men is dead. It is cold and we have no blankets. The little children are freezing to death. My people, some of them, have run away to the hills and have no blankets, no food; no one knows where they are—may be freezing to death. I want time to look for my children and see how many of them I can find. May be I shall find them among the dead. Hear me my chiefs; I am tired. My heart is sick and sad. From where the sun now stands I will fight no more forever. (Qtd. in Aoki 1989, 17)

The two earliest versions of the single-sentence speech follow below. The first appeared in the Chicago *Times* on the same date as the first publication of the longer speech, October 26, 1877. It was supplied by Wood. The second is from the *North American Review* article of 1879 signed by Joseph. It is from the translation by Arthur Chapman as surely edited by others. I give these versions as well, as reprinted by Aoki (1989, 18).

1. "From where the sun stands, forever and ever, I will never fight again."
2. "From where the sun now stands I will fight no more."

Notes

Introduction

1. This perspective allowed me to write the essay Professor Weisman had requested, "'That the People Might Live': Notes toward a Study of Native American Elegy." It is that essay that inspired this book. I am very grateful to Professor Weisman for her persistence and subsequent help.

2. It has also found some differences as well, e.g., what has been called "ghost fright" (Hittman 1997, 180) among southwestern tribal nations, who (in this like the Nez Perce people of the Plateau and the Kiowa of the Southern Plains) do *not* (contrary to the practice of many other tribal nations) speak the names of the dead and bestow them soon on the living.

3. See Peter Sacks's chapter 4 on "Lycidas" for a full and persuasive account of that poem.

4. But even those Native nations that were able, physically, to stay where they were suffered what Vine Deloria Jr. called an "exile." See below.

5. Sacks's brief remarks on Whitman throughout his book, and in particular in his "Epilogue" are very helpful. Max Cavitch's chapter "Retrievements out of the Night: Whitman and the Future of Elegy" (2007) is a valuable recent study.

6. Without substantial revisions and the particular "depathologizing" of the term I have noted above, it is not possible to use the term "melancholia" as it is presented in Freud's 1917 essay to name anything positive. Sacks's 1985 study largely retained the distinction between mourning and melancholia but complicated it fruitfully, importantly influencing Ramazani's "melancholic mourning" (xi). I'll use Ramazani's phrase on several occasions in what follows. See also Clewell.

7. See, for example, Simon Ortiz's terse evocation of exile in the first lines of his poem "A Designated National Park": "This morning / I have to buy a permit to get back home" (1992, 235).

8. For this, see the two-volume *Encyclopedia of American Indian Removal* edited by Daniel Littlefield and James Parins.

9. Vizenor has from the 1980s to the present offered the terms "continuance" and "survivance" (survival through resistance) as substitutes for what he sees as the dominant Euramerican terms "progress" and "dominance." See his account of survivance in "Aesthetics of Survivance: Literary Theory and Practice" (2008).

10. Freud's essay "Mourning and Melancholia" referred not only "to the loss of a loved person," but "to the loss of some abstraction which has taken the place of one, such as one's country, liberty, an ideal, and so on" (243). W. David Shaw has called elegiac responses to such losses "apocalyptic"; they offer "a lament not just for a dead person, but for the passing of a world" (155).

11. To be sure, we speak of Darwin's *theory* of evolution, but that theory operates as a *law,* like the law of gravity or the law of relativity.

12. See, for example, Johannes Fabian, *Time and the Other: How Anthropology Makes Its Object.* It "makes" it in part by "distancing those who are observed from the Time of the observer" (25).

13. It will be clear that "modern" as I use it here is a descriptive term, just as "traditional" is a broadly descriptive term. "Modern" doesn't mean "new" or "up-to-date," in the same way that "traditional" doesn't mean "old" or "out-of-date," with an implicit evaluation.

14. See Krupat 2002a.

15. This is, once more, only a glance at the poem. A very fine and finely detailed reading can be found in Peter Sacks's chapter 7, "Tennyson: *In Memoriam.*"

16. On this, see the discussion of Ginsberg in Ramazani's chapter *"American Family Elegy I."*

17. It had, for a time, been the fashion to present translations from oral literature—narrative as well as song—as verse on the printed page (see Parker 2003b), so that one could not tell from looking at the translation whether the original performance did or did not have an "underlying metric sub-structure." Apart from the tastes of the translator, it is only the presence of an "underlying metric sub-structure" in the original that justifies speaking of "oral poetry."

18. A brief autobiography had been composed in the eighteenth century by the Reverend Samson Occom, a Mohegan, but it was not published until the last quarter of the twentieth century.

1. Oral Performances (i)

1. These names are spelled differently by different authors. What I have given above are the most usual spellings.

2. It was Deganawidah who first named the fifty chiefs. Condolence rites of a less extensive character were performed ten days after the death of someone who was not a chief, and, in the recent past, the tendency has also been to allow ten days before formally condoling the death of a chief in order that appropriate preparations may take place. See Woodbury, p. xxxiii, n. 71.

3. I have discussed this particular sort of exile in the introduction.

4. The Tuscaroras entered the League in the eighteenth century, the Five Nations becoming, thus, the Six Nations.

5. In similar fashion, Sergei Kan considers the Tlingit memorial potlatch, which I will discuss below, to be "double obsequies" (1989, 13)—not a funeral ceremony, but rather a ritual that connects people to what has gone before and what will come after. For some of the rites and customs pertaining to deaths among the Iroquois, see Shimony.

6. Long ago these were indeed deer antlers. See, for example, the following from the "Chiefs' Version" (see below and note 16) of the origins of the League: "Then De-ka-nah-wi-deh said, We shall now adopt these signs (or emblems) deer's horns by placing them upon the head of each other. It shall be thus then, that these horns shall be placed upon the head of every man who shall be called a 'Lord' by his people and he shall have the power to rule his people" (Scott 219). On this, see also Fenton's translation of Chief Gibson (1998, 91). At some undetermined more recent date, the horns came to be represented by special wampum strings.

7. Jay Miller (1998) has noted something similar for the Tshimshian, a continent away to the west. He writes: "Tsimshian say that people are given to the names rather than the reverse because the names are immortal and each can convey benefits to its 'holder' who treats it with respect by leading an honorable and generous life." These names "are not just remembered, they are inherited to 'live again' by another mortal body" (670). He notes "the Iroquoian parallel" (671).

8. Some accounts of the Condolence Council speak of the *Two* Brothers even after the addition of the Tuscaroras to the League, while other accounts refer to the *Four* Brothers, including the Tuscaroras along with one of the associated tribes. Hewitt spoke of the moieties as two "sisterhoods," with each addressing "the other sisterhood as 'our cousins.'" The "sisterhood" made up of Senecas, Onondagas, and Mohawks, however, is the sisterhood "on the *father's* side," while the Oneidas and Cayugas constitute the sisterhood "on the *mother's* side" (Hewitt 1977, 164; my emphases; 1928, 91ff.).

9. Woodbury notes that some of the English names for parts of the Condolence Council that have appeared in the scholarly literature do not accord very well with the Native language originals. Thus, for example, what has been called the welcome "At the Woods' Edge" is more accurately called "Near the Thorny Bushes," probably wild raspberry bushes on the outskirts of a cleared settlement. See in particular Woodbury xxxii and xxxiii on this matter.

10. Although I have cited Fenton's dating of the League from 1570, this first element of the Condolence Ritual, the greeting "at the wood's edge," as both Fenton (1998, 180) and Gunther Michelson (among others) remark, "is described in an entry of Jacques Cartier's journal in 1535" (G. Michelson 66). Fenton notes the "first recorded performance of the Requickening Address to open the proceedings of a treaty" council with the French was an address by "Kiotsaeton...a Mohawk speaker in 1645" (1998, 181). That a fire is kindled may suggest that the ceremony did not take place in the late spring or summer. Indeed, Hewitt writes that the ceremony "is so deeply concerned with the dead and with the powers that requicken and preserve the living from the power of the Destroyer [death]...it was thought to be deadly and destructive to growing seeds and plants and fruits were it held in the spring or summer" (1973, 165). But as I have noted above in note 2, there is also the prescription that the Rites be held within three or ten days after a chief's death—which might indeed be in the spring or summer.

Taiaiake Alfred points to the Condolence Rites as a model "to consecrate a new relationship," so that instead of condolers, "the other party to a *treaty*" might come to "the woods edge" (xx; my emphasis). Michael Foster's essays "On Who Spoke First at Iroquois-White Councils: An Exercise in the Method of Upstreaming" and "Another Look at the Function of Wampum in Iroquois-White Councils" show in great detail the manner in which the Condolence Ceremony served to shape the interaction of whites and Iroquois peoples in treaty-making councils particularly in the eighteenth century. See also Pomedli.

11. I believe this must be Foster, although the chapter, called "Glossary of Figures of Speech in Iroquois Political Rhetoric," does not carry an author's name.

12. See also Woodbury, p. 601, n. 4.

13. This exists only in an English-language version, and it is not known (Woodbury xvi) whether the Chiefs dictated it in English or made an English translation from one or several Native-language versions. See Scott.

14. Hewitt's manuscript has never been published, and I have not been able to see it. We can, however, compare Hewitt's 1916 text with Fenton's 1944 revision. Both are stiffly formal and archaic in feel, although it is altogether possible that John Gibson's language would also have felt formal and old-fashioned to his contemporaries. The Fenton version is a bit less verbose and tangled than Hewitt's original. I'll offer just one example from what is called the "Seventh Wampum String" in Hewitt (1973, 172), and "The Seventh Article of Burden: The Loss of the Sky" in Fenton (1944, 74). Hewitt: "Now, another thing, (I say). That it comes to pass where a direful thing befalls a person, the sky, the firmament, becomes lost to that person, and that person knows nothing of what is taking place in the heavens. This very thing, moreover, has befallen thy person, this

one [*indicating*], my offspring, thou noble one, thou whom I have been wont to hold in my bosom, (I say)." Fenton: "Oh, my offspring, now there is another matter to be considered at this time. It is that, then, that where a great calamity has befallen a person it invariably comes to pass that the sky is lost to the senses of that person; invariably he does not know anything of what is taking place in the sky (I say)."

15. This involved going through the Gibson-Goldenweiser MS with contemporary Onondaga speakers who repronounced each word and offered thoughts on its proper translation. See p. xii, n. 6, and pp. xv-xvii for further information on Woodbury's method for "re-elicitation." Karin Michelson had engaged in a similar, though less extensive, project a bit earlier, publishing in 1980. See below.

16. Carrie Dyck's comment that Woodbury's "*Concerning the League* is the only *complete* version published in an Iroquoian language" is correct (37; my emphasis), although her subsequent observation that only Woodbury's "version is *by* the Iroquois, rather than being *about* them" (37) is mistaken. If nothing else, the 1912 "Chiefs' Version" is entirely *by* the Iroquois—but this is true as well for, say, Gibson and Hewitt, if not also for some of the other texts I have mentioned.

17. See Woodbury lviii-lix and passim for a full account of the available sources.

18. La Fort was not just an interpreter. According to Thomas Abler, he was "the most influential Onondaga chief" of the 1880s (1984, 90–91). The first part of Hale's earlier Mohawk text was re-elicited by Karin Michelson, who worked with three speakers of Mohawk in 1976 and 1979. Michelson's 1980 publication presents "Hale's Mohawk text exactly as it was published in 1883, with the modern Mohawk version as spoken at the Caughnawaga Reserve near Montreal, Quebec below it," along with an English translation done by her Mohawk consultants (26).

19. Among many sources on this, see Fenton 1998, 26, 29, and 32; and Richter 1992, 19. An important aspect of reciprocity is what Michael Foster has called "the Iroquoian emphasis on the channel of communication" (1985, 103), through which reciprocal acts of condolence or, as in Foster's discussion here, treaty proposals may pass from one side to the other.

20. Fenton, summarizing from the Gibson-Goldenweiser MS, lists eleven matters to be addressed (1998, 728), several of which I take up below.

21. After actually attending a Condolence Ceremony, Horatio Hale noted "what [he] had not before understood—that this portion [the chant of welcome] of the Book of Rites was intended to be, not spoken, but sung" (1895, 52). Other portions, too, were more nearly sung ("chanted" and "intoned" are words often used) than spoken.

22. Woodbury's literal translation of Gibson's later dictation differs remarkably little in substance. The condolers will wipe "your tears with this white, soft cloth.... Then, moreover, you will look around calmly, and you will see them all about you, roaming around, your nephews and nieces, and then you will see the land again. Thereupon you will begin to think calmly again; moreover for at least one day, you should be thinking peacefully" (Woodbury 607–8).

23. The "person" referenced alludes to individual persons who are grieving but importantly to the collective or social person of the bereaved moiety.

24. Beauchamp translates from Daniel La Fort's Onondaga version, in which the Younger Brothers condole the Older Brothers, saying: "Now we will open your ears, and also your throat, for there is something that has been choking you, and we will also give you water which shall wash down all the troubles you have in your throat. We shall hope that then your mind will recover its cheerfulness. This we say and do, we three brothers" (1907, 384).

25. See, for example, my discussion of Tlingit potlatch oratory, Arapaho Ghost Dance songs, and Black Hawk's and Black Elk's autobiographies below.

26. Hale: "We will also give you the water that shall wash down all the troubles in your throat. We shall hope that after this your mind will recover its cheerfulness. This we say and do, we three brothers" (1883, 111); Woodbury: "It happens in this way, and it is dreadful that thus it should happen to them, that repeatedly there is a great twisting around within one's body, there being much

bile in addition to the displacement of the organs within the body, and eventually it will fail, one's spirit and one's strength" (652); "Therefore the Three Brothers will say, 'Now we are pouring in the liquid...when the liquid settles down, it will begin to work in your body; it will strengthen your mind, and it will wipe away the widespread jaundice and readjust the twisted organs within your body. Thereupon you will begin to be happy again'" (653–54).

27. Beauchamp, from Daniel La Fort's Onondaga: "Now another thing we will say, we younger brothers. You are mourning in the deep darkness. I will make the sky clear for you, so that you will not see a cloud. And also I will cause the sun to shine upon you, so that you can look upon it peacefully as it goes down. You shall see it when it is going. Yea! the sun shall seem to be hanging just over you, and you shall look upon it peacefully as it goes down. Now I have hope that you will yet see the pleasant days. This we say and do, we three brothers" (1907, 384); Woodbury: "It has become dark for you...and you can no longer see the light of day. So now the Three Brothers will say, 'Now we are making it bright for you again.' Then, moreover, you will see the daylight, you will notice them again,...your nephews and nieces, and you will see the earth and you will be happy from then on" (657).

28. Cf. Woodbury: "Again there is another matter: 'Every day it threatens us with a pole raised to the level of our heads, the Great Destroyer, who lurks in darkness near the house, overpowering us with magic, scattering things about'" (664). Indeed, "the [Great Destroyer], this is what [cavorted] there, and from the fire container it caused the firebrands [i.e., the Confederacy chiefs] to scatter...it is dreadful that thus it has happened to you. Moreover, we, the Three Brothers, say 'we are gathering together firebrands again for your fire container.' Moreover, when we rekindle it, smoke will rise again, beautiful smoke will pierce the sky again..." (667), so that "'you will think peacefully in future'" (668), with the full complement of chiefs once more in place.

29. Woodbury: "Moreover they will say, the Three Brothers, 'Now, moreover, show us our new colleague. Moreover, we shall keep in mind that it has happened according to our custom....' Now, moreover, the Three Brothers have completed their speech" (684). "'Now your words are completed, my father's kinsmen.... From among the people they will raise him up in front of the chiefs, who will call him by the name of the dead chief'" (693).

30. *Potlatch* is a Chinook jargon word that derives from Nootka. Spelled a variety of ways in the nineteenth century, it means to make a gift, or gift-giving. See Shaw, Gibbs, and, more recently, Lang. Edward Curtis noted: "The Indians usually apply to the festival names that signify an assemblage, or, referring to the general invocation sent out by the prospective host, a convocation" (69). There are also variant spellings of the term *ḵoo.'eex'*, which basically means "to invite" (see below). "Tlingit," the Dauenhauers write, "is pronounced Klink-it in English, and Lingít in Tlingit, with a voiceless 'L'" (1990, 150). One of the earliest outsiders to write about these people was Charles Erskine Wood, who, in 1882, published "Among the Thlinkits in Alaska," getting the pronunciation approximately right. We will meet Wood again in our discussion of Nez Perce Joseph's "farewell" speech. Although I cite authors who refer to Tlingit potlatch oratory, I have found no full examples of it—unlike the case with Iroquoian Condolence performances—apart from those given by the Dauenhauers.

31. Tlingit people occupy territories in the southeast of what is now Alaska, and in northern British Columbia, as well as lands a bit farther south. They speak an Athabaskan language.

32. And perhaps as well similar ceremonies among other Northwest Coast nations, as I have noted, e.g., the Tsimshian (J. Miller 1998).

33. The Raven People are sometimes known as the Crows, a close enough parallel. But the Eagle People are sometimes known as the Wolves, and I haven't found an explanation of that parallelism. Jay Miller (1998) notes that Coast and Southern Tshimshians recognize four paired clans, which have parallels among the "inland Gisksan and Nishga," who, however, "substitute Frog for Tsimshian Raven," and "Grizzly or Fireweed for Orca," the whale (661).

34. Cf. Kan: *"ḳu: eex'*, 'invitational ceremony,' from the verb *ya-eex'*, 'to call out, to invite'" (1989, 196). De Laguna, citing Boas, notes a derivation of the term for a major potlatch "from *qu 'ix tlen*, 'big invitation'" (1972, 610).

35. The Dauenhauers affirm that "*respect* is the single, major concept that most Tlingit elders place at the top of their list of imperatives to know, understand, and practice in the study of Tlingit culture" (1990, xxix).

36. The ceremony began at 5:00 p.m. and concluded at 5:00 a.m. (Dauenhauer and Dauenhauer 1990, 82), thus taking longer than the Condolence Rites we know of.

37. The Dauenhauers give a complete analysis of Dalton's speech (1990, 94–107), and my own brief account is heavily dependent on theirs.

38. In their contribution to Brian Swann's volume *Coming to Light: Contemporary Translations of the Native Literatures of North America* (1994), the Dauenhauers had reprinted Jessie Dalton's oratorical performance of 1968, preceding it with a myth story called "Glacier Bay History," as told by Amy Marvin in 1984. Unable to see this story as performing the function in Ms. Dalton's speech specified by Kan—I couldn't, that is to say, see it as a "mythological tragedy" containing a "protagonist" whose behavior could be "likened to the helping actions and words of the guests" (Kan 1983, 52)—I contacted Richard Dauenhauer who generously explained that, in fact, it had not been included for that purpose. Rather, it appeared as one of a group of stories generally taken to be about (among other things) the origins of the potlatch.

39. In a discussion "rethinking" the Tsimshian potlatch, Christopher Roth makes clear the importance of the redistribution of names among the Tsimshian People. See in particular his reflections on names on p. 134.

40. William Beauchamp had noted that this was also true for parts of the Condolence Rites that preceded the Requickening Address, when "The forest paths were *symbolically* cleared, [and] thorns were taken out of the feet," before "the tears were wiped away, the throat and ears were cleansed," and "the heart...restored to its right place, and clouds were removed from the sun in the sky" (1907, 393; my emphasis).

41. We will soon note Jeffrey Anderson's description of a very similar procedure at work in Arapaho Ghost Dance songs.

42. In his 1909 publication, *Tlingit Myths and Texts,* John Swanton recorded a similar speech, which, in addition to a transition from wet to dry, and cold to warm, also employs a metaphorical transition similar to the one in David Kadashan's speech, from being unmoored to being anchored and stable again. Swanton says that one of the bereaved rises and says: "I thank you, my grandfathers, for your words. It is as if I had been in a great flood. My uncles' houses and my uncles' poles went drifting about the world with me. But now your words have made [the flood] go down from me. My uncles' houses have drifted ashore and have been left at a good place. Your kind words have put down my floor planks. We have been as if we were cold. But now that you have made a fire for us with my grandfathers' emblem [*at.oow*] we shall be very warm. Thank you for what you have done. On account of your words we will not mourn any more" (377).

Like the oratory of the Iroquois Condolence Rites, Tlingit potlatch oratory, it would seem, has not much changed, at least between 1909 and 1968.

43. Nor, so far as I have been able to learn, did the various parts of the Iroquois Condolence Council have an underlying metric structure. Hewitt wrote of the Requickening Address he published that "it is sometimes delivered in the form of blank verse; but the text from which the following translation is not in such form" (1977, 166). I suspect Hewitt meant to elevate the importance of his material by claiming that it might appear in the meter of Shakespeare: but there is nothing like "blank verse" in the chants of the Condolence Council.

44. "The Farewell Song," Hinton writes, was first sung in the nineteenth century "by an ancestor of [Mr. Hanna] named Horned Heart" (1994, 690). Dan Hanna learned the song from his father, Henry Hanna, who "learned [it] from his sister's husband, Kit Jones"; Hinton recorded

his version when Henry Hanna "was in his eighties...and had recently had a serious operation" (Hinton 1984, 147). It appears, in Havasupai and in English in Hinton and Watahomigie 1984, 148–53. An unattributed fragment of this song is also included in Hinton 1984, 275–76. Hinton writes that the song "was not ceremonial in nature, nor magical, nor spiritually powerful or dangerous" (personal communication, June 22, 2008).

45. Dan Hanna explained to her, Hinton writes, "that although [the *ha na*'s] are indeed vocables, they are not meaningless." (Vocables, as we will see further, are usually syllables—not words—used to fill out the rhythm.) Something like *ha na* "always bear[s] the connotation of mourning." A parallel, Hinton notes, is the way in which "the vocables *tra-la-la* in English bear a connotation of happiness" (1994, 691).

46. In 1999, an interlinear translation was prepared by Ida Mae Valdez, a Yerington Paiute tribal elder, along with Jeanette Allen and Ralph Burns of the Pyramid Lake Paiute Language Project. The free translation from which I quote with his permission is by Professor Michael Hittman of Long Island University and Mrs. Wright.

47. I will later consider elegies for a squirrel, other small animals, and also a tree in the work of some contemporary Native writers.

48. Where material appears in both the 1965 and the 1973 reissues of Mooney's work, I cite the former because, as I've noted, it is more widely available. Although he does not explicitly refer to Mooney, Thomas Overholt, asking the question, "What did [the Ghost Dance movement] *mean* to the people who were involved in it?" writes that "an historian of religion" might conclude that it meant to them a "*return* to paradise" (57; my emphases).

49. Americans have for long narrated the progress of "civilization" as a *comic* story. This requires that inevitable Indian decline before this progress be narrated as *tragic,* a story sad but just. "We" rise to the heights of civilization while "they" tragically fall, victims of their own "savagery." See my "Representing Indians in American Literature, 1820–1870" (Krupat 2009a) for a fuller account along these lines.

50. This was very much the view of Charles Alexander Eastman, a Santee Sioux and a medical doctor who tended to the Indians wounded by army fire at Wounded Knee. In his autobiography, *From the Deep Woods to Civilization* (1916), Eastman wrote: "A religious craze such as that of 1890–91 was a thing foreign to the Indian philosophy.... It meant that the last hope of race entity [*sic*] had departed, and my people were groping blindly after spiritual relief in their bewilderment and misery" (1977, 92). Except for the unfortunate characterization of the People "groping blindly," the latter part of Eastman's statement is correct, although the former part is quite mistaken.

51. "Relative deprivation" is David Aberle's term, as developed in his "The Prophet Dance and Relations to White Contact" (1959). Anthony F. C. Wallace had earlier introduced the concept of revitalization movements in his "Revitalization Movements" (1956).

52. Or even earlier. Hittman, commenting on what he calls the "rigidity of Spier's position" (1990, 104), briefly summarizes other positions (95–96). On this matter, see Deward Walker's "New Light on the Prophet Dance Controversy" (1969) and Christopher Miller's somewhat more recent *Prophetic Worlds* (1985).

53. Hittman (1990) makes clear that although the Paiutes had suffered drought around 1889, they were not, in 1890, in the sort of crisis situation that had prevailed before 1870. Wovoka seems generally to have taught not that the dead would come back to earth, but rather that the living would join them in heaven. Apart from this distinction, I know of no fully satisfactory explanation as to why, in 1890, Wovoka's community would have put aside its traditional "ghost fright."

54. The Ghost Dance religion among the Paiute was called *nanigukwa,* "dance in a circle."

55. Hittman reports Wovoka's commentary "that ecstatic seizures"—trances—"by followers were not part of his religion," and he cites a contemporary, Mrs. George Plummer, to the effect that trances Wovoka himself experienced had no connection to the Ghost Dance. The Cheyenne,

Arapaho, and Lakota ghost dancers, however, did experience trances "on home reservations" (Hittman 1990 82).

56. This was not what Mooney reported. To the contrary, what Hittman calls Mooney's "plains bias" appears "to have led him to recapitulate what his beloved Kiowa, etc. told him, rather than what he heard from Wovoka and others in Nevada with his own ears, and also read in Chapman" (1990, 98). Hittman is referring to Arthur Chapman's "Report to the Secretary of War," published in 1891, and based on an 1890 interview with Wovoka, which is reprinted as an appendix to Hittman's book. Chapman wrote that Wovoka had told him the Indians "must not fight with the white people or one another; that we were all brothers, and must remain in peace" (qtd. in Hittman 1990, 234). I will return to Mooney's Plains-based or Plains-biased view below, and in a later chapter I will have more to say about Chapman's earlier career.

57. This Sitting Bull was a much younger man than the great Lakota chief of that name killed in December 1890.

58. Not only because of the whites' attempts to forbid it, but also because of the extreme scarcity of buffalo bulls, whose skulls were extremely important to Sun Dance ritual. This scarcity is an aspect of exile described by Vine Deloria Jr.

59. As late as 1989, Alice Kehoe would still write that Kicking Bear and the Lakota "distorted" (7) and "perverted" (39) Wovoka's message. As I have tried to show, this oversimplifies a complex matter. Thomas Overholt's work (1974) is useful in presenting the views of Porcupine, the Arapaho Sitting Bull, and Kicking Bear, with reference to earlier reports of Wovoka's message by a Paiute man known as Captain Dick. See in particular Overholt 42–56.

60. This was certainly the position of the important Sahaptin prophet Smohalla, of the upper Columbia River. "His doctrine was that the world, and particularly the Whites, would be destroyed and the old way of life would be restored complete with the resurrection of the dead" (Suttles 1957, 354).

61. One of the most important of these has to do with "ghost shirts," which were said to have the power to protect the wearer from bullets. After Lakotas clad in ghost shirts died from gunfire at Wounded Knee, Wovoka was asked whether he had indeed claimed that the ghost shirts would protect the wearers. He said that any comment of his to that effect was a "joke" (Hittman 1990, 83–84). But we know that he had indeed made demonstrations of his own imperviousness to bullets shot at him (Hittman 192), a standard feature of Paiute shamanic power (i.e., Wovoka's father was said to have been impervious to bullets), and that he had also sold protective Ghost Dance shirts to other Indians—although his Paiute People did not wear them.

62. Of the third song he publishes, Mooney says only that "this song may refer to something in Paiute mythology" (1965, 290), which does not help a great deal.

63. Both Mooney and Anderson transcribe the Arapaho language versions of the songs; Anderson's transcriptions are interlined with the English, while Mooney gives the Arapaho first and then the English. I have left out the Arapaho. I suspect that Anderson's transcriptions, conforming to the state of current linguistic knowledge, are more accurate than Mooney's, but I am not able to judge or compare the two.

64. The Plains Indians generally considered Wovoka to be the *wanekia,* the son of God or Christ, and as late as 1917, Wovoka wrote: "I am the only living Jesus there is" (qtd. in Hittman 1990, 190). The degree to which Christianity influenced his or any of the other Ghost Dances has not been established—although the idea of reunion with the dead in heaven seems quite obviously Christian. Hittman notes that Paiutes of the late twentieth century claim that there were not many Christian elements in Wovoka's message, and William Powers insists that "there is simply no empirical evidence that in 1889–90 most Lakotas participating in the Ghost Dance were Christianized" (1990, 61). In any case, what Powers says of Christianity among the Lakota—that it underwent a "*Lakotification process*" (10; my emphasis)—may be observed generally: where Native people involved in the dances seem clearly to have adopted elements of Christianity (e.g., some

tribes held the dances on Sunday, and some dancers—the Klamath, for example—made the sign of the cross before they danced), it was surely an *Indianized* Christianity consonant with traditional religious beliefs.

65. On the subject of vocables, see Powers, who summarizes existing work up to 1992 and recommends Charlotte Frisbie's "Vocables in Navajo Ceremonial Music" as "the most definitive article on the place of the vocable in song of a singular [*sic*] tribe" (1999, 31).

66. Powers lists many published versions of this song, including a performance by "Jerome Wolf Ears, collected by [him], Summer, 1950, Pine Ridge" (1990, 74). Here is Powers's retranslation of that song: "'Mother **he** come back home, / Mother **he** come back home, / My little brother, crying, is going around, / My little brother, crying, is going around, / Mother **he** come back home, / Mother **he** come back home,' / Father said it so, / Father said it so" (1999, 35). The **he** is a vocable. Mooney gives a version of this song "composed by a young *woman* who saw her dead mother in the other world, and on waking out of her trance vision implores the mother to come back" (1965, 305; my emphasis).

67. Mooney remarks that Grant Left-hand had been a student at the Carlisle Institute and that "notwithstanding several years of English education, . . . [he] is a firm believer in the doctrine and the dance, and the principal organizer of the auxiliary 'crow dance' in his own tribe." His wife "is as prominent in the Ghost dance among the Cheyenne" (1965, 278).

68. Mooney called Dr. McGillycuddy "a man of most positive character" (1965, 93). McGillycuddy strongly urged Christianity and agriculture on the Sioux, something that put him at odds with the eminent traditionalist chief Red Cloud. But when McGillycuddy told the Indians that a change of administration would require him to leave as their agent, Red Cloud is said to have addressed him as "Wasichu Wakan" (wise or holy white man), "a young man with an old man's head on his shoulders." McGillycuddy is buried on Harney Peak in the sacred Black Hills (where Black Elk had his vision) with Red Cloud's words "Wasichu Wakan" as his epitaph. www.coldsplinters.com/2010/02/harney-peak-valentine-mcgillycuddy (accessed August 15, 2011).

69. The Ghost Dance was once more invoked as a metaphor of Indian renewal in a 1992 report by the Indian Nations at Risk Task Force, which proposed "a *new* Ghost Dance" that, after the manner of Wovoka, called on "Native and non-Native people to join together and take action" (qtd. in Krupat 2002c, 102–3). A bit later in the 1990s, Sherman Alexie's novel *Indian Killer* reimagined a different sort of Ghost Dance, one in which whites would be destroyed. See the chapter "The 'Rage Stage'" in my *Red Matters: Native American Studies* (2002c).

2. Oral Performances (ii)

1. Murray's full sentence refers not only to surrender speeches, but also to "protest speeches by Indians." He suggests that the "often devastating criticism of white actions" contained in many of the latter is part of an "already overdetermined" context in which "*what* [the Indians] are saying is actually less important than the fact and manner of their saying it" (36).

2. There are some important exceptions. As John Coward has shown, in the years 1820–90, wild Indians could be presented as analogous to other "wild" groups. For the *Herald*, a staunchly Democratic paper, "Indians, African Americans, radicals, Catholics, foreigners, and lower-class whites were all connected in [the paper's] rehash of Custer and the Little Bighorn, so much so that Sitting Bull's persona became a part of the paper's ongoing explanation of election year issues!" (166). Coward properly credits Richard Slotkin's *The Fatal Environment* for earlier work on these connections.

3. In a study of Indian autobiography published in 1985, I claimed that "the Indian autobiography has no prior model in the collective practice of tribal cultures" (31). Strictly speaking, that remains true. But it has subsequently been shown that aspects of what the West includes under the broad heading of autobiographical expression do certainly exist among tribal cultures.

4. Brief as it is, the best account of Indian-to-Indian oratory, mortals speaking to mortals, remains that of Donald Bahr (1994).

5. We will again see how what *may* have been a communication sent as a *message* was transformed into a face-to-face oration or a *speech* when we consider Chief Joseph's "farewell" at the end of this chapter.

6. When some claimed that the speech was a fraud, Jefferson responded by printing twenty-three pages of affidavits testifying to its authenticity in the 1801 edition of *Notes on the State of Virginia*. The question remains open more than two hundred years later.

7. See Edward Seeber's "Chief Logan's Speech in France" (1946).

8. See Edward Seeber's "Critical Views on Logan's Speech" (1947). Roosevelt also admired Chief Joseph's speech and met with Joseph himself.

9. Louis Jones includes it in his *Aboriginal American Oratory: The Tradition of Eloquence among the Indians of the United States* (1965), along with a confused and confusing discussion that I will note just below. It appears in the version given by Jefferson in Armstrong's collection (1971) and in the textbook by Sanders and Peek (1973); Moquin and Van Doren (1973) reprint it, using as their source the first edition of Samuel Drake's *Biography and History of the Indians of North America* (1832). The speech is shrewdly discussed by David Murray (1991) and is mentioned several times by Clements (2002).

10. Its relation to romantic notions of the "noble savage" has been abundantly discussed. See, in particular, Seeber 1947 and Murray.

11. Merrell acknowledges that none of the information he offers is beyond dispute. Wallace, publishing three years later than Merrell (whom he does not cite), calls Logan "a son of the notable *Cayuga* chief Shikellamy" (1999, 5; my emphasis). Much earlier, in 1947, Edward Seeber had written that Logan was born "of a White father—a Frenchman" (135), while William Clements, in 2002, in a very brief notice of Logan, refers to his father as "S*k*ikellamy, an Oneida" (235; my emphasis). McElwain notes that although Logan is usually said to be "the son of a Cayuga mother and a French father," he was "undoubtedly the son of Chief Shickellamy [an Oneida] (the Iroquois vice regent in Pennsylvania, 1728–1748)" (2001, 111). McElwain does not consider the possibility that Shickellamy might have been a Frenchman adopted by the Oneida.

12. McElwain (2001, 111) thinks there may have been a third son.

13. The brothers' English names derive from a connection to James Logan, who had been the governor of Pennsylvania. Jefferson's Logan has most often been identified as Tahgahjute, meaning "his eyelids stick out," with the implication that "he spies." This identification derives from a book published in 1851 by Brantz Mayer, and it has been repeated many times. Seeber (1947), for example, identified Logan as Tahgahjute, as I did, too, in introducing Logan's speech in the seventh edition of the *Norton Anthology of American Literature*. But Armstrong, in 1971, referred to the orator as Tachnechdorus or John Logan (32), and she is supported by the work of Wallace (1999, 1) and Richter (2001, 213). Meanwhile, McElwain, who identifies himself as a Mingo, continues to refer to Logan as Tahgajute (2001, 108ff.).

14. Mingo was the term used for Iroquoian people living away from their traditional homelands, in particular, those of the Ohio Valley. McElwain writes that Mingo "is originally of derogatory origin," coming from the word '*mengwe*', meaning 'sneaky people'" (2001, 108). *Mengwe* is a Delaware word, thus an Algonkian, not an Iroquoian term, and it may once have been used in a derogatory manner. William Bright gives both a Munsee and an Unami Delaware form of the word, noting that Vogel (1983) had translated it as "treacherous" (Bright 2004, 285), pretty much as McElwain had said. In volume 17 of the 1978 edition of *The Handbook of North American Indians,* Ives Goddard wrote: "From Delaware came the name Mingo, applied to the non-League Senecas, Cayugas, and other Iroquoians in the Ohio Valley in the eighteenth century" (320–21). But, as Professor Goddard kindly wrote me, "The name has *no literal meaning* except as a tribe name" (personal communication, November 4, 2009; my emphasis). Gordon Whittaker (personal

communication, October 29, 2009) supports this, noting that "according to John O'Meara's Delaware-English/English-Delaware Dictionary published in 1996, the word *meengweew* simply means 'Oneida Indian' today." If there was a negative connotation to Mingo—and there may have been—it seems to have dropped away. I am grateful to Michael Foster, Ives Goddard, and Gordon Whittaker for their generous help with this matter.

15. McElwain gives Girty's Indian name as Katepakomen and believes that whether the speech was "delivered by Girty or Gibson,...[it] should have been transmitted word for word," because either "man was eminently capable linguistically and would not have misrendered Tahgajute's [sic] words" (2001, 112). Yet on the same page McElwain writes: "It is in the translation that the real trouble begins." If so, that would suggest *neither* Gibson *nor* Girty as the likely translator.

16. And, later, as Lieutenant C.E.S. Wood did as well, transforming what may have been a *message* sent by Chief Joseph into a *speech*.

17. McElwain, however, notes that because Logan's father had "worked with Moravians and been previously baptized by the Jesuits" (2001, 114), Logan might well have been familiar with the Bible. And see Sheehan, in note 19 below.

18. Stevenson had made this point as well in disparaging the "speech" (157).

19. See Murray 40–42 on Jefferson's use of Logan as natural nobleman. Sheehan writes: "Though Logan's speech may be eloquent, it is an eloquence of the Biblical rather than the Indian sort [sic]. It should be used not to illustrate the peculiar talents of the noble savage, as it was by Jefferson, but to point up the Indian's extraordinary facility in absorbing the white man's culture" (351n). Thus Stevenson dismisses Logan's "eloquence" because he couldn't have known the Bible well, and Sheehan dismisses it because Logan had perhaps "absorbed" it too well! Sheehan is also determined to see Logan as a degenerate drunkard.

20. There are a great many valuable observations in McElwain's attentive reading, some of which I have already cited, and others that I will cite below. But there is also a fair amount of silly carping, e.g., that no Indian would call his dwelling a "cabin." Logan may well have used a very specific term for dwelling place that had either no close English equivalent or one the translator failed to produce. The word "cabin" is certainly inaccurate as a literal translation of whatever word Logan used, but it is hardly evidence of inauthenticity. McElwain also indulges in unhelpful fancy when, for example, he conjectures that the "author" of Logan's speech may have regarded him as "a resting cotton-picker...strumming a banjo, and showing gleaming white teeth" (2001, 115).

21. I strongly suspect it also would not be an accurate translation of terms used to identify the People in other Native languages.

22. Sheehan, in what I find a deeply uninformed, indeed a nasty commentary, is determined to show that Logan "will not do as a noble savage; he represents, rather, the unfortunate culturally disintegrated Indian." Sheehan claims that Logan "was closely connected with the whites, [and] drank heavily" (351n). There are, however, a great many possibilities between the extremes of "noble savage" and "culturally disintegrated Indian"—neither of which expressions would have been meaningful to Mingo people.

23. Chaetar is not an identifiable Winnebago name. Nancy Lurie, using an early twentieth-century manuscript by a Winnebago man named John Blackhawk, identifies "Chaetar" as "Chasja-ka, or Wave...Chaashjan-ga in modern orthography" (164). She points out that he was the brother of the half-Sauk, half-Winnebago prophet, Wabokieshiek or White Cloud, who surrendered to Agent Street along with Black Hawk.

24. Black Hawk was not present at the treaty making. The treaty, signed by General Winfield Scott and Illinois governor John Reynolds for the American side, with Keokuk as the first Sauk signatory, concludes: "Done at Fort Armstrong, Rock Island, Illinois" (Whitney 1184). But that is not the case. Although the treaty was *supposed to* have been drawn up at Fort Armstrong, because "an epidemic of cholera was raging..., and there were many ill at the Fort,...the big treaty tent was pitched in what is now Davenport, at Fifth and Farnam streets" (C. Snyder 95).

25. John Allen Wakefield's *History of the War between the United States and the Sac and Fox Nations of Indians,* also published in 1834, gives only the brief paraphrase from the *Galenian* (148). In a preface to the eleventh edition of his *Biography and History of the Indians of North America,* dated 1841 but printed in 1851, Drake wittily remarks that the "word *edition* in the title-page of a book now-a-days may mean anything or nothing when a number stands before it" (n.p.).

26. This is probably Henry Atkinson. Colonel Taylor, who ultimately praised Atkinson's efforts, had earlier sent criticisms of him to Washington.

27. As I have noted in regard to Logan's apparent use of it, "countrymen" is not a term a traditionally raised Native person would use, because it derives from affiliative, abstract, and social-contract thinking. Black Hawk—like Logan—would have spoken in filiative—family or kinship—terms.

28. The spelling Sealth means to suggest the way the name would be pronounced in Lushootseed, the central coast Salishan language of Sealth's people; the name comes from the root words for "Puget Sound region" and "language" (Suttles and Lane 501). Vi Hilbert, a Lushootseed elder and linguist, noted that a "phonetic spelling that approximates the correct pronunciation is **See**-ahth, with the accent on the first syllable" (259). Old Man House "was the old potlatch house... on the Indian reservation at Suquamish, across from Point Agate on Bainbridge Island" (Bagley 256; see also Suttles 1991, 219). Unlike the practice among the more northerly Tlingit people, for whom the potlatch functioned importantly to console the living who had suffered a death, potlatches among the Puget Sound tribes could also be held to "transfer names to children, announce a daughter's coming-of-age" (Suttles 1991, 219), or even to erase an embarrassment. Jay Miller, in a discussion of the ceremony that avoids the word "potlatch" entirely, speaks of the inviting-meetings as marking changes in status or, indeed, "stages in life such as puberty, marriage and death" (Shelton 81). Potlatch, as we have noted, is a Chinook jargon word originally from Nootka. As with the Tlingit people, who call it *ḵoo.'eex'*, the ceremony in Lushootseed is called *sgwi'gwi,* a word that also means "inviting people" (Waterman 80). See also Barnett, Drucker, Suttles and Lane, and Waterman 75–82. Waterman's sense that "the central feature [of the potlatch] on Puget Sound, as in the north, is the pecuniary one" (75) seems to me mistaken.

29. Cf. Bagley: when "Seattle was twenty or twenty-two years old, news reached the various tribes in this vicinity that a large number of mountain or Upper Green and White Rivers Indians were preparing to make a raid upon the saltwater tribes" (246). Sealth presented a plan for defense. He "was victorious and... was chosen head chief of the six tribes" (247). Carlson identifies these tribal nations as the Duwamish, Suquamish, Samahmish, Skopahmish, Stakahmish, and Sktahhmish, although his spelling sometimes varies (preface, n.p. Buerge (online, 3) writes that it was Sealth's uncle Kitsap who was in charge "of Puget Sound forces against the powerful Cowichans of Vancouver Island," although it was indeed Seattle who "succeeded in ambushing and destroying a party of raiders coming down the Green River."

30. Bagley's 1931 reprinting of Sealth's speech is generally said to be the first to have added this ending, and with no indication that these final words are his, not Sealth's. Roberta Frye Watt, who is rarely cited (e.g., Kaiser—see below—does not include her in his extensive bibliography), in her *Four Wagons West,* published the same year as Bagley's essay, also includes these words as the conclusion to her reprinting of Sealth's speech (182). It is possible that Watt's book preceded the publication of Bagley's essay, so she may, in fact, have been the "first" to append these words to the end of the speech. In 1932, John Rich also used the same thirteen words in the conclusion of his reprinting of the speech (41). Rich puts the words in italics but does not say why he has italicized them. (I suspect all three of these Washington writers may have been in contact with one another.) This ending, although it does *not* appear in the original 1887 publication of Sealth's speech, has been much remarked, and, although it derives entirely from the work of three white writers of the 1930s, it is not, as I hope to demonstrate, inconsistent with the general tenor of Sealth's address.

31. The fullest account of these matters remains Rudolf Kaiser's "Chief Seattle's Speech(es): American Origins and European Reception" (1987). Appearing just before Kaiser's work, "Thus Spoke Chief Seattle: The Story of an Undocumented Speech," by Jerry L. Clark of the National Archives and Records Administration, also gives a detailed account of the speech. Denise Low's essay "Contemporary Reinventions of Chief Seattle" (1995) and Albert Furtwangler's *Answering Chief Seattle* (1997) are also useful.

32. Kaiser's essay prints and compares all four versions. Albert Furtwangler writes that "there is only one surviving copy of the [October 29, 1887 *Seattle Sunday] Star*, and it is a damaged sheet with missing or half-legible lines in some places" (12). Furtwangler gives the text "as it appears in the *Star*, with phrases in brackets from the reprint in Grant's *History*," and it is his version that I present in the appendix and reference in my discussion. Sealth's speech appears on pp. 433–36 in Grant.

33. Roberta Frye Watt had written that "the second treaty arranged by Governor Stevens—the Treaty of Point Elliott—was attended with great pomp and ceremony. It was made in January, 21–3, 1855, at Mukilteo" (183). Mukilteo, a name that occurs in the records with various spellings, was the Native term for Point Elliott. Watt considers this "a spectacle of savage pageantry" (184). But, as Seeman writes, "the effect of these treaties was the decimation of the Northwest Indian tribes" (19).

34. Hilbert notes that "there is a record of two short speeches delivered by [Sealth] at Mukilteo in 1855 on the occasion of the signing of the Treaty of Point Elliot" (259). These exist in the National Archives in Washington, D.C., and have been reprinted by Kaiser and Clark, among others. Hilbert presents one of these speeches "as remembered by a Suquamish elder, Amelia Sneatlum," who was recorded on tape in 1955, in Lushootseed, and she provides a literal translation into English (259, 261, and 262). "Only two other speeches by [Sealth] are known, a fragment of a speech recorded by B. F. Shaw in 1850, and a lament...in May 1858 that the Treaty of Point Elliott had not been ratified by the U.S. Senate" (259). Carlson (21) and Kaiser (525) print the latter.

35. Clark (see just below) has him arriving in October, not November.

36. Buerge estimates the total number of white residents at the time to have numbered no more than 120, while the Puget Sound Indians in attendance numbered some 1,200! (1991, 28). Carlson writes that there were "about two thousand three hundred Indians" assembled at Mukilteo (18) in January 1855.

37. Watt makes clear that Governor Stevens's first meeting with the Puget Sound Indians—she dates it, as I have noted, in December 1854—was very much intended to "prepare the way for the treaty making" (178); and Buerge—who uses the January 1854 date—concurs (1988 28). Main Street is now blocked off from the waterfront, but it did continue down to the water in Sealth's time. Point Elliott is north of Seattle and almost to Everett, on Puget Sound. Port Madison is also on Bainbridge Island, northwest of Seattle. I am grateful to Duane Niatum for help with these matters.

38. Among these scholars are Jerry Clark, of the National Archives and Records Administration, and the historian Carole Seeman, both of whom conflate the brief remarks on record and sections of Dr. Smith's published speech (Clark 61; Seeman 28ff.).

39. For one example, while "counts taken in the 1850s...total about 5000" Lushootseed speakers, "by 1885 numbers appear to have dropped to less than 2000" (Suttles and Lane 501).

40. See an entry from the diary of William Fraser Tolmie, Hudson's Bay Company surgeon in 1833: "Sialth was a brawny Suquamish with a Roman countenance and black curley hair, the handsomest Indian I have ever seen" (qtd. in Buerge 1992, n.p.). In the only known photograph of Sealth his hair appears to be more nearly straight than "curley."

41. In the photograph referred to above, Sealth is seated, and it does not appear to me that he would be six feet tall if he stood. But this was taken in 1865, when he was almost eighty years old, eleven years after Dr. Smith heard him speak, and it may not be a good representation of his

stature as a younger man. One cannot tell from this photo or from any of the physical descriptions of Sealth that I have found that he would have had a flattened forehead, but "except for slaves and the very poor, all [Puget Sound Indians] had their heads flattened in infancy" (Suttles and Lane 493). Perhaps this was not particularly noticeable later in Sealth's life.

42. Cf. Amelia Sneatlum: "Chief Seattle had Thunderbird power.... Thunderbird was the power of Seattle. Thunderbird was the greatest power. When Seattle would be angry at someone, he would shout angrily at him. The one he was angry at would shake" (qtd. in Buerge 1992, n.p.).

43. As Sealth, in Dr. Smith's description (and that of some others), is about six feet tall, and Isaac Stevens has consistently been described as of considerably less than average height—perhaps not quite five feet tall—the hand-on-the-head business might produce a rather comic portrait if it were true (but I think it is not).

44. W. C. Vanderwerth, who mistakenly dates Sealth's speech as having been delivered in 1853, writes that Dr. Smith had "mastered the Duwamish language in about two years" (117), something earlier attested to by Roberta Frye Watt, who wrote that Seattle "spoke in his native Duwamish," and that "Dr. Smith had learned this tongue and was able to take notes" (179). There is no "Duwamish language," and I am certain that Dr. Smith did not understand Lushootseed. There is, however, a considerable likelihood that he had a fair grasp of Chinook jargon. Just as some of Sealth's remarks from Point Elliott have been back-translated into Lushootseed by the Suquamish elder Amelia Sneatlum, so, too, have "excerpts" from Dr. Smith's version been "transcribed into Northern Lushootseed" by Vi Hilbert.

45. We know from Tulalip elder "Gram" Ruth Sehome Shelton that at Mukilteo it was "a white man named Simmons... who was brought... by Governor Stevens to interpret for him," translating Stevens's English into Chinook jargon. It was a man named John Taylor "who interpreted for the people (Native Americans)," translating the "Chinook Jargon to Lushootseed" (Shelton 19).

46. Such a collation might explain the rather loose structure of Sealth's lengthy speech. But this looseness of structure may also serve as evidence of a certain accuracy in Dr. Smith's reconstruction of the speech. Toby Langen, for example, has noted that "recursive structures of discourse" (Langen and Moses 124) that operate in Lushootseed narrative—"conversations that repeatedly leave and return to a topic" (123)—may also "operate as a successful process for consensus decision-making" (123). Although Langen's Tulalip Lushootseed-speaking consultant Marya Moses felt strongly that "repetition" and "business" did not go together, they may well have done that "recursively" in Chief Sealth's speech. Ruth Shelton's narrative (q.v.), while not concerned with decision making, most certainly "repeatedly leave[s] and return[s] to a topic" (Langen and Moses 123).

47. This is not to say that it renders Sealth very literally. I'll let a few examples stand for many. Thus Dr. Smith has Sealth begin by saying: "Yond[er] sky that has wep[t] tears of compassion on our fathers for centuries untold, and which, to us, looks et[erna]l, may change" (qtd. in Furtwangler 12). Sealth probably just said "the sky"; "tears of compassion" and "centuries untold" are abstractions unlikely to have an equivalent in any oral performance. Smith has Sealth say: "When our young men grow angry at some real or imaginary wrong, and disfigure their faces with black, their hearts, also, are disfigured and turn black." (qtd. in Furtwangler 13). Black was the face paint for war; red for more peaceful endeavors. If he were speaking for peace, it is not likely that black face paint would please him, but it is unlikely Sealth would have described either color as "disfiguring." There are many other places in the speech where Dr. Smith's language may convey the gist of what Sealth said while not literally reproducing his actual words.

48. Sealth's language here uncannily reproduces Chief Justice Roger Taney's decision in the Dred Scott case of 1857, i.e., that blacks "had no rights which the white man was bound to respect." Taney's opinion was delivered after Sealth spoke, but well before Smith's publication of Sealth's speech.

49. I've taken the spelling in brackets from Coll Thrush's 2008 book. Thrush writes of "Dookweebathl, the Changer, [who] brought order to things" (24).

50. Roberta Frye Watt speaks of Sealth as "among the white people whom he loved," and she ascribes this "love" to Sealth's having, as a boy of six, "gazed with wonder upon Captain Vancouver's great 'bird-ship,' the *Discovery*," and then being shown "kindness" by Vancouver and his men (178). Watt's account of these matters is paternalistic, "savagist," and from a contemporary perspective thoroughly obnoxious (as is that of John Rich). I think it would nonetheless be unwise to reject out of hand everything she (and he) says.

51. This would probably have been sometime after 1848, "when the Oblate priest Father Pascal Ricard founded the first permanent mission on Puget Sound" (Suttles and Lane 500). But Catholic missionaries had been in the area since 1839–40 (499).

52. According to Edward Curtis, the "third name [on the Medicine Creek treaty] is 'Leshhigh'" (9: 17), although Leschi insisted that he never did sign, something affirmed by all the Indians who had been there. For further information on Leschi, his opposition, and his execution in 1858, see the Nisqually historian Cecilia Svinth Carpenter and the early pioneer Ezra Meeker.

53. See Womack: "I wish to posit an alternative definition of traditionalism as anything that is useful to Indian people in retaining their values and worldviews, no matter how much it deviates from what people did one or two hundred years ago" (42). And Ortiz: "In every case where European culture was cast upon Indian people... there was similar creative response and development,... a nationalistic impulse to make use of foreign ritual, ideas, and material in their own— Indian—sense (2006, 254). There is, however, a tipping point: once "anything" "deviates" too greatly "from what people did one or two hundred years ago," we are going to need a term other than "traditional" to describe it. In the same way, Native people can indeed "make use of foreign ritual, ideas, and material" to fortify their Indian sense of themselves—I have earlier cited William Powers's sense of the *Lakotification* of Christianity—but this is true only up to a point. Beyond that point, however we may determine it, it's not clear how best to describe their sense of themselves.

54. "Ashes" is probably not a word Sealth would have used, as his people did not cremate the dead. I'd guess he said something like their "remains." From a traditional Lushootseed perspective, the notion that the remains of the dead were "sacred" or that their resting place "is hallowed ground" is unlikely. But Sealth was a Catholic convert at this point and may well have said words like these.

55. See Suttles and Lane: "Death was given greater ritual attention than other life crises" (496). What Miller terms the "shamanic odyssey" is described by Suttles and Lane as the "soul-recovery ceremony" (498).

56. Watt's 1931 reprinting of Sealth's speech makes some unacknowledged additions to Dr. Smith's original at this point. Watt adds to what I have quoted that the dead also love their homelands' "verdant lined lakes and bays"; as for their yearning for the living, she has the dead "often return from the *Happy Hunting Ground* to visit, guide, console, and comfort" the living (181; my emphasis). She seems unaware of the fact that these amiable revenants might often kill their descendants because they were lonely in the land of the dead and wished for their company (J. Miller 1999, 88).

57. His Apache name was Cheis, which means something like "oak," indicating "the strength and quality of oak rather than the wood itself" (Ball 23). White soldiers or settlers added the prefix.

58. A more recent chronicler of these matters, David Roberts, quotes the Ellis version of Cochise's speech and says it was delivered in September 1871 (66). Ball and Armstrong seem to believe that it was in September 1871 that both Ellis and Turrill heard Cochise speak. Only Sweeney places both Ellis and Turrill at the parley in March 1872.

59. Turrill of Granger: "He continued this kind of talk for some time, thinking no doubt that he was making quite an impression on his Indian audience, which might have been so, but

certainly not on his white hearers, and I for one was hoping that he would finish and let the Indian have his say" (19).

60. Sweeney notes, however, that Jeffords "in early 1869 [had] received a license to trade with the Southern Apaches" (1991, 5). It was in part through the Indian trade that Jeffords met Cochise some time in 1870.

61. While Turrill may have had less patience for long-windedness than Ellis did, I'll venture to guess that if Granger did this time go on at length, it could have been because he thought that his earlier brevity—in Ellis's judgment—might possibly have displeased the Indians and thus contributed to the bad outcome of the encounter. But it was clearly *what* he proposed—a reservation at Tularosa or possibly Canada Alamosa—rather than *how* he proposed it that was deficient.

62. As late as 1967, Thrapp repeats this geographical determinism, e.g., "The tribes of Apacheria were a product of their habitat, harsh, cruel, and pitiless" (x). With Indians it always comes down to nature!

63. Roberts offers some particularly bizarre commentary on the first two paragraphs of Ellis's version, which he cites. "For once," Roberts writes, "the interpreter must have been competent, for he could hardly have invented Cochise's eloquence" (67). But "Cochise's eloquence" is strictly a function of Ellis's memory and reconstruction. We have no idea what Cochise or his interpreter actually said. Roberts remarks that "the speech the chief made that September day is the longest single utterance of Cochise's ever recorded" (67). Turrill's account, however, is considerably longer. Roberts further comments that "something of the formal beauty, of the strophes and antistrophes, of Apache oratory transcended the gulfs of culture and language" (67). Strophes and antistrophes are, of course, elements of Greek classical drama, and involve the dance of a chorus! They are unlikely to be found in "Apache oratory," about which, I suspect, Roberts knows absolutely nothing. How "the formal beauty...of Apache oratory" can be deduced from Ellis's prose is a mystery; any notion that it "transcended the gulfs of culture and language" is a standard universalist fantasy.

64. Obviously it was not his to "give," nor was American permission for Cochise's people to live where they had lived for many generations a "gift." This sort of language persists in dominant history writing about Indian affairs in the nineteenth century, and in the twentieth century in some measure as well, e.g., that the reservation lands to which tribal nations were confined somehow constituted an expression of American generosity.

65. Second Lieutenant George Bascom, a twenty-five-year-old officer just two years out of West Point, in February 1861 asked Cochise to report to him regarding the kidnapping or disappearance of a twelve-year-old mixed-blood boy known as Felix Ward. (Some years later, about 1874, this fellow reappeared under the name of Mickey Free and went on to a rather notorious career.) Cochise may well have come "to Bascom's tent in an amicable mood, bringing with him his brother, two nephews, his wife and two young children," as Roberts dramatically expresses it (22). Be that as it may, Cochise denied any knowledge of the boy's whereabouts but offered "to find out who the perpetrators were and to negotiate for the return of the boy" (Roberts 22). Bascom refused this offer, announcing that Cochise and his relatives would be held hostage. At that point, Cochise pulled out a knife he had hidden, and cut through the canvas of the tent, fleeing up a hill to escape, although wounded in the leg or thigh by the soldiers' fire (Sweeney 151). Cochise and his men had earlier captured nine Mexicans, part of a wagon train, and they also held four Americans. Perhaps on Tuesday, February 5, Cochise left a white flag, or some say a note he had had one of the Americans write, which pleaded for the release of his family, still held captive by Bascom, and repeated his offer to look for the missing boy. Bascom refused. Cochise had the Mexicans burned to death, and his men then killed and mutilated the Americans. In retaliation, Bascom hung several of his Apache captives, among them Coyuntera, Cochise's brother, and his two nephews (all asked to be shot, but Bascom refused). Cochise's wife and two children were freed. It has been said that the fiercest period of Apache warfare began with the Bascom affair, and contemporary Apache people

continue to have a vivid recollection of the episode in their history known as "cuts the tent" or "cutting the tent." See Thrapp's account for some variant details (15–18). See also the recollections of this event narrated by Asa (or Ace) Daklugie, son of the great chief, Juh (pronounced Whoa or Ho), who was about four when Cochise was near the end of his life (Ball 25).

66. It seems to have been fairly common knowledge that Cochise was ill at this time, perhaps with stomach cancer. Roberts, once more with a touch of dramatic excess, writes that when Cochise met with General Howard in the Dragoon Mountains in October 1872, he "was in constant physical agony. The pain centered in his stomach; it sharpened whenever he ate, and for days at a time he could swallow only water.... Day after day, the pain grew worse, and the chief of the Chokonen grew weaker" (103). Sweeney writes that in October 1872 "the fact that most of Cochise's men had grown weary of war and preferred to remain home with their families surprised Sladen [Howard's loyal aide]" (1997, 22). Surely the fact that these men had been constantly at war for more than a decade would also have had its effect at the earlier meeting in March.

67. My thanks to Professor Cameron Afzal for this observation. Professor Afzal also referred me to Psalm 110, whose last verse is "He shall drink of the brook in the way: therefore shall he lift up the head."

68. It was to the Dragoon Mountains that Jeffords took General Howard to meet with Cochise in October 1872.

69. The name has also been spelled Tu-ela-kas, and an 1855 drawing of Old Joseph by Gustav Sohon spells his name Toowe-tak-hes. Professor Patricia Penn Hilden kindly asked Professor Haruo Aoki about this; he directed her to Jewie Davis and Albert Andrews of the Chief Joseph Band of the Colville Reservation, both Nez Perce speakers. Mr. Davis gave Tukeke?s as the name, while Mr. Andrews thought it best spelled Tuwe'ke?s (Hilden, personal communication, November 20, 2010). Neither they nor any other source I have consulted offered a translation of the name. Curtis gives Old Joseph's name as Walamuitkin—as have others, using various spellings—meaning "hair knotted in front," something permitted only to a seasoned warrior (8: 8).

70. This is the spelling and translation used by the linguist Haruo Aoki (1979). David Michael Liberty, a great-great-great-great-nephew of Chief Joseph, spells Joseph's Nimipu name Hinmatooyalatkekt and translates it as "thunder rolling over the mountains" (96). As noted above, there are many variant spellings and translations of Nez Perce names.

71. Howard had lost his arm in the Civil War at the Battle of Fair Oaks. He had earlier negotiated with Cochise and the Chiricahuas, although none of the sources I consulted reported the Apaches distinguishing him by reference to his missing arm.

72. I am for the most part using Aoki's 1979 account of this incident, which not only references the major historical sources available at the time (Bailey, Brown, Curtis, Fee, Haines, Howard and McGrath, Josephy, and McDermott) but also includes the personal recollections of Mrs. Agnes Moses, a Nimipu woman who was nine years old in 1877. (Mrs. Moses was tape-recorded in 1961.) Curtis wrote that "the beginning of the war was the act of a boy [Walaitits] crazed with the white man's whiskey, avenging the white man's killing of his father" (8: 24). He later gives the Nez Perce warrior Yellow Bull's account, which confirms this (164).

73. He also erroneously blamed Joseph for the murder of a white woman and her baby. The full title of his 1881 memoir—not always cited in full, e.g., Josephy's bibliography lists only *Nez Perce Joseph*—is *Nez Perce Joseph, an Account of His Ancestors, His Lands, His Confederates, His Enemies, His Murders, His War, His Pursuit and Capture* (my emphasis). After his negotiations with Cochise, Howard had learned that too great a concern for Indians was not conducive to career advancement. Nonetheless, he had initially written the War Department: "I think it is a mistake to take from Joseph and his band of Nez Perces [sic] that valley [the Wallowa]" (qtd. in Venn 2005, 40). When that "mistake" became government policy, it does seem to be the case that as Venn has written, Howard "turned the peaceful Lapwai council" with Joseph and his band "from a legitimate treaty rights forum into a bellicose, ethnocentric, and racist assault" (41). Yellow Wolf said

of Howard's behavior at the council that it constituted "showing the rifle" (40) or indicating a desire to commence hostilities.

74. In an article published in 1972, Colonel Mark Brown, whose earlier and more substantial work I will reference below, refers to this as Joseph's "pathetic little speech" (14). In this estimate he stands as a minority of one. In his 1908 study of the Nez Perce, the anthropologist Herbert Spinden, in a brief section called "Oratory," cites the speech as having "a great deal of power and pathos" (243). Later, Armstrong (1971), Vanderwerth (1971), and Nabokov (1991) all include it in their anthologies, and Clements (2002) refers to it favorably among other speeches recorded in "Soldier's Memoirs." It is also cited by Dee Brown (1971), and it appears in the Sanders and Peek textbook (1973). The 1975 film *I Will Fight No More Forever* closes movingly with Joseph's speech. In his 1982–83 long poem *Chief Joseph of the Nez Perce Who Called Themselves the Nimipu, "The Real People,"* Robert Penn Warren cites Joseph's speech (45–46) as a tragic-heroic address. The Nez Perce view of the speech may perhaps be conveyed by Allen Slickpoo Sr.'s 1973 quotation of it as justly "famous" (193), and I will note just below its back-translation into Nimipu by Elizabeth Wilson. Not one of these editors, authors, and translators mentions that the speech's authenticity, as we will see, is highly questionable.

75. This directly echoes Curtis, who wrote that on their crossing of the mountains the Indians "moved as if they were on their customary journey to the buffalo country" (8: 30).

76. The "Crows rebuffed them," McCoy writes, "because they did not want to anger the United States government and cause trouble for themselves" (123). Miles was aided by Cheyenne and Sioux scouts (McCoy 124; D. Walker 1998, 435).

77. As Josephy (among others) has made clear, Joseph might well have thought that Miles would let his people return to the Wallowa Valley. Miles, with the support of Howard, who was his superior, seems to have had in mind the Idaho Lapwai reservation that had been agreed on earlier. But, as Josephy writes, "there was no question that Joseph could count, at least, on a return to the Northwest" (1965, 627). This was not to be. As Yellow Wolf made clear, "We were not captured. It was a draw battle. We did not expect being sent to Eikish Pah [Hot Place, Indian Territory]. Had we known this we never would have surrendered. We expected to be returned to our own homes" (225). Slickpoo's phonetic spelling is "A-kheese-pa, the hot place" (192). Joseph and other survivors returned to the Northwest in 1885, where they were settled on the Colville Reservation in Washington.

78. The Nez Perce names for these two convey Joseph's band's view of them far better than their English names do. In a footnote, McWhorter writes that Captain John was known as Jokais, Block or Worthless, or Chojykies, Lazy. Old George, curiously, was Meopkowit, Baby or Know Nothing (Yellow Wolf 222n3). In *Hear Me, My Chiefs* McWhorter gives only Jokais for Captain John (493). It has often been pointed out that these two had daughters in Joseph's camp whom they wished to persuade to leave.

79. Howard was Miles's superior, but he magnanimously allowed Miles to accept the "surrender." Reports Miles subsequently wrote of the end of the Nez Perce "War," however, entirely obscured Howard's role and even his presence—prompting a number of what might be called damage-control maneuvers on the part of Howard and his aide-de-camp, Lieutenant C. E. S. Wood, whom we will meet in a moment.

80. But not his last account. As I note below, he repeated much of this account in a letter to Edward Lyman dated January 17, 1939. Most of it is quoted in E. Wood 16–20. See also Venn, "Brief Chronology."

81. We will soon return to the distinction between a *reply* from Joseph relayed by Captain John and a *speech* delivered by Joseph himself. It was Wood, as we will note further, who inserted the speech into Howard's report. Howard does not mention a surrender speech by Joseph either in his 1881 memoir, cited above, or in a later memoir, *My Life and Experiences among Our Hostile Indians* (1907).

82. Mark Brown calls Sutherland "a generally reliable newspaper correspondent" (1972, 7). Sutherland soon published his own account of these events called *Howard's Campaign against the Nez Perce Indians, 1877*. It mentions no speech by Joseph.

83. Armstrong (1971), Vanderwerth (1971), Dee Brown (1971), and Nabokov (1978 and 1991), for example, all give Howard's *Report* as the source for their reprinting of the speech in their anthologies.

84. Both Captain John and Old George were members of treaty bands; thus Joseph was not in any regard Captain John's "chief." Wood might not have found Captain John's tears—if indeed there were such tears—quite so moving had he known the meaning of his Nez Perce names.

85. Erskine Wood states that his father "never saw the proofs" of this article, that "the speech is badly garbled, and is incorrectly described as a *mere message* from Joseph to General Howard" (20; my emphasis). This is because, as Venn has explained, Lieutenant Wood had some time ago "decided to use the 'face to face oration by Joseph in the afternoon' motif" (BC). I will return briefly to the ideological reasons for preferring a speech to a message, something we have earlier noted in regard to Thomas Jefferson and Chief Logan.

86. Wood died in 1941. Venn writes that the last "of Wood's written versions" of the speech was contained in a letter dated January 17, 1939, "sent to the publisher [Edward D. Lyman] of Prof. Francis Haines' *Red Eagles of the Pacific Northwest*" (BC). This particular version of the Chief Joseph speech did not appear in print until 1978, when Wood's son, Erskine Wood, included it in a biography of his father called *Life of Charles Erskine Scott Wood*. Venn believes that this is the only version that should be reprinted because it represents the culmination of Wood's efforts to make the Chief Joseph speech a masterful "literary text" (Venn 1998; personal communication, July 6, 2010). For the purposes of this book, however, earlier versions seem preferable precisely because they may be closer to things Wood actually heard from Joseph, with less time for "literary" revision. I reprint the earliest version of the long speech from October 26, 1877, in the appendix.

87. The speech in a sense became Joseph's when Elizabeth Wilson back-translated it from English into Nimipu. She was taped reciting it by Aoki in 1966 (Aoki 1979, 123–25). Thanks to the generosity of my friend the Nez Perce scholar Professor Patricia Penn Hilden, I have been able to listen to a CD of Wilson's recitation.

88. Louis Jones once more goes one better, announcing that Joseph's words, "written in scrawled English, were brought to General Howard" (111). Joseph did not speak English and most certainly could not have "scrawled" it. Nor does it seem likely that either Old George or Captain John could have written English. Jones finds the speech—it is a speech, despite its having been written or "scrawled"—"one of the finest examples of Indian eloquence.... The gripping power of these words is matched only by those which fell from the lips of the Galilean on Golgotha's hill!" (111). Lieutenant Wood might well be proud.

89. As noted earlier, he would drift south and conduct an interview with Wovoka that was then sent to John Gibbon, on December 6, 1890, who by this time was a general commanding the Division of the Pacific. The full text of the interview is reproduced in Hittman 1997.

90. Born in what is now West Virginia in 1848, Lucullus Virgil McWhorter moved his family to the Yakima Valley of Washington in 1903. He was a cattle rancher, an intense critic of federal Indian policy, a photographer, and an amateur historian. He worked on land rights issues for the Yakima Nation and published a book on the Yakima War of 1855–56. In 1907 he met the Nez Perce warrior Yellow Wolf and pursued research into the events of 1877, visiting various battlefields, collecting artifacts, and taking photographs. He interviewed many of the Native survivors of the 1877 encounter with the U.S. Army, as he also interviewed many of the surviving army veterans. He was the editor of *Yellow Wolf: His Own Story*, published in 1940, and his collection of interviews and writings on Nez Perce history and legend, *Hear Me, My Chiefs*, edited by Ruth Bordin, appeared in 1944, after his death. Among literary scholars, he is best known for the work he did (for better or worse) with Humishima or Mourning Dove on the novel she published in 1927, *Cogewea*.

91. This is mistaken. Josephy writes that Joseph mounted his horse to give up his rifle to Miles "about 2 o'clock in the afternoon" (1965, 629), while Fee had the army officers "summoned by a sentry" that "Joseph was coming" at "four in the afternoon" (262). Wood's 1939 letter to Lyman, presumably an eyewitness account, states that "*not long before sunset,* the two old Indians [Old George and Captain John] took back a final message *and after considerable delay* Joseph was seen coming toward us mounted on his horse" (qtd. in E. Wood 18; my emphasis). Sutherland wrote that "at sunset Joseph rode into camp, surrounded by a few warriors on foot" (44). But although he had been present throughout much of the campaign, Sutherland was *not* present at the surrender (Venn, personal communication, July 6, 2010). In any case, it surely did not take place at ten in the morning.

92. Joseph's self-reference in the third person on this occasion is probably a late "literary" touch introduced by Wood. We have noted many other instances of Indian orators using third-person self-reference in English that almost surely would not have been present when they spoke in their own languages.

93. E.g., Deward Walker's statement that among the Nez Perce "the deceased's name was not mentioned" (424).

94. Erskine Wood speculated that Joseph might have been "addressing the spirits of those dead chiefs" (20)—that is, Looking Glass and others he had just mentioned. The 1975 film has Joseph quite effectively turning away from Miles and Howard to shout these words (they are delivered in English in the film) in the direction of his camp—although he would have known that there were no chiefs there either.

3. Authors and Writers

1. Indian autobiographies, as I have said, are bicultural, composite compositions; they are produced by a Native subject and a non-Native editor (also, and most commonly, with a translator). Autobiographies by Indians are texts written by a Native American person. Black Hawk's *Life* is the first Indian autobiography. Although the Reverend Samson Occom, a Mohegan, composed a brief autobiography in the eighteenth century (which was not published until late in the twentieth century), Apess was the first Native writer to produce a full-length autobiographical text.

2. All further references to Black Hawk's autobiography are to the 2008 edition by J. Gerald Kennedy. Anthony F. C. Wallace quotes from an 1831 memo in which Black Hawk's remarks to Gaines and also to Governor Reynolds of Illinois are quoted as follows: "You asked, 'Who I am'—I am a Sauk; my fathers were great men, and I wish to remain where the bones of my fathers are laid. I desire to be buried with my fathers. Why then should I leave their fields?" (Wallace 1982, 280). We will consider below the importance Black Hawk attaches to being buried with his "fathers."

3. See Krupat, "Native American Autobiography and the Synecdochic Self" (1992).

4. See Christopher Miller writing about Native people of the Columbia Plateau: "Even the most private aspects of the individual's identity were conceived as being the product of a social relationship" (19).

5. A fuller account of these matters appears in Krupat 2010a.

6. It will be apparent to the reader that some of these patterns and powers were general to Native prophets, whether Wodziwob and Wovoka or the "Dreamer" prophet of the Northwest, Smohalla. I consider some other prophetic figures of the nineteenth century just below.

7. Nonetheless, any "common understanding" there may have been among these various leaders did not necessarily lead to common courses of action. Thus, Handsome Lake, as Alice Kehoe points out, considered himself to be a "peace prophet"; he was opposed to the military resistance of Tenskwatawa and Tecumseh (120).

8. Caring for and honoring medicine bundles appropriately could be quite demanding. According to Alanson Skinner, "When a war bundle is to be taken from its repository to another

lodge on the occasion of a feast or other ceremony, it must be rewrapped and tied." Further: "All sacred bundles should be opened at least four times a year"; "Tobacco sacrifices are made to them at intervals, and the feasts are religiously given for them" (1925, 84).

9. Keokuk was the accomodationist leader appointed by white authorities to a position of authority among the Sauks. Throughout the *Life* Black Hawk shows dislike and disdain for him.

10. Black Hawk had concluded his story with a wish that "the watchword between the Americans and Sacs and Foxes, ever be—*Friendship!*" and that "the Great Spirit keep our people and the whites always at peace" (154). Neil Schmitz considers this "final apostrophe [to be] surely...Patterson's" (2001b, 70), not Black Hawk's. He reads the *Life* as "defiant, litigious, maledictory" (70). Similarly, Gerald Kennedy, in the introduction to his new edition of the *Life*, considers it to be "the first thoroughly *adversarial* account of frontier hostilities between white settlers and native people" (vii; my emphasis).

11. No manuscript or notes of LeClaire's work with Black Hawk have been found, nor has my examination of the catalogue of LeClaire's papers, held at the Putnam Archives in Davenport, Iowa, yielded any record of their collaboration—although LeClaire's September 1833 bill to Patterson for translation work, almost surely on the Black Hawk life story, does exist. I am very grateful to Ms. Eunice Schlichting of the Putnam Archives for providing the catalogue and responding to my questions.

12. This and similar phrases have been used by many Native people to explain their decision to tell of their lives and their peoples' ways. See my book by this title (Krupat 1985).

13. As I noted in the introduction, Vizenor in a variety of publications has proposed the values of *continuance* and *survivance* (survival through resistance) as an alternative to the Euramerican values of *progress* and *dominance*. See Vizenor, "Aesthetics of Survivance: Literary Theory and Practice" (2008).

14. One might guess that the Indian "messiah" Neihardt had in mind was Wovoka, but this is not the case. Neihardt's Indian "messiah" is, instead, Sitanka or Big Foot, the Minneconjou leader killed along with many of his people in the massacre at Wounded Knee in 1890. On Neihardt's poem, see Rice chap. 3.

15. It is also the best-documented: the transcripts of the interviews have been edited by Raymond J. DeMallie and published as *The Sixth Grandfather: Black Elk's Teachings Given to John G. Neihardt*. The manuscripts have more recently been examined by Brian Holloway.

16. For this it is necessary to consult Demallie 229–35.

17. In *The Sixth Grandfather*, DeMallie notes that although *Black Elk Speaks* does date this in 1883, when Black Elk would have been twenty, it is more likely that the event took place in 1885 (242).

18. Rice's work on *Black Elk Speaks* offers readings that most nearly parallel my own view of it as Native American elegy—indeed Rice has strongly influenced my view. But Rice, DeMallie, and Holloway, to mention only those three, all differ considerably in their views of Neihardt's intentions and the effects of his editing.

19. Wasichu is the term by which the whites were known in Lakota. The word has nothing to do with skin color but, rather, means something like "fat eaters" or "those who take the best part."

20. Neihardt does not include anything about Black Elk's Catholicism in *Black Elk Speaks*, although, as can be seen in *The Sixth Grandfather,* Black Elk did mention it several times.

21. For example, Neil Schmitz's (2001c) chapter "Ponca Testimony, Lakota Elegies," does not discuss elegiac expression *by* the Lakota, but rather elegies *for* the Lakota in the pages of Elaine Goodale Eastman's books. Goodale, the wife and editor-collaborator of the Santee Sioux Dr. Charles Alexander Eastman, Schmitz demonstrates, like the "Friends of the Indian" and others who saw "civilization" and assimilation as the only route to Indian survival, writes frequently of traditional Lakota life as already dead and gone.

22. In *From Sand Creek,* Ortiz writes: *"It's almost inexplicable that black Elk would say the dream ended; we know why now, and we know it did not end and will not end"* (1981, 40). I think he means that we now know Neihardt himself wrote those words, and that Black Elk in fact did not say them. See just below.

23. My view is more or less shared by Rice and Holler, but this was not at all what McCluskey meant when she made public Neihardt's communication to her. Brian Holloway offers support for her view. There is no question that Neihardt was much taken with Black Elk, and, moreover, that he was fascinated by Lakota religion. But—and I think Rice makes the best case for this—even his positive view of Lakota religion subsumes it to the mystical Christianity in which he himself believed. In the manner of many a Western-supremacist before him, Neihardt meant, I think, to flatter Black Elk by showing that his traditional Lakota beliefs were valuable steps on the way to a "higher" religion.

24. I've only belatedly discovered that Alice Kehoe had earlier (1989) juxtaposed Black Elk's apparent conclusion to *Black Elk Speaks* with his actual final words from *The Sixth Grandfather* to make the point that this is "hardly a 'pitiful old man' speaking" (62). It is Kehoe's view—which I share—that as Black Elk "himself prospered through his collaboration with John Neihardt," so, too, would his Lakota People "find means to prosper" (62). Kehoe is interested in establishing affinities among "prophets" who revitalize their people: Wovoka, Black Elk, and Handsome Lake. She does not attend to the elegiac dimension of *Black Elk Speaks* or to its persistence in "The Author's Postscript" to that volume and also in *The Sixth Grandfather's* concluding section called "Ceremony on Harney Peak," which I will note below.

25. Irving's presentation of Philip as a tragic hero was not the first such nor was it to be the last. As Cheryl Walker has noted, Jedediah Morse and Elijah Parish, in their *Compendious History of New England* (1804), had already presented Philip sympathetically "as a tragic hero" (C. Walker 168). Irving's essay, originally published in the *Analectic* magazine in 1814, became more widely known when he reprinted it in the 1819–20 serial publication of his *The Sketch-Book of Geoffrey Crayon, Gent.,* in which Irving also reprinted another of his *Analectic* essays, "Traits of Indian Character." In 1820, James Wallis Eastburn and Robert Sands's *Yamoyden, A Tale of the Wars of King Philip: In Six Cantos* was published, while the end of the decade saw the publication of James Fenimore Cooper's *The Wept of Wish-ton Wish* (1829), set in the period of King Philip's War, and, importantly, the first performance in New York of John Augustus Stone's *Metamora; or, the Last of the Wampanoags: An Indian Tragedy in Five Acts as Played by Edwin Forrest.* One of many plays of the period in which Indians said good-bye, it was enormously popular for decades. Further references to early nineteenth-century works treating King Philip and his period may be found in Gordon Sayre's *The Indian Chief as Tragic Hero,* in particular chap. 1, "From Enemy to Hero," which begins with Philip. See also Lepore.

Apess knew Irving's "Traits," which is cited by Elias Boudinot in his 1816 text, *A Star in the West,* from which Apess borrowed freely in the appendix to the first edition of his autobiography, *A Son of the Forest, The Experience of William Apess, a Native of the Forest* (1829). It is not clear whether Apess knew Irving's reflections on King Philip.

26. Everett had been a professor of Greek at Harvard and the editor of the influential *North American Review.* He would be elected governor of Massachusetts in 1836. The words I've quoted from Jill Lepore were actually written to describe portions of a letter Chief Justice John Marshall sent Justice Joseph Story in 1828. I think they aptly describe Everett's effort in this address. Everett would not have known Marshall's letter.

27. The footnote appears in the published text of the address. I don't know how Everett would have made this point to his audience when he originally spoke.

28. Everett had staunchly opposed Cherokee removal in a speech he made before the House of Representatives on May 19, 1830. He developed his argument in "The Cherokee Case," published in the *North American Review* in 1831.

29. Nor would a few others, in particular, Lydia Maria Child and Sarah Savage, opponents of Cherokee removal who wrote histories of the colonial period for young readers that took the Puritans to task. See Lepore 105ff; and Sayre 2005.

30. The full title of Everett's address is *An Address Delivered at Bloody Brook in South Deerfield, September 30, 1835, in Commemoration of the Fall of the 'Flower of Essex,' at That Spot in King Philip's War, September 18, (O[ld].S[tyle], 1675)*. The "Flower of Essex" refers to the town's bravest young men. In "Philip of Pokanoket," Irving had earlier written of Philip and an ally "having drawn up the *flower* of their forces" (1996a, 259; my emphasis). Everett may have had Irving's essay in mind, although I suspect this was a common-enough metaphor of the time. See Krupat 2009b, 92–101, for a detailed comparison of Everett's and Apess's texts. See also Sayre 2005, 95–99; and Wolfe 15–18.

31. Apess's full sentence compares Philip to Washington, who "lives endeared and engraven on the hearts of every white in America, never to be forgotten in time—even such is the *immortal* Philip honored, as held in memory by the *degraded but yet grateful* descendants who appreciate his character" (1992a, 277; my emphasis). As others have noted and as I note further below, while all Indians may broadly be considered the "descendants" of King Philip, Apess had on two occasions specified a blood relation between himself and Philip, making him very much one of Philip's "descendants." Apess seems to use "degraded" in two senses: first, that Philip and all Indian people have been scorned as inferior by the whites, denigrated; and, second, that the introduction by the whites of strong liquor among the Indians has often led to their degradation.

32. Cf. Wolfe: the notion that "present-day Indians [are] always-already anachronistic" (5).

33. Thus Apess, as Wolfe writes, "insists on a sustained melancholy that refuses to let go [or mourn] the losses of the past," which he "links...with the political project of reclaiming Indian sovereignty in the future,...rewriting the texts of Euroamerican mourning as Indian melancholy" (15). Not to put too fine a point on it, I will nonetheless repeat that Freud's classic 1917 essay, "Mourning and Melancholia," is adamant that melancholia is a pathological condition. As noted earlier, Freud revised his notions of mourning and melancholia in *The Ego and the Id* (1923); as also noted, something like what Wolfe wishes to describe was called "melancholic mourning" by Jahan Ramazani in 1994 (xi, 4, and passim), who dilutes "Freud's overly rigorous distinction between 'mourning' and 'melancholia' to a matter of *emphases within mourning*" (29; my emphasis). Recall here as well Eng and Han's "depathologizing of melancholia" (363) in the Eng and Kazanjian book that Wolfe knows; a mention of this "depathologizing" would have been useful to Wolfe's otherwise powerful argument. Tammy Clewell's important essay of 2004 is also much to the point.

34. Quite literally, it should be said, for the Puritans had had Philip drawn and quartered, and severed his head from his body. See the brief discussion of Wendy Rose's "Retrieving Osceola's Head" (1994).

35. Roumiana Velikova writes that "the pan-Indian dimension of the *Eulogy on King Philip* is easily noticeable in the strikingly low number of tribal names" appearing in it (327), and pointedly refers to Apess as "an Indian rather than a Pequot" (329). Gordon Sayre writes of "Apess' inability to learn Pequot culture as a child," asserting that "he learned his culture only later, inspired by the Mashpee and he learned it in English" (1996, 15). Whether Apess understood or could speak Pequot is also not clear. In his Introduction to *On Our Own Ground: The Complete Writings of William Apess, a Pequot*, Barry O'Connell wrote that Apess's work with Sally George for his book *The Experiences of Five Christian Indians of the Pequot Tribe* had to have been done in the Native language because she "probably spoke only broken English. Pequot was unquestionably her first language" (O'Connell 1992, lx-lxi). Sayre finds O'Connell's case "weaker" than his own counter-conjecture that Apess's failure as a child to comprehend what his grandmother was saying to him—in a powerful early scene of *A Son of the Forest*—resulted from the simple fact that she was speaking to him in Pequot, which he did *not* understand (1996, 15). In an error or possibly a strategy much commented on, Apess made Philip a Pequot—and a blood relation—on the first page of the second

edition (1831) of his autobiography. Velikova's essay is focused on this "error." By the time he composed the *Eulogy*—in which he neither names Philip's tribe nor refers to any relationship to him—Apess had himself become a Wampanoag in that he had been adopted by the Mashpees of Cape Cod, whose ancestors, however, had fought against Philip. In an early commentary on Apess's *Eulogy,* I called Apess "an Indian member of the colorblind saved" (Krupat 1992, 229) as a way of describing what Velikova might call his "pan-Indianness."

36. A draft of a fifth elegy for her son appears in an unpublished essay by Schoolcraft's husband, Henry, called "Dawn of Literary Composition by Educated Natives of the Aboriginal Tribes." See Schoolcraft, in Parker 2007, 251.

37. Rollin Ridge, as he was usually called, was the son of John Ridge and the grandson of Major Ridge, who, under relentless pressure from Georgia and the Jacksonians, in 1835 signed the Treaty of New Echota assenting to Cherokee "removal" to lands west of the Mississippi River. This was regarded as an act of treason by the followers of principal chief John Ross, still strongly opposed to removal. In 1839, after the Cherokees had been forcibly driven west on the Trail of Tears into Indian Territory, members of the Ross faction assassinated Major Ridge, John Ridge, and other members of their family. Rollin and his mother fled to Arkansas. Ten years later, Rollin—possibly in self-defense—killed David Kell, another Cherokee, in a dispute over a horse. Not long after, he joined a wagon train to California, never to return to the Cherokee Nation. See Foreman; and Wilkins. The fullest study of Rollin Ridge is Parins.

38. Parker takes the title of his collection from Carlos Montezuma's 1916 poem assertively called "Changing Is Not Vanishing" (Parker 2011, 287–88). The distinguished Seneca ethnologist, Arthur C. Parker (no relation to Robert Dale Parker), titled a 1914 poem of his "My Race Shall Live Anew" (284). Obviously neither one of these poems is elegiac. But, as I will note further, the Native American poetic elegies of this period do not *both* mourn *and* also envision the Peoples' ongoing life.

39. Curiously, the first poem to be published by an Indian—which appeared in Latin and Greek—was the composition of a Harvard student known as Eleazar and was an elegy for Thomas Thacher, a Puritan minister. See Parker 2011, 47–50.

40. This is not true, however, of Alex Posey and Lynn Riggs. Some of the poets included, like Arthur C. Parker, Carlos Montezuma, and Mary Spotted Elk, were well known for achievements other than poetry.

41. Parker says this was "written perhaps around 1831, published 1875" (2011, 67).

42. See also Jesse Bushyhead's poem just below and Ruth Muskrat's "Trail of Tears," among others.

43. It appeared first, apparently, in Wyandot, although the Wyandot version has not survived (Parker 2011, 66).

44. Parker publishes another, very different sort of elegy by Muskrat called "Nunih Waiyah." This is the name by which a sacred Choctaw mound is known, but in this poem it is also the name of the deceased young woman, a "Redman's child," loved by the "paleface" speaker of the poem, who mourns her, believing that "She waits [his] coming out in that eternal space" (Parker 2011, 325). I'll use this note also to recognize the elegy D'Arcy McNickle (Dahlberg) composed for his grandfather, Isidore Parenteau, called "Old Isidore" (1925). In what I hope will not be too enigmatic a shorthand, let me say that it seems to commemorate Old Isidore so that Montana might live. The poem won a contest sponsored by the *Sunday Missoulian,* one of whose judges praised it because in it "the poet and his reader stand with uncovered heads in the presence of the mystery of Montana" (qtd. in Parker 2011, 363).

45. Parker's note makes clear that Clinton is specifically responding to "the Curtis Act of 1898 [which] took power from Indian nations, including the Cherokee nation, and prepared the path for Indian Territory and Oklahoma Territory to become the state of Oklahoma in 1907" (2011, 203).

4. Elegy in the "Native American Renaissance" and After

1. Momaday has received a great deal of critical attention. As early as 1973 a monograph on his work by Martha Trimble appeared in the Boise State College Western Writers Series, and in 1975 Abraham Chapman's *Literature of the American Indian* reprinted Momaday's lecture "The Man Made of Words," along with a critical essay on his work by Barbara Strelke. By 1982 Alan Velie had included Momaday in his book *Four American Indian Literary Masters*, while Kenneth Lincoln treated him as a major figure in his 1983 work, *Native American Renaissance*. A book-length study of Momaday's work by Matthias Schubnell appeared in 1985. In 1988, Kenneth Roemer edited a volume of essays called *Approaches to Teaching Momaday's "The Way to Rainy Mountain"* for the Modern Language Association's series Approaches to Teaching World Literature, thus putting Momaday in the company of Chaucer, Shakespeare, Milton, and Dickens, among others, as a world-canonical author.

2. This is simply to say that epics are not autobiographies, nor are autobiographies usually prose poems, and so on. H. David Brumble treated *The Way to Rainy Mountain* as autobiography in an essay in Roemer's 1988 book and in a longer study in his own book, *American Indian Autobiography*, also published in 1988. I treated Momaday's work as an autobiography in the chapter "Monologue and Dialogue in American Indian Autobiography" in *The Voice in the Margin*, published in 1989, as did Hertha Wong, who also considered Momaday's full-length autobiography *The Names* in her 1992 study, subtitled "Tradition and Innovation in Native American Autobiography." More recently, Kendall Johnson included *The Way to Rainy Mountain* (and also *The Names*) in his contribution to *The Columbia Guide to American Indian Literatures of the United States since 1945* (2006), titled "Imagining Self and Community in American Indian Autobiography." Momaday himself called his journey to his grandmother's grave a "pilgrimage" on p. 7 of *The Way to Rainy Mountain* (he calls the Kiowas' migration onto the Southern Plains a "quest" on p. 118). Kimberly Blaeser's beautifully admiring account of *The Way to Rainy Mountain* in "Sacred Journey Cycles" (2003) also treats the book as both a journey and a pilgrimage. The latter term appears in Heidi Oberholtzer's recognition of Momaday in her "Pilgrimage in Literature of the Americas" (2003), as well as in many other essays. The "poetic" quality of Momaday's prose and the description of *The Way to Rainy Mountain* as a "prose poem" occurs in too many essays to cite.

3. In a very early essay (1970) on *The Way to Rainy Mountain*, Kenneth Fields described the three sections of Momaday's chapters as "the legendary, the historical, and the personal or contemporary," noting that "the tone of the contemporary passages is nearly always elegiac" (199).

4. See Schubnell 147. Helen Jaskoski is one of the few to attempt specific commentary on the poem, much of which remains to me incomprehensible.

5. I find much of this poem also unclear: how, for example, can "the mind to be" "inhere" in whatever the "nominal unknown" is? Jaskoski notes that "although the word *name* is repeated in the poem four times within ten lines, that name is never spoken; it remains the 'nominal unknown'" (76). It will be necessary to return to the matter of names in *The Way to Rainy Mountain*, if only in passing.

6. See Schubnell: "Aho was born around 1880" (152); Roemer: "1880: Aho and Mammedaty born" (157). If a Kiowa Sun Dance was held in 1887, however constrained by circumstances, it is hard to understand how Kiowa culture could already be gone by 1875 (Momaday 1969, 114). The Kiowas also gathered for a Sun Dance in August 1890 that was disrupted by rumors of army patrols en route to prevent it. As noted in section 4 of chapter 1, it was shortly after this that the Kiowas held their first Ghost Dance.

7. But Momaday, as I noted many years ago (Krupat 1989), also—repeatedly and insistently—claims that these things inhere in the blood, in "racial memory." Schubnell quotes him, for example, as saying "the Kiowa carries in his blood the meaning and full development of the plains culture" (148), a remark I will let stand without comment. Barbara Strelke's early essay (1975)

uses the phrase "racial memory" in thoroughly untroubled fashion. Gary Kodaseet, a Kiowa man two years younger than Momaday, would seem to demystify this sort of thing when, noting Momaday's claim that although she had never been there, Aho knew "the continental interior...like memory in her blood" (1969, 7), he explained that he feels the same way about places he's never seen because he's heard about them "*all my life, since I was very small*" (149; my emphasis). Kodaseet does add, however, his belief that when he gets to see Devil's Tower, "probably somewhere in our genetic makeup [there is] something [that] says, 'You know, you're home. This is where you're from'" (149). I continue to argue that that sort of feeling comes from cultural experience not our "genetic makeup."

8. Although most of the Kiowas camped on the Staked Plains on that rainy autumn day would be driven *back* to the Fort Sill Reservation by 1875, they would not have been "driven" *onto* them. Nor is it likely that they were there "preeminently [as] a matter of disposition rather than of survival" (Momaday 1969, 6), for, short of rations for the coming winter, and very much concerned with survival, some were hunting the remaining buffalo ("Of the 3,700,000 buffalo destroyed from 1872 through 1874, only 150,000 were killed by Indians" [D. Brown 254]). Having for long conducted raids into Texas and Mexico and attacked army and civilian supply caravans, the Kiowas had very specifically made it a point to "pillage" white buffalo hunters—who often pillaged Indian stock themselves. Satanta surrendered, but not at Fort Sill. Rather, he brought his People "in to the Cheyenne and Arapaho agency" (Hoig 219) on October 4—only to be delivered in chains to Fort Sill nonetheless. See Maggie Smokey's account of "The Battle of Palo Duro Canyon" in Boyd 2: 247–48. Maggie Smokey was six years old in 1874 and told her story in 1956. See also Charley Buffalo's account recorded in 1933. Mr. Buffalo was twenty-three when he "rode in that war party with Lone Wolf" in 1874 (qtd. in Boyd 2: 249).

9. Momaday's uncle Jimmie Mamaday was a descendant of both Lone Wolf and Mamanti. See Boyd 1: 80. Momaday does say, late in the book, that his grandfather "Mammedaty was the grandson of Guihpago" (1969, 102), but I doubt many readers would understand that this was Lone Wolf, a leader of Kiowa resistance, and the plaintiff in Lone Wolf v. Hitchcock, which was decided by the Supreme Court in 1903.

10. In section 19 of the book, Momaday writes: "After the fight at Palo Duro Canyon, the Kiowas came in, a few at a time, to surrender at Fort Sill.... In a field just west of the post, the Indian ponies were destroyed. Nearly 800 horses were killed outright; two thousand more were sold, stolen, given away" (1969, 90). This account may derive from Kiowa oral tradition, and it may be accurate. It differs, however, from the standard historical account as I've given it, which has the destruction of the Indians' horses—over a thousand of them—occurring immediately after the battle and in the area of Palo Duro Canyon. See the book by Captain R. G. Carter for an eyewitness account (494).

11. Of course Momaday's conception of written literature also privileges its "realization of the imaginative experience," so it is hard to see how oral literature—which, he says, does exactly the same thing—is a less "mature condition of expression."

12. Kroeber's sentence continues: "*particularly in its cultural functions*" (1983, 323; my emphasis)—a point I have tried to make in the epigraph to this section of the chapter. The anonymous second reader of this book in manuscript wrote that "Kroeber's use of 'our' and 'ours' makes me shiver" in its assumption "that he writes only for and about non-Indian readers." Both the reader and I find Kroeber's point a valuable one, although I would also question the disquieting use of "our" and "ours." But, then, look just above at Momaday's use of the first-person plural in his remark about what "*we* call literature!"

13. In Freud's early model of mourning—one that has been criticized on ethical and political grounds—these texts, like the successful mourner, would finally release the lost other in favor of a fully compensating replacement, in this case, themselves. But one can only experience the consolation these texts provide by reengaging with their evocation of what has been lost. Most usually

that evocation is a painful one. I see no pain for what has been lost in Momaday's text. Rather than "melancholic mourning" (Ramazani xi), "the dominating feeling of...the whole book [*The Way to Rainy Mountain*]," as Kenneth Fields notes, "is nostalgia, the desire for what cannot be had." Fields continues: "The landscape...embodies the spirit of a vanished race" (202). Obviously the Kiowa "race" has not "vanished," nor has Kiowa culture.

14. Schubnell does, however, claim that recognizing "the extent of the deterioration in the tradition of American Indian poetry and mythology," Momaday accepted "the imperative for speedy research to *salvage* what was still in reach" (144; my emphasis). Maurice Boyd's two volumes called *Kiowa Voices* (1981 and 1983), produced with the help of the Kiowa Research and Historical Society, and Gus Palmer Jr.'s *Telling Stories the Kiowa Way* (2003), for example, testify to the fact that Momaday may have overestimated the "deterioration" of Kiowa oral tradition.

15. Clements almost surely means that Momaday's work takes its place *within* that oral heritage. But his sentence can also be read to mean that Momaday's work takes the place *of* that oral heritage.

16. Momaday was on the faculty of the University of California at Santa Barbara from 1963 to 1969, at which time he joined the faculty at Berkeley. (He was at Amherst on a Guggenheim Fellowship in the fall of 1966.) It was in the winter of 1968–69 that the National Indian Youth Council issued its statement of Indian "self-determination," and in the fall of 1969 that Indians of many nations, citing an old federal law, occupied the former prison on Alcatraz Island and held it for nineteen months. In 1969 as well, Vine Deloria Jr.'s strong attack on anthropologists and other "friends" of the Indian, *Custer Died for Your Sins: An Indian Manifesto,* was published. There is nothing of this ferment in *The Way to Rainy Mountain, House Made of Dawn* (which is, of course, set much earlier), or Momaday's major address, "The Man Made of Words," delivered at the First Convocation of American Indian Scholars at Princeton University in March 1970. Alan Velie's chapter on *House Made of Dawn* in his 1982 work is called "Nobody's Protest Novel" (51). For more on this period, see Smith and Warrior.

17. If Angel is seventeen in 1972, when the novel begins, she would have been born in 1955, and taken from Bush a few years later. It was not until 1978 and the passage of the Indian Child Welfare Act that federal law acknowledged tribal control over Indian children, "establishing guidelines for their adoption" (Krupat and Elliott 174n24).

18. My account untangles and oversimplifies Hogan's richly woven text. I've offered this linear version of the "facts" of the novel only to contextualize the "Prologue," which I will be reading as a contemporary example of Native American elegiac writing.

19. I say "perhaps" because it is by no means certain that condolence rites such as those of the Iroquois or Tlingit People studied earlier did *not* have the dimension I will discuss. No one today—myself very much included—knows every nuance of those rites, and one can safely speculate that very few *then*—whatever early date is chosen for "then"—knew them all either.

20. See Krupat and Elliott 152; and Tarter for a fuller account.

21. In an essay that pays considerable attention to Bush's "mourning feast" for Angel, Catherine Kunce repeatedly refers to Hannah as "insane." Of course, one could hardly claim that Hannah's behaviors are "sane." But Hogan goes to great lengths to show that such a binary—sane/insane—is totally inadequate for understanding what it is that grips Hannah. Kunce makes a point of approving the ways in which Western binaries are undone in *Solar Storms* all the while herself working with this particular one. In telling her dream of Hannah, Agnes has also said that "what was wrong with her we couldn't name and we distrusted such things as had no name. She was like the iron underground that pulls the needle of a compass to false north" (12). Along with her reference to traditional tales of the Windigo, Agnes's metaphor here suggests that another way to think about Hannah's disease may have something to do with "false" readings of nature—something that is very clearly at the root of the James Bay Project's evil. But the novel never does answer the question of how to "name" Hannah's problems.

22. There is a very brief later version of this material that I will treat just below.

23. Steiner also writes: "At its intimate centre, in the zone of familial or totemic [sic] immediacy, our language is...most dense with intentionality and compacted implication. Streaming outward it thins, losing energy and pressure as it reaches an alien speaker" (qtd. in Vizenor 1987, 108). This might seem to privilege Native American traditional, oral expression, but if so, that is only because Steiner views this "intimate" discourse from a romantic, evolutionary perspective that regards it as a paradise inevitably to be lost. Vizenor's elegies for the red squirrel may eventually "reach" "alien" readers, but they seek to do so in a manner that retains the "dense...intentionality and compacted implication" of language directed to "those nearest to us" in a "kinship" that is not based on blood alone.

24. I've argued for an autobiographical reading of *Dead Voices* in "*Dead Voices*, Living Voice: On the Autobiographical Writing of Gerald Vizenor" (1996).

25. I have found no source for the term *wanaki* in relation to a game of any sort. *Wanaki*, an Ojibwe word that does not appear in any contemporary Ojibwe dictionaries, does appear, however, in Bishop Fredric Baraga's *Dictionary of the Otchipwe Language* (1853). The definition is "I inhabit a place in peace, undisturbed, I live somewhere in peace" (398). Professor Scott Lyons pointed out that the Baraga dictionary "lists a whole lot of 'wan' words," such as "*Wanakia*, I make him live in peace...*Wanakiwendam*, I am appeased in my thoughts, in my mind, I am out of danger, out of trouble" (398). Professor Lyons, who has helped me greatly with these matters, notes that not only has *wanaki* become a nearly ubiquitous signifier of "indigenous," as, for example, in the names of golf courses in Ojibwe campgrounds and in Papua, New Guinea, but it has also made its way "as part of the standard Na'vi greeting in the movie *Avatar*, e.g., 'Wanaki Kamayu,' 'I see you'" (personal communication, March 5, 2010).

26. A brief but very useful account of these matters is given in Kathryn Milun's review of *Dead Voices* (1994).

27. Thus it would seem that the event has been moved forward more than twenty years in time.

28. The somewhat baffling repetition of the phrase *coup de grace*—strictly speaking, it refers to the single act that puts the sufferer out of his or her misery—is perhaps explained in *Fugitive Poses* where Vizenor writes: "The Boy Scouts of America and the Izaak Walton League taught me and other hunters of my generation the monomercies of the coup de grace. We learned as hunters and later as authors never to let a wounded animal suffer" (1998, 130). Thus when "the first mercy bullet" does not dispatch the animal, Vizenor fires a second and then two more shots before the squirrel finally dies.

29. A brief return to this material a little later is more nearly consistent with the earliest accounts. In chapter 3 of *Fugitive Poses* (1998), entitled "Literary Animals," a section called "Escape Distance" returns to the more individual and vocational use of the killing of the red squirrel. The penultimate page of Kimberly Blaeser's book-length study of Vizenor (1996) discusses the variant tellings to that point (203), and Kathryn Hume's discussion of Vizenor's "metaphysics" (2007) considers all of them.

30. It is a subject for further study whether this commitment to reciting the names of the dead is equally prominent among writers from the Southern Plains, the Plateau, and importantly, the Southwest, where there was what Gladys Reichard called a marked "phobia of the dead" (40) and what Hittman called—as I quoted him earlier—"ghost fright" (1990, 180). I've found texts by Luci Tapahonso, Della Frank, and Nora Yazzie Hunter, three Navajo women, and by Ofelia Zepeda, who is Tohon'o O'odham (Papago), that do indeed speak of the dead. Adrian Louis, whom we shall consider below, is Numu (Paiute), and Numu people also did not like to talk of the dead, although it was the Numu man Wovoka who initiated the Ghost Dance religion, which promised the return of the Indian dead! (Louis for many years, however, lived and worked among the Lakota.)

31. Kicking Bird had long advocated the adoption of farming among his Kiowa people, and education by the whites. A portrait of this complex and interesting Kiowa leader by someone who knew him well may be found in Battey; see also Hoig.

32. And earlier, as, for example, in John Dos Passos's "anti-elegiac," "mock elegy" (Ramazani 89; see below) "'They Are Dead Now': Eulogy for Sacco and Vanzetti" (1927), which begins: "This isn't a poem / This is two men in grey prison clothes."

33. This provides a lesson in Cherokee history before removal (1830/1838) and, in several instances, after. John Ross was principal chief of the Cherokees in the 1830s. Tsali was a Cherokee farmer forced with his family onto the Trail of Tears in 1838. He resisted, leading to the death of an American soldier. Eventually, Tsali gave himself up upon General Winfield Scott's promise not to pursue other resisting Cherokees and was executed by firing squad. About 1821, Sequoia invented a syllabary in which the Cherokee language could be written. Tagwadahi, Itaguni, and Ayunini (Swimmer or The Swimmer) were all traditional healers; the latter worked with the anthropologist James Mooney toward the end of the nineteenth century, who published many of his healing charms and spells.

34. A different sort of recitation of names but in the same interest of survivance occurs in Simon Ortiz's "Some Indians at a Party." The poem begins: "'Where you from?' / Juneau / Pine Ridge / Sells / Tahlequah"; and, after the listing of sixteen more place-names, it concludes: "Acoma / the other side, ten miles from Snow Bird. / That's my name too. / Don't you forget it" (1992, 220).

35. Ralph Salisbury conveys a different and perhaps more complex sense of Joseph—in the conditional tense. His poem "For Joseph, Great Peace Chief, Great War Chief, of the Nez Perce" begins: "You'd have liked our Cherokee / Tennessee autumn rain" (1983, 34).

36. Other of Revard's family elegies, which have been published in his 2001 and 2005 collections, include "Aunt Jewell as Powwow Princess," "Ponca War Dancers," "My Right Hand Don't Leave Me No More," "And Don't Be Deaf to the Singing Beyond," among others. As I note below, Wendy Rose has published a number of poems that might be considered variants of the family elegy. See also Ralph Salisbury's "For Uncle Jimmy Harkin" (1983, 58) and "Family Stories, and the One Not Told" (1980, n.p.).

37. In its second section, Auden's "In Memory of W. B Yeats" includes the line "For poetry makes nothing happen" (209). The third and final section of the poem, however, has Auden writing: "Follow, poet, follow right / To the bottom of the night, / With your unconstraining voice / Still persuade us to rejoice; / With the farming of a verse / Make a vineyard of the curse" (210).

38. Many of Ortiz's poems express sentiments of this kind, although they are not necessarily elegiac. The poem following "Mama's and Daddy's Words," for example, is called "Returning It Back, You Will Go On." In "Juanita, Wife of Manuelito," the nineteenth-century Navajo war chief, Ortiz memorializes her, and, as often in his work, turns from the past to the present and the future: "I can see, Navajo woman / that it is possible for dreams / to occur, the prayers full of the mystery / of children, laughter, the dances, / my own humanity, so it can last unto forever. / *That is what I want to teach my son*" (1992, 133; my emphasis).

39. Rose's *Itch Like Crazy* contains a number of poems representing deceased members of her family. They might, as I noted above, be called "family elegies" in that they memorialize members of her family who have passed on, although they seem to me more oriented toward self-knowledge than toward sustaining the community. One could, of course, read them differently.

Works Cited

Aberle, David. 1959. "The Prophet Dance and Reactions to White Contact." *Southwestern Journal of Anthropology* 15: 74–78.
Abler, Thomas. 1984. "The Kansas Connection: The Seneca Nation and the Iroquois Confederacy Council." *Extending the Rafters*. Ed. Michael Foster, Jack Campisi, and Marianne Mithun. Albany: State University of New York Press. 81–93.
———. 2000. "Iroquois Policy and Iroquois Culture: Two Histories and an Anthropological Ethnohistory." *Ethnohistory* 47: 484–91.
Afzal, Cameron. Personal communication. August 24, 2009.
Alexie, Sherman. 1993. *First Indian on the Moon*. Brooklyn: Hanging Loose Press.
———. 2000a. *One Stick Song*. Brooklyn: Hanging Loose Press.
———. 2000b. "The Unauthorized Autobiography of Me." *One Stick Song*. 13–25.
Alfred, Taiaiake. 1999. *Peace, Power, Righteousness: An Indigenous Manifesto*. Ontario: Oxford University Press.
Allen, Chadwick. 1999. "Blood (and) Memory." *American Literature* 71: 469–84.
Allen, Paula Gunn. 1997. *Life Is a Fatal Disease: Collected Poems, 1962–1995*. Albuquerque: West End Press.
Anderson, Jeffrey. 2005. "Arapaho Ghost Dance Songs." *Algonquian Spirit: Contemporary Translations of the Algonquian Literatures of North America*. Ed. Brian Swann. Lincoln: University of Nebraska Press. 448–71.
Aoki, Haruo. 1979. *Nez Perce Texts*. Berkeley: University of California Press.

214   Works Cited

———. 1989. "Chief Joseph's Words." *Idaho Yesterdays*. Boise: Idaho Historical Society. 16–21.
Apess, William. 1829. *A Son of the Forest: The Experience of William Apes, a Native of the Forest, Comprising a Notice of the Pequot Tribe of Indians*. New York: By the author.
———. 1992a. *Eulogy on King Philip* [1836]. O'Connell, *On Our Own Ground* 277–310.
———. 1992b. *A Son of the Forest: The Experience of William Apess, a Native of the Forest* [1831]. O'Connell, *On Our Own Ground* 3–97.
Armstrong, Virginia, ed. 1971. *I Have Spoken: American History through the Voices of the Indians*. New York: Swallow Press.
Arnold, Elliott. 1947. *Blood Brother*. New York: Duell, Sloan, and Pearce.
Auden, W. H. 1965. "In Memory of W. B. Yeats." *Modern Poetry*. Ed. Maynard Mack, Leonard Dean, and William Frost. 1940. Englewood Cliffs, NJ: Prentice-Hall. 208–10.
Bagley, Clarence. 1931. "Chief Seattle and Angeline." *Washington Historical Quarterly* 22: 243–75.
Bahr, Donald. 1994. "Oratory." *Dictionary of Native American Literature*. Ed. Andrew Wiget. New York: Garland. 107–18.
Bahr, Donald, Lloyd Paul, and Vincent Joseph. 1997. *Ants and Orioles: Showing the Art of Pima Poetry*. Salt Lake City: University of Utah Press.
Bahr, Donald, Juan Smith, William Smith Allison, and Julian Hayden. 1994. *The Short Swift Time of Gods on Earth: The Hohokam Chronicles*. Berkeley: University of California Press.
Ball, Eve. 1980. *Indeh: An Apache Odyssey*. Provo, UT: Brigham Young University Press.
———. 2000. *Apache Voices: Their Stories of Survival as Told to Eve Ball*. Ed. Sherry Robinson. Albuquerque: University of New Mexico Press.
Baraga, Fredric. 1992. *A Dictionary of the Ojibway Language*. St. Paul: Minnesota Historical Press. Rpt. of *Dictionary of the Otchipwe Language* (1853).
Barnes, Jim. 1997. *On Native Ground: Memoirs and Impressions*. Norman: University of Oklahoma Press.
Barnett, H. G. 1966. "The Nature of the Potlatch." *Indians of the North Pacific Coast*. Ed. Tom McFeat. Seattle: University of Washington Press. 81–91.
Basso, Keith. 1971. *Apachean Culture, History, and Ethnology*. Tucson: University of Arizona Press.
———. 1984. "'Stalking with Stories': Names, Places, and Moral Narratives among the Western Apache." *Cultural Anthropology* 1: 19–54.
———. 1990. *Western Apache Language and Culture*. Tucson: University of Arizona Press.
Battey, Thomas C. 1972. *The Life and Adventures of a Quaker among the Indians*. 1875. Williamstown, MA: Cornerhouse Publishers.
Beal, Merrill. 1963.*"I Will Fight No More Forever": Chief Joseph and the Nez Perce War*. New York: Ballantine.
Beauchamp, William. 1895. "An Iroquois Condolence." *Journal of American Folklore* 8: 313–16.
———. 1907. "Civil, Religious, and Mourning Councils and Ceremonies of Adoption of the New York Indians." *New York State Museum Bulletin* 113, *Archeology* 13: 341–451.
Ben-Amos, Dan. 1969. "Analytical Categories and Ethnic Genres." *Genre* 2: 275–301.

Berkhofer, Robert, Jr. 1971. "The Political Context of a New Indian History." *Pacific Historical Review* 40: 357–82.
Bevis, William. 1987. "Native American Novels: Homing In." Swann and Krupat, *Recovering the Word* 580–620.
Bierhorst, John. 1974. "The Ritual of Condolence: An Iroquois Ceremonial." *Four Masterworks of American Indian Literature*. By Bierhorst. New York: Farrar, Straus and Giroux. 108–83.
Bierwert, Crisca, ed. 1996. *Lushootseed Texts: An Introduction to Puget Sound Narrative Aesthetics*. Lincoln: University of Nebraska Press.
———. 1998. "Remembering Chief Seattle: Reversing Cultural Studies of a Vanishing Native American Author(s)." *American Indian Quarterly* 22: 280–304.
Black Elk. 1979. *Black Elk Speaks*. Ed. John G. Neihardt. 1932. Lincoln: University of Nebraska Press.
Black Hawk. 1964. *Black Hawk: An Autobiography* [1833]. Ed. Donald Jackson. 1955. Urbana: University of Illinois Press.
———. 1999. *Black Hawk's Autobiography*. Ed. Roger Nichols. Ames: Iowa State University Press.
———. 2008. *Life of Black Hawk, or Ma-ka-tai-me-she-kia-kiak*. Ed. J. Gerald Kennedy. New York: Penguin.
Blaeser, Kimberly. 1996. *Gerald Vizenor: Writing in the Oral Tradition*. Norman: University of Oklahoma Press.
———. 2002. *Absentee Indians and Other Poems*. East Lansing: Michigan State University Press.
———. 2003. "Sacred Journey Cycles: Pilgrimage as Re-Turning and Re-Telling in American Indigenous Literatures." *Religion & Literature* 35: 83–104.
———. 2006. "Cannons and Canonization: American Indian Poetries through Autonomy, Colonization, Nationalism, and Decolonization." Cheyfitz 183–287.
Blair, Emma Helen. 1969. *The Indian Tribes of the Upper Mississippi Valley and Region of the Great Lakes*. 2 vols. 1911. New York: Kraus.
Blaisdell, Robert. 2000. *Great Speeches by Native Americans*. Mineola, NY: Dover.
Bourke, John. 1891. *On the Border with Crook*. New York: Scribners.
Boyd, Maurice. 1981–83. *Kiowa Voices: Ceremonial Dance, Ritual, and Song*. 2 vols. Fort Worth: Texas Christian University Press.
Brady, Cyrus T. 1974. *Northwestern Fights and Fighters*. 1907. Williamstown, MA: Corner House.
Bright, William. 2000. "The Sociolinguistics of the 'S-Word': 'Squaw' in American Placenames." MS.
———. 2004. *Native American Placenames of the United States*. Norman: University of Oklahoma Press.
Brightman, Robert. 1989. *Acaoohkiwina and Acimowina: Traditional Narratives of the Rock Cree Indians*. Mercury Series Paper 113. Hull, Quebec: Canadian Museum of Civilization.
Bross, Kristina. 2001. "Vanishing Savages: 'Dying Indian Speeches' in Colonial New England Literature." *Early American Literature* 36: 325–52.

Brown, Dee. 1978. *Bury My Heart at Wounded Knee: An Indian History of the American West.* 1971. New York: Bantam.
Brown, Mark H. 1967. *The Flight of the Nez Perce.* New York: Putnam.
———. 1972. "The Joseph Myth." *Montana, the Magazine of Western History,* January: 2–17.
Brumble, H. David. 1988. *American Indian Autobiography.* Berkeley: University of California Press.
Buerge, David. 1991. "Seattle's King Arthur." *Seattle Weekly,* July 17, 1991: 27–29.
———. 1992. *Chief Seattle.* Seattle: Sasquatch Books.
———. "Chief Seattle and Chief Joseph: From Indians to Icons." Accessed December 8, 2009. <http://content.lib.washington.edu/aipnw/buerge2.html>.
Butler, Judith. 2003. "After Loss, What Then?" Afterword. Eng and Kazanjian 467–73.
Campisi, Jack. Personal communication. May 21, 2009.
Carlson, Frank. 1903. "Chief Sealth." *Bulletin of the University of Washington, the State University,* ser. 3, no. 2 (December).
Carpenter, Cecelia Svinth. 1996. *Tears of Internment: The Indian History of Fox Island and the Puget Sound Indian War.* Tacoma, WA: Tahoma Research Service.
Carter, Captain R. G. 1961. *On the Border with Mackenzie; or, Winning West Texas from the Comanches.* 1935. New York: Antiquarian Press.
Cave, Alfred. 2006. *Prophets of the Great Spirit: Native American Revitalization in Eastern North America.* Lincoln: University of Nebraska Press.
Cavitch, Max. 2007. *American Elegy: The Poetry of Mourning from the Puritans to Whitman.* Minneapolis: University of Minnesota Press.
———. 2010. "American Constitutional Elegy." Weisman 224–37.
Chapman, Abraham, ed. 1975. *Literature of the American Indians: Views and Interpretations.* New York: New American Library.
Cheyfitz, Eric, ed. 2006a. *The Columbia Guide to American Indian Literatures of the United States since 1945.* New York: Columbia University Press.
———. 2006b. "The (Post)Colonial Construction of Indian Country: U.S. American Indian Literatures and Federal Indian Law." Cheyfitz 1–126.
Child, Lydia Maria. 1829. *The First Settlers of New England, or Conquest of the Pequods, Narragansetts, and Pokanokets.* Boston: Monroe and Francis.
Clark, Jerry. 1985. "Thus Spoke Chief Seattle: The Story of an Undocumented Speech." *Prologue Magazine* 18: 58–65.
Clements, William. 1985. "Folk Historical Sense in Two Native American Authors." *MELUS* 12: 65–78.
———. 2002. *Oratory in Native North America.* Tucson: University of Arizona Press.
Clewell, Tammy. 2004. "Mourning beyond Melancholia: Freud's Psychoanalysis of Loss." *Journal of the American Psychoanalytic Association* 52: 43–67.
Cook, Barbara. 2003. *From the Center of Tradition: Critical Perspectives on Linda Hogan.* Boulder: University of Colorado Press.
Coward, John. 1999. *The Newspaper Indian: Native American Identity in the Press, 1820–90.* Urbana: University of Illinois Press.
Curtis, Edward. 1976. *The North American Indian.* 20 vols. 1907–30. Reprint. New York: Johnson Reprint Corporation.
Curtis, Natalie, ed. 1968. *The Indians' Book: Songs and Legends of the American Indians.* 1907. New York: Dover.

Cushman, H. B. 1999. *History of the Choctaw, Chickasaw, and Natchez Indians.* 1899. Norman: University of Oklahoma Press.

Dauenhauer, Nora Marks, and Richard Dauenhauer, eds. 1987. *Haa shuká, Our Ancestors: Tlingit Oral Narratives.* Seattle: University of Washington Press; Juneau: Sealaska.

——. 1990. *Haa Tuwunaagu Yis, for Healing Our Spirit: Tlingit Oratory.* Seattle: University of Washington Press/Sealaska Heritage Foundation.

——. 1994. "'Glacier Bay History' Told by Amy Marvin and 'Speech for the Removal of Grief' Delivered by Jessie Dalton [Tlingit]." Swann 151–75.

Dauenhauer, Richard. Personal communication. May 11, 2009.

Davis, Christopher. 1969. *North American Indians.* Middlesex, Eng.: Hamlyn House.

De Laguna, Frederica. 1952. "Some Dynamic Forces in Tlingit Society." *Southwestern Journal of Anthropology* 8: 1–12.

——. 1972. *Under Mount Saint Elias: The History and Culture of the Yakutat Tlingit.* 2 vols. Washington, DC: Smithsonian Institution Press.

——. 1990. "Tlingit." *Handbook of North American Indians.* Vol. 7. Ed. Wayne Suttles. Washington, DC: U.S. Government Printing Office. 203–28.

Deloria, Vine, Jr. 1969. *Custer Died for Your Sins: An Indian Manifesto.* New York: Avon.

——. 1989. "Out of Chaos." *I Become Part of It: Sacred Dimensions in Native American Life.* Ed. D. M. Dooling and Paul Jordan-Smith. New York: Parabola Books. 256–69.

DeMallie, Raymond. 1982. "The Lakota Ghost Dance: An Ethnohistorical Account." *Pacific Historical Review* 51: 385–405.

——, ed. 1985. *The Sixth Grandfather: Black Elk's Teachings Given to John G. Neihardt.* Lincoln: University of Nebraska Press.

Dodge, Robert, and Joseph McCullough, eds. 1985. *New and Old Voices of Wah'kon-Tah.* New York: International Publishers.

Dowd, Gregory E. 1992. *A Spirited Resistance: The North American Indian Struggle for Unity, 1745–1815.* Baltimore: Johns Hopkins University Press.

Drake, Samuel. 1834. *Biography and History of the Indians of North America from Its First Discovery.* 3rd enl. ed. Boston.

——. 1841. *Biography and History of the Indians of North America from Its First Discovery.* 11th enl. ed. Boston.

Drucker, Philip. 1966. "Some Variations on the Potlatch." *Indians of the North Pacific Coast.* Ed. Tom McFeat. Seattle: University of Washington Press. 102–7.

Dunn, Carolyn, and Carol Comfort, eds. 1999. *Through the Eye of the Deer: An Anthology of Native American Women Writers.* San Francisco: Aunt Lute Books.

Durham, Jimmie. 1983. *Columbus Day: Poems, Drawings, and Stories about American Indian Life and Death in the Nineteen-Seventies.* Albuquerque: West End Press.

Duthu, N. Bruce. 2008. *American Indians and the Law.* New York: Viking/Penguin.

Dyck, Carrie. 2011. "Should Translation Work Take Place? Ethical Questions Concerning the Translation of First Nations Languages." *Born in the Blood: On Native American Translation.* Ed. Brian Swann. Lincoln: University of Nebraska Press. 17–42.

Eastman, Charles Alexander. 1977. *From the Deep Woods to Civilization: Chapters in the Autobiography of an Indian.* 1916. Lincoln: University of Nebraska Press.

Edmunds, R. David. 1978. *The Potawatomis, Keepers of the Fire.* Norman: University of Oklahoma Press.

———. 1983. *The Shawnee Prophet*. Lincoln: University of Nebraska Press.
———. 1985. "Main Poc: Potawatomi Wabeno." *American Indian Quarterly* 9: 259–72.
Ellis, Anderson Nelson. 1913–14. "Recollections of an Interview with Cochise." *Kansas State Historical Society Collections* 13: 387–92.
Eng, David, and Shinhee Han. 2003. "A Dialogue on Racial Melancholia." Eng and Kazanjian 343–71.
Eng, David, and David Kazanjian, eds. 2003a. *Loss: The Politics of Mourning*. Berkeley: University of California Press.
———. 2003b. "Mourning Remains." Introduction. Eng and Kazanjian 1–25.
Everett, Edward. 1831. "The Cherokee Case." *North American Review* 33: 136–53.
———. 1835. *An Address Delivered at Bloody Brook in South Deerfield, September 30, 1835, in Commemoration of the Fall of the 'Flower of Essex,' at That Spot in King Philip's War, September 18, (O[ld]. S[tyle], 1675.* Boston.
Fabian, Johannes. 1983. *Time and the Other: How Anthropology Makes Its Object*. New York: Columbia University Press.
Fee, Chester. 1936. *Chief Joseph: The Biography of a Great Indian*. New York: Wilson-Erickson.
Fenton, William. 1944. "Simeon Gibson: Iroquois Informant, 1889–1943." *American Anthropologist* 44: 231–34.
———. 1946. "An Iroquois Condolence Council." *Journal of the Washington Academy of Sciences* 36: 110–27.
———. 1950. "The Roll Call of the Iroquois Chiefs: A Study of a Mnemonic Cane from the Six Nations Reserve." *Smithsonian Miscellaneous Collections* 111: 1–73.
———, ed. 1968. *Parker on the Iroquois*. Syracuse, NY: Syracuse University Press.
———. 1998. *The Great Law and the Longhouse: A Political History of the Iroquois Confederacy*. Norman: University of Oklahoma Press.
Fenton, William, and Gertrude Kurath. 1951. "The Feast of the Dead, or Ghost Dance at Six Nations Reserve, Canada." *Symposium on Local Diversity in Iroquois Culture*. Bureau of American Ethnology Bulletin 149. Washington: U.S. Government Printing Office. 139–65.
Fields, Kenneth. 1970. "More than Language Means." *Southern Review* 6: 196–204.
Foley, Dennis. 1973. "The Iroquois Condolence Business." *Man in the Northeast* 5: 47–53.
Foreman, Carolyn. 1936. "Edward W. Bushyhead and John Rollin Ridge." *Chronicles of Oklahoma* 14: 295–311.
Forsyth, Thomas. 1969. "An Account of the Manners and Customs of the Sauk and Fox Nations of Indians Traditions [sic]." Blair 2: 182–245.
Foster, Michael K. 1984. "On Who Spoke First at Iroquois-White Councils: An Exercise in the Method of Upstreaming." *Extending the Rafters: Interdisciplinary Approaches to Iroquoian Studies*. Ed. Michael K. Foster, Jack Campisi, and Marianne Mithun. Albany: State University of New York Press. 183–208.
———. 1985a. "Another Look at the Function of Wampum in Iroquois-White Councils." *The History and Culture of Iroquois Diplomacy: An Interdisciplinary Guide to the Treaties of the Six Nations and Their League*. Ed. Francis Jennings et. al. Syracuse, NY: Syracuse University Press. 99–114.

———— [?]. 1985b. "Glossary of Figures of Speech in Iroquois Political Rhetoric." Jennings 115–24.

———. Personal communication. October 23, 2009.

Francis, Lee. 2002. *On the Good Red Interstate: Truck Stop Tellings and Other Poems.* San Francisco: Taurean Horn Press.

Freud, Sigmund. 1986. "Mourning and Melancholia." *The Standard Edition of the Complete Psychological Works of Sigmund Freud.* Ed. James Strachey, with Anna Freud, Alix Strachey, and Alan Tyson. Vol. 14. 1917. London: Hogarth Press. 237–58.

Frow, John. 2006. *Genre.* London: Routledge.

Furtwangler, Albert. 1997. *Answering Chief Seattle.* Seattle: University of Washington Press.

Garroutte, Eva Marie. 2003. *Real Indians: Identity and the Survival of Native America.* Berkeley: University of California Press.

Geronimo. 1906. *Geronimo's Story of his Life.* Ed. S.M. Barrett. New York: Duffield.

Gibbs, George. 1863. *A Dictionary of the Chinook Jargon, or Trade Language of Oregon.* New York: Cramoisy Press.

Gibson, John A. 1992. *Concerning the League: The Iroquois League Tradition as Dictated in Onondaga by John Arthur Gibson.* Ed. and trans. Hanni Woodbury. Memoir 9, Algonquian and Iroquoian Linguistics. Winnipeg: Algonquian and Iroquoian Linguistics.

Gilbert, Sandra, ed. 2001. *Inventions of Farewell: A Book of Elegies.* New York: Norton.

Glancy, Diane. 1991. *Lone Dog's Winter Count.* Albuquerque: West End Press.

Goddard, Ives. 1978. "Classification of Native Languages." *Handbook of North American Indians,* vol. 17. Ed. I. Goddard. Washington, DC: U.S. Government Printing Office. 320–21.

———. Personal communication. November 4, 2009.

Gould, Philip. 1996. *Covenant and Republic: Historical Romance and the Politics of Puritanism.* New York: Cambridge University Press.

Grant, Frederic. 1891. *History of Seattle, Washington.* New York: American Publishing and Engraving Co.

Greene, Jerome. 2000. *Nez Perce Summer, 1877: The U.S. Army and the Nee-Me-Poo Crisis.* Helena: Montana Historical Society Press.

Hale, Horatio. 1883. *The Iroquois Book of Rites.* Philadelphia: Brinton's Library of Aboriginal American Literature.

———. 1895. "An Iroquois Condolence Council." *Proceedings and Transactions of the Royal Society of Canada* ser. 2, vol. 1: 45–65.

Hallwas, John. 1981. "Black Hawk: a Reassessment." *Annals of Iowa* 45: 599–619.

Harjo, Joy. 2002. *How We Became Human.* New York: Norton.

Harrington, M. R. 1914. *Sacred Bundles of the Sac and Fox Indians.* University Museum Anthropological Publications, vol. 4. Philadelphia: University of Pennsylvania. 123–262.

Henson, Lance. 1976. *Naming the Dark: Poems for the Cheyenne.* Norman, OK: Point Riders Press.

———. 1985. *Selected Poems, 1970–1983.* Greenfield Center, NY: Greenfield Review Press.

———. [1992?]. *Another Distance: New and Selected Poems.* Norman, OK: Point Riders Press.
———. 1992. *A Cheyenne Sketchbook: Selected Poems, 1970–1991.* Rev. ed. Greenfield Center, NY: Greenfield Review Press.
Hewitt, J. N. B. 1928. "John Deserontyon. A Mohawk Form of Ritual Condolence, 1782." *Indian Notes and Monographs* 10: 83–110.
———. 1944. "The Requickening Address of the Iroquois Condolence Council." Ed. William Fenton. *Journal of the Washington Academy of Sciences,* March 15: 65–85.
———. 1977. "The Requickening Address of the League of the Iroquois." *Holmes Anniversary Volume: Anthropological Essays Presented to William H. Holmes in Honor of His Seventieth Birthday December 1, 1916, by His Friends and Colaborers.* 1916. New York: AMS Press. 163–79.
Hilbert, Vi. 1991. "When Chief Seattle (Si AL) Spoke." *A Time of Gathering: Native Heritage in Washington State.* Ed. Robin K. Wright. Seattle: Burke Museum/University of Washington Press. 259–66.
Hilden, Patricia Penn. Personal communication. November 20, 2010.
Hinton, Leanne. 1984. *Havasupai Songs: A Linguistic Perspective.* Tubingen: G. Narr.
———. 1994. "The Farewell Song [Havasupai]." Swann 690–703.
———. Personal communication. June 22, 2008.
Hinton, Leanne, and Lucille Watahomigie, eds. 1984. *Spirit Mountain: An Anthology of Yuman Story and Song.* Tucson: Sun Tracks/University of Arizona Press.
Hittman, Michael. 1973. "The 1870 Ghost Dance at the Walker River Reservation: A Reconstruction." *Ethnohistory* 20: 247–78.
———. 1990. *Wovoka and the Ghost Dance.* Carson City, NV: The Grace Dangberg Foundation.
———. 1997. *Wovoka and the Ghost Dance.* Ed. Don Lynch. Expanded ed. Lincoln: University of Nebraska Press.
———. Personal communication. August 1, 2010.
Hogan, Linda. 1995. *Solar Storms.* New York: Scribner.
Hoig, Stan. 2000. *The Kiowas and the Legend of Kicking Bird.* Boulder: University of Colorado Press.
Holler, Clyde, ed. 2000. *The Black Elk Reader.* Syracuse, NY: Syracuse University Press.
Holloway, Brian. 2003. *Interpreting the Legacy: John Neihardt and "Black Elk Speaks."* Boulder: University of Colorado Press.
Horsman, Reginald. 1975. "Scientific Racism and the American Indian in the Mid-Nineteenth Century." *American Quarterly* 27: 152–68.
Howard, O. O. 1877. *Report of the Secretary of War, Being Part of the Message and Documents Communicated in the Two Houses of Congress at the Beginning of the Second Session of the Forty-fifth Congress, 1877.* Washington, DC: Government Printing Office.
———. 1881. *Nez Perce Joseph, an Account of His Ancestors, His Lands, His Confederates, His Enemies, His Murders, His War, His Pursuit and Capture.* Boston: Lee and Sheperd.
———. 1907. *Famous Indian Chiefs I Have Known.* New York: Century.
Hume, Kathryn. 2007. "Gerald Vizenor's Metaphysics." *Contemporary Literature* 48: 580–612.

Hutchinson, William, and William Rachal, eds. 1962. *The Papers of James Madison*. Vol. 1. Chicago: University of Chicago Press.

Irving, Washington. 1996a. "Philip of Pokanoket." *The Sketch-Book of Geoffrey Crayon, Gent.* 1819–20. New York: Oxford University Press. 250–64.

———. 1996b. "Traits of Indian Character." *The Sketch-Book* 240–49.

Jackson, Donald. 1964. Introduction. *Black Hawk*. By Black Hawk. Ed. Donald Jackson. Urbana: University of Illinois Press.

Jaskoski, Helen. 1988. "Image and Silence." Roemer 69–77.

Jefferson, Thomas. 2007. "Notes on the State of Virginia." *Norton Anthology of American Literature*. Ed. Nina Baym et. al. 7th ed. Vol. A. New York: W.W. Norton. 444–45.

Jennings, Francis. 1993. *The Founders of America: From the Earliest Migrations to the Present*. New York: Norton.

Johnson, Kendall. 2006. "Imagining Self and Community in American Indian Autobiography." Cheyfitz 357–404.

———. 2007. "Peace, Friendship, and Financial Panic: Reading the Mark of Black Hawk in the *Life of Ma-ka-tai-me-she-kia-kiak*." *American Literary History* 19: 771–99.

Jones, Louis T. 1965. *Aboriginal American Oratory: The Tradition of Eloquence among the Indians of the United States*. Los Angeles: Southwest Museum.

Josephy, Alvin. 1961. *The Patriot Chiefs: A Chronicle of American Indian Resistance*. New York: Penguin.

———. 1965. *The Nez Perce Indians and the Opening of the Northwest*. New Haven, CT: Yale University Press.

Jung, Patrick. 2007. *The Black Hawk War of 1832*. Norman: University of Oklahoma Press.

Kaiser, Rudolph. 1987. "Chief Seattle's Speech(es): American Origins and European Reception." Swann and Krupat, *Recovering the Word* 497–536.

Kan, Sergei. 1983. "Words That Heal the Soul: Analysis of the Tlingit Potlatch Oratory." *Arctic Anthropology* 20: 47–59.

———. 1986. "The 19th-Century Tlingit Potlatch: A New Perspective." *American Ethnologist* 13: 191–212.

———. 1989. *Symbolic Immortality: The Tlingit Potlatch of the Nineteenth Century*. Washington, DC: Smithsonian Institution Press.

Kehoe, Alice. 1989. *The Ghost Dance: Ethnohistory and Revitalization*. Fort Worth: Holt, Rinehart, and Winston.

Kenny, Maurice. 1992. *Tekonwatonti/Molly Brant: Poems of War*. Fredonia, NY: White Pine Press.

Kodaseet, Gary. 1988. "Interview with Kenneth Roemer." Roemer 145–52.

Konkle, Maureen. 2004. *Writing Indian Nations: Native Intellectuals and the Politics of Historiography, 1827–1863*. Chapel Hill: University of North Carolina Press.

Kracht, Benjamin. 1992. "The Kiowa Ghost Dance, 1894–1916: An Unheralded Revitalization Movement." *Ethnohistory* 39: 452–77.

Kroeber, Karl. 1983. "Poem, Dream, and the Consuming of Cultures." *Smoothing the Ground: Essays on Native American Oral Literature*. Ed. Brian Swann. Berkeley: University of California Press. 323–33.

———. 1989. "Technology and Tribal Narrative." *Narrative Chance: Postmodern Discourse on Native American Indian Literatures.* Ed. Gerald Vizenor. Albuquerque: University of Arizona Press. 17–38.

Krupat, Arnold. 1985. *For Those Who Come After: A Study of Native American Autobiography.* Berkeley: University of California Press.

———. 1989. "Monologue and Dialogue in Native American Autobiography." *The Voice in the Margin: Native American Literature and the Canon.* By Krupat. Berkeley: University of California Press. 132–201.

———. 1992. "Native American Autobiography and the Synecdochic Self." *Ethnocriticism: Ethnography, History, Literature.* By Krupat. Berkeley: University of California Press. 201–31.

———. 1996a. "*Dead Voices,* Living Voice: On the Autobiographical Writing of Gerald Vizenor." *The Turn to the Native: Studies in Criticism and Culture.* By Krupat. Lincoln: University of Nebraska Press. 70–87.

———. 1996b. "*Ratio-* and *Natio-* in Gerald Vizenor's *Heirs of Columbus.*" Krupat, *The Turn to the Native* 56–69.

———. 2002a. "Nationalism, Indigenism, Cosmopolitanism: Three Perspectives on Native American Literatures." *Red Matters: Native American Studies.* By Krupat. Philadelphia: University of Pennsylvania Press. 1–23.

———. 2002b. "On the Translation of Native American Song and Story: A Theorized History." Krupat, *Red Matters* 24–47.

———. 2002c. "The 'Rage Stage': Contextualizing Sherman Alexie's *Indian Killer.*" Krupat, *Red Matters* 98–121.

———. 2009a. "Representing Indians in American Literature, 1820–1870." *All That Remains: Varieties of Indigenous Expression.* By Krupat. Lincoln: University of Nebraska Press. 103–29.

———. 2009b. "Resisting Racism: William Apess as Public Intellectual." Krupat, *All That Remains* 73–101.

———. 2010a. "Patterson's *Life;* Black Hawk's Story; Native American Elegy." *American Literary History* 22: 527–52.

———. 2010b. "'That the People Might Live': Notes toward a Study of Native American Elegy." Weisman 343–63.

Krupat, Arnold, and Michael Elliott. 2006. "American Indian Fiction and Anticolonial Resistance." Cheyfitz 127–82.

Kunce, Catherine. 2009. "Feasting on Famine in Linda Hogan's *Solar Storms.*" *Studies in American Indian Literatures* 21: 50–70.

Lang, George. 2008. *Making Wawa: The Genesis of Chinook Jargon.* Vancouver: University of British Columbia Press.

Langen, Toby, and Marya Moses. 2001. "Reading Martha Lamont's Crow Story Today." *Native American Oral Traditions: Collaboration and Interpretation.* Ed. Larry Evers and Barre Toelken. Logan: University of Utah Press. 92–129.

LeClaire, Antoine. Catalogue of His Papers. Putnam Archive. Davenport, IA.

Lepore, Jill. 1999. *The Name of War: King Philip's War and the Origins of American Identity.* New York: Vintage.

Lewis, James. 1988. "Shamans and Prophets: Continuities and Discontinuities in Native American New Religions." *American Indian Quarterly* 12: 221–28.

Liberty, David Michael. 2004. "It's Never too Late to Give Away a Horse." *Oregon Historical Quarterly* 105: 96–107.

Lincoln, Kenneth. 1983. *Native American Renaissance*. Berkeley: University of California Press.

Littlefield, Daniel, and James Parins, eds. 2011. *Encyclopedia of American Indian Removal*. 2 vols. Westport, CT: Greenwood Press.

Louis, Adrian. 1989. *Fire Water World*. Albuquerque: West End Press.

———. 1992. *Among the Dog Eaters: Poems*. Albuquerque: West End Press.

———. 1994. *Blood Thirsty Savages*. St. Louis: Time Being Books.

Low, Denise. 1995. "Contemporary Reinventions of Chief Seattle: Variant Texts of Chief Seattle's 1854 Speech." *American Indian Quarterly* 19: 407–21.

Lowenstein, Tom, ed. 1973. *Eskimo Poems from Canada and Greenland*. Pittsburgh: University of Pittsburgh Press.

Lurie, Nancy. 1988. "In Search of Chaetar: New Findings on Black Hawk's Surrender." *Wisconsin Magazine of History* 71: 162–83.

Lyons, Scott. Personal communication. March 5, 2010.

Maddra, Sam. 2006. *Hostiles? Lakota Ghost Dancers and Buffalo Bill's Wild West*. Norman: University of Oklahoma Press.

Madison, James. 1962. *The Papers of James Madison*. Ed. William Hutchinson and William Rachal. Vol. 1. Chicago: University of Chicago Press.

Marino, Cesare. 1990. "History of Western Washington since 1846." *Handbook of North American Indians*. Vol. 7. Ed. Wayne Suttles. Washington, DC: US Government Printing Office. 169–85.

Marston, Morrell. 1969. "Memoirs Relating to the Sauk and Foxes." Blair 2: 136–82.

Mayer, Brantz. 1851. *Tah-Gah-Jute or Logan and Captain Michael Cresap, a Discourse Delivered in Baltimore, before the Maryland Historical Society, on Its Sixth Anniversary*. Baltimore: Maryland Historical Society.

McClennan, Catharine. 1954. "The Interrelation of Social Structure with Northern Tlingit Ceremonialism." *Southwestern Journal of Anthropology* 10: 76–96.

McCoy, Robert. 2004. *Chief Joseph, Yellow Wolf, and the Creation of Nez Perce History in the Pacific Northwest*. New York: Routledge.

McElwain, Thomas. 2001. "'Then I Thought I Must Kill Too': Logan's Lament; A Mingo Perspective." *Native American Speakers of the Eastern Woodlands: Selected Speeches and Critical Analyses*. Ed. Barbara Mann. Westport, CT: Greenwood Press. 107–21.

———. "The Use of the Mingo Language in the Last Half of the Twentieth Century." Accessed October 19, 2009. <http://www.mingolanguage.org/texts/tom/20c_mingo.html>.

McGloughlin, William. 1984. "The Cherokee Ghost Dance Movement of 1811–1813." *The Cherokee Ghost Dance: Essays on the Southeastern Indians, 1789–1861*. By McGloughlin. Macon, GA: Mercer University Press. 111–51.

———. 1990. "Ghost Dance Movements: Some Thoughts on Definition Based on Cherokee History." *Ethnohistory* 37: 25–44.

McWhorter, L. V. 1992. *Hear Me, My Chiefs: Nez Perce Legend and History*. Ed. Ruth Bordin. 1952. Caldwell, ID: Caxton.

Meeker, Ezra. 1905. *Pioneer Reminiscences of Puget Sound and the Tragedy of Leschi*. Seattle: Lowman and Hanford.

Merrell, James. 1996. "Shickellamy, 'A Person of Consequence'." *Northeastern Indian Lives, 1632–1816*. Ed. Robert Grumet. Amherst: University of Massachusetts Press. 227–57.

Meserve, Walter. 1956. "English Works of Seventeenth-Century Indians." *American Quarterly* 8: 264–76.

Michelson, Gunther. 1988. "An Account of an Iroquois Condolence Council." *Man in the Northeast* 36: 61–75.

Michelson, Karin. 1980. "Mohawk Text: The Edge of the Forest Revisited." *Northern Iroquoian Texts*. Ed. Marianne Mithun and Hanni Woodbury. International Journal of American Linguistics Native American Texts Series, No. 4. Chicago: University of Chicago Press. 27–40.

Michelson, Truman. 1927. *Contributions to Fox Ethnology—I*. Smithsonian Institution Bureau of American Ethnology Bulletin 85. Washington, DC: Smithsonian Institution Press.

———. 1929. *Observations on the Thunder Dance of the Bear Gens of the Fox Indians*. Smithsonian Institution Bureau of American Ethnology Bulletin 89. Washington, DC: Smithsonian Institution Press.

———. 1930. *Contributions to Fox Ethnology—II*. Smithsonian Institution Bureau of American Ethnology Bulletin 95. Washington, DC: Smithsonian Institution Press.

———. 1932. *Notes on the Fox Wapanowiweni*. Smithsonian Institution Bureau of American Ethnology Bulletin 105. Washington, DC: Smithsonian Institution Press.

Miles, Nelson. 1896. *Personal Recollections and Observations of General Nelson A. Miles*. Chicago: Werner.

———. 1911. *Serving the Republic*. New York: Harper.

Miller, Christopher. 1985. *Prophetic Worlds: Indians and Whites on the Columbia Plateau*. New Brunswick, NJ: Rutgers University Press.

Miller, Jay. 1988. *Shamanic Odyssey: The Lushootseed Salish Journey to the Land of the Dead*. Menlo Park, CA: Ballena Press.

———. 1997. "Back to Basics: Chiefdoms in Puget Sound." *Ethnohistory* 44: 375–87.

———. 1998. "Tsimshian Ethno-Ethnohistory: A 'Real' Indigenous Chronology." *Ethnohistory* 45: 657–74.

———. 1999. *Lushootseed Culture and the Shamanic Odyssey: An Anchored Radiance*. Lincoln: University of Nebraska Press.

Milun, Kathryn. 1994. "*Dead Voices: Natural Agonies in the New World* by Gerald Vizenor." *Ethnohistory* 41: 481–84.

Momaday, N. Scott. 1969. *The Way to Rainy Mountain*. Albuquerque: University of New Mexico Press.

———. 1975. "The Man Made of Words." Chapman 96–110.

———. 1976. *The Names*. New York: Harper.

Mooney, James. 1965. *The Ghost-Dance Religion and the Sioux Outbreak of 1890*. Ed. and abr. Anthony F. C. Wallace. Chicago: University of Chicago Press.

———. 1973. *The Ghost-Dance Religion and Wounded Knee*. 1896. New York: Dover.

———. 1979. *Calendar History of the Kiowa Indians*. 1898. Washington, DC: Smithsonian Institution Press.

Moquin, Wayne, and Charles Van Doren, eds. 1973. *Great Documents in American Indian History*. New York: Praeger.

Morgan, Lewis Henry. 1972. *League of the Iroquois*. 1851. Secaucus, NJ: Citadel.
Moses, Marya, and Toby C. S. Langen. 2001. "Reading Martha Lamont's Crow Story Today." *Native American Oral Traditions: Collaboration and Interpretation*. Ed. Larry Evers and Barre Toelken. Logan: Utah State University Press. 92–129.
Mulder, Jean. 1994. "Structural Organization in Coast Tsimshian Music." *Ethnomusicology* 38: 81–125.
Murray, David. 1991. *Forked Tongues: Speech, Writing, and Representation in North American Indian Texts*. Bloomington: Indiana University Press.
Nabokov, Peter, ed. 1991. *Native American Testimony: A Chronicle of Indian-White Relations from Prophecy to the Present, 1492–1992*. New York: Penguin.
Niatum, Duane. Personal communication. November 24, 2009.
Norman, Howard. 1972. *The Wishing Bone Cycle: Narrative Poems from the Swampy Cree Indians*. Santa Barbara: Ross Erickson.
Oberholtzer, Heidi. 2003. "Pilgrimage in Literature of the Americas: Spiritualized Travel and Sacred Place." *Religion & Literature* 35: 1–9.
O'Connell, Barry, ed. 1992. *On Our Own Ground: The Complete Writings of William Apess, a Pequot*. Amherst: University of Massachusetts Press.
Opler, Morris. 1941. *An Apache Life-Way: The Economic, Social, and Religious Institutions of the Chiricahua Indians*. Chicago: University of Chicago Press.
Ortiz, Simon. 1981. *From Sand Creek: Rising in This Heart Which Is Our America*. Oak Park, NY: Thunder's Mouth Press.
———. 1992. *Woven Stone*. Tucson: University of Arizona Press.
———. 2006. "Towards a National Indian Literature: Cultural Authenticity in Nationalism." *American Indian Literary Nationalism*. Ed. Jace Weaver, Craig Womack, and Robert Warrior. Albuquerque: University of New Mexico Press. 253–60.
Overholt, Thomas. 1974. "The Ghost Dance of 1890 and the Nature of the Prophetic Process." *Ethnohistory* 21: 37–63.
Palmer, Gus, Jr. 2003. *Telling Stories the Kiowa Way*. Tucson: University of Arizona Press.
Parins, James. 1991. *John Rollin Ridge: His Life and Works*. Lincoln: University of Nebraska Press.
Parker, Robert Dale. 2003a. "The Existential Surfboard and the Dream of Balance, or 'To be there, no authority to anything': The Poetry of Ray A. Young Bear." *The Invention of Native American Literature*. By Parker. Ithaca, NY: Cornell University Press. 101–27.
———. 2003b. "Text, Lines, and Videotape: Reinventing Oral Stories as Written Poems." Parker, *The Invention of Native American Literature* 80–100.
———, ed. 2007. *The Sound the Stars Make Rushing through the Sky: The Writings of Jane Johnston Schoolcraft*. Philadelphia: University of Pennsylvania Press.
———, ed. 2011. *Changing Is Not Vanishing: A Collection of American Indian Poetry to 1930*. Philadelphia: University of Pennsylvania Press.
Peter, Susie Sampson. 1995. *Huchooseda: The Wisdom of a Skagit Elder*. Seattle: Lushootseed Press.
Peterson, John A. 1998. *Utah's Black Hawk War*. Salt Lake City: University of Utah Press.
Pferd, William, III. 1987. *Dogs of the American Indians*. Ed. William Denlinger and R. Annabel Rathman. Fairfax, VA: Denlinger's.

Pomedli, Michael. 1995. "Eighteenth-Century Treaties: Amended Iroquois Condolence Rituals." *American Indian Quarterly* 19: 319–39.
Powers, William K. 1994. *Testimony to Wounded Knee: A Comprehensive Bibliography.* Kendall Park, NJ: Lakota Books.
———. 1999. *Voices from the Spirit World: Lakota Ghost Dance Songs.* Kendall Park, NJ: Lakota Books.
Ramazani, Jahan. 1994. *Poetry of Mourning: The Modern Elegy from Hardy to Heaney.* Chicago: University of Chicago Press.
Reichard, Gladys. 1963. *Navaho Religion: A Study of Symbolism.* Princeton, NJ: Princeton University Press.
Revard, Carter. 2001. *Winning the Dust Bowl.* Tucson: University of Arizona Press.
———. 2005. *How the Songs Come Down.* Cambridge: Salt Publishing.
Rice, Julian. 1991. *Black Elk's Story: Distinguishing Its Lakota Purpose.* Albuquerque: University of New Mexico Press.
Rich, John. 1977. *Chief Seattle's Unanswered Challenge.* 1932. Fairfield, WA: Ye Galleon Press.
Richter, Daniel. 1992. *The Ordeal of the Longhouse: The Peoples of the Iroquois League in the Era of European Colonization.* Chapel Hill: University of North Carolina Press.
———. 2001. *Facing East from Indian Country: A Native History of Early America.* Cambridge, MA: Harvard University Press.
Rifkin, Mark. 2008. "Documenting Tradition: Territoriality and Textuality in Black Hawk's Narrative." *American Literature* 80: 677–705.
Robbins, Bruce. 2007. Afterword. *PMLA* 5: 1644–51.
Roberts, David. 1993. *Once They Moved Like the Wind: Cochise, Geronimo, and the Apache Wars.* New York: Simon and Schuster.
Roemer, Kenneth, ed. 1988. *Approaches to Teaching Momaday's "The Way to Rainy Mountain."* New York: The Modern Language Association.
Rose, Wendy. 1994. *Bone Dance: New and Selected Poems, 1965–1993.* Tucson: Sun Tracks/University of Arizona Press.
———. 2002. *Itch Like Crazy.* Tucson: University of Arizona Press.
Roth, Christopher. 2002. "Goods, Names, and Selves: Rethinking the Tsimshian Potlatch." *American Ethnologist* 29: 123–50.
Sacks, Peter. 1985. *The English Elegy: Studies in the Genre from Spenser to Yeats.* Baltimore: Johns Hopkins University Press.
Salisbury, Ralph. 1972. *Ghost Grapefruit and Other Poems.* Ithaca, NY: Ithaca House.
———. 1980. *Pointing at the Rainbow: Poems from a Cherokee Heritage.* Marvin, SD: Blue Cloud Quarterly Press.
———. 1982. *Spirit Beast Chant.* Marvin, SD: Blue Cloud Quarterly Press.
———. 1983. *Going to the Water: Poems of a Cherokee Heritage.* Eugene, OR: Pacific House Books.
———. 2000. *Rainbows of Stone.* Tucson: Sun Tracks/University of Arizona Press.
Sandefur, Ray. 1960. "Logan's Oration—How Authentic?" *Quarterly Journal of Speech* (October): 289–96.
Sanders, Thomas, and Walter Peek, eds. 1973. *Literature of the American Indian.* New York: Glencoe Press.

Savage, Sarah. 1827. *Life of Philip the Indian Chief.* Salem, MA.
Sayre, Gordon. 1996. "Defying Assimilation, Confounding Authenticity: The Case of William Apess." *A/B: Autobiography Studies* 11: 1–18.
———. 2005. *The Indian Chief as Tragic Hero: Native Resistance and the Literatures of America from Moctezuma to Tecumseh.* Chapel Hill: University of North Carolina Press.
Schlichting, Eunice. Personal communication. February 15, 2010.
Schmitz, Neil. 2001a. "Black Elk Enters American Literature." *White Robe's Dilemma: Tribal History in American Literature.* By Schmitz. Amherst: University of Massachusetts Press. 112–36.
———. 2001b. "Black Hawk and Indian Irony." Schmitz 69–85.
———. 2001c. "Ponca Testimony, Lakota Elegies." Schmitz 86–111.
Schoolcraft, Jane Johnston. 2007. *The Sound the Stars Make Rushing through the Sky: The Writings of Jane Johnston Schoolcraft.* Ed. Robert Dale Parker. Philadelphia: University of Pennsylvania Press.
Scott, Duncan Campbell. 1912. "Traditional History of the Confederacy of the Six Nations, Prepared by a Committee of the Chiefs." *Proceedings and transactions of the Royal Society of Canada,* ser. 3, vol. 5.
Schubnell, Matthias. 1985. *N. Scott Momaday: The Cultural and Literary Background.* Norman: University of Oklahoma Press.
Seeber, Edward. 1946. "Chief Logan's Speech in France." *Modern Language Notes* 61: 412–16.
———. 1947. "Critical Views on Logan's Speech." *Journal of American Folklore* 60: 130–46.
Seeman, Carole. 1986. "The Treaties of Puget Sound." *Indians, Superintendents, and Councils: Northwestern Indian Policy, 1850–1855.* Ed. Clifford Trafzer. Lanham, MD: University Press of America. 19–36.
Shaw, George C. 1909. *Chinook Jargon and How to Use It.* Seattle: Rainier.
Shaw, W. David. 1994. *Elegy and Paradox: Testing the Conventions.* Baltimore: Johns Hopkins University Press.
Sheehan, Bernard. 1969. "Paradise and the Noble Savage in Jeffersonian Thought." *William and Mary Quarterly* 26: 327–59.
Shelton, Ruth Sehome. 1995. *Huchoosedah Siastenu: The Wisdom of a Tulalip Elder.* Seattle: Lushootseed Press.
Shimony, Annemarie. 1961. *Conservatism among the Iroquois at the Six Nations Reserve.* Yale University Publications in Anthropology, no. 65. New Haven, CT: Yale University Press.
Silko, Leslie Marmon. 1977. *Ceremony.* New York: Viking.
Skinner, Alanson. 1923. "Observations on the Ethnology of the Sauk Indians, Part I." *Bulletin of the Public Museum of the City of Milwaukee* 5.1: 3–59.
———. 1925. "Observations on the Ethnology of the Sauk Indians, Part II." *Bulletin of the Public Museum of the City of Milwaukee* 5.2: 63–119.
Sladen, Joseph Alton. 1997. *Making Peace with Cochise: The 1872 Journal of Captain Joseph Alton Sladen.* Ed. Edwin Sweeney. Norman: University of Oklahoma Press.
Slickpoo, Allen P., Sr. 1973. *Noon Nee-Me-Poo (We, the Nez Perces): Culture and History of the Nez Perces.* Vol. 1. Lapwai, ID: The Nez Perce Tribe of Idaho.
Slotkin, Richard. 1985. *The Fatal Environment: The Myth of the Frontier in the Age of Industrialization, 1800–1890.* New York: Atheneum.

Smith, Paul Chaat, and Robert Warrior. 1996. *Like a Hurricane: The Indian Movement from Alcatraz to Wounded Knee.* New York: Norton.
Smith, Sherry. 1996. "Reimagining the Indian: Charles Erskine Scott Wood and Frank Linderman." *Pacific Northwest Quarterly* 87: 149–58.
Snyder, Charles. 1941–42. "Antoine LeClaire, the First Proprietor of Davenport." *Annals of Iowa* 23: 79–117.
Snyder, Sally. 1975. "Quest for the Sacred in Northern Puget Sound: An Interpretation of Potlatch." *Ethnology* 14: 149–61.
Spier, Leslie. 1935. *The Prophet Dance of the Northwest and Its Derivatives: The Source of the Ghost Dance.* General Series in Anthropology, no. 1. Menasha: University of Wisconsin Press.
Spier, Leslie, Wayne Suttles, and Melville Herskovits. 1959. "Comment on Aberle's Theory of Deprivation." *Southwestern Journal of Anthropology* 15: 84–88.
Spinden, Herbert. 1908. "The Nez Perce Indians." *American Anthropological Association Memoirs* vol. 2, no. 3: 167–274. Rpt. 1964.
Stevenson, M. Louise. 1903. "Cresap and Logan." *Virginia Historical Magazine Quarterly* 3: 144–62.
Strelke, Barbara. 1975. "N. Scott Momaday: Racial Memory and Individual Imagination." Chapman 348–57.
Sutherland, Thomas. 1980. *Howard's Campaign against the Nez Perce Indians, 1877.* 1878. Fairfield, WA: Ye Galleon Press.
Suttles, Wayne. 1957. "The Plateau Prophet Dance among the Coast Salish." *Southwestern Journal of Anthropology* 13: 352–96. Rpt. in *Coast Salish Essays* (Vancouver: Talonbooks/Seattle: University of Washington Press, 1987), 152–98.
———. 1991. "The Shed-Roof House." Wright 212–22.
Suttles, Wayne, and Barbara Lane. 1990. "Southern Coast Salish." *Handbook of North American Indians,* vol. 7. Ed. Suttles. Washington, DC: US Government Printing Office. 485–502.
Swann, Brian, ed. 1994. *Coming to Light: Contemporary Translations of the Native Literatures of North America.* New York: Random House.
———, ed. 1996. *Wearing the Morning Star: Native American Song-Poems.* New York: Random House.
———, ed. 2005. *Algonquian Spirit: Contemporary Translations of the Algonquian Literatures of North America.* Lincoln: University of Nebraska Press.
Swann, Brian, and Arnold Krupat, eds. 1987. *Recovering the Word: Essays on Native American Literature.* Berkeley: University of California Press.
Swanton, John. 1909. *Tlingit Myths and Texts.* Bureau of American Ethnology Bulletin 39. Washington, DC: Government Printing Office.
Sweeney, Edwin. 1991. *Cochise: Chiricahua Apache Chief.* Norman: University of Oklahoma Press.
———. Personal communication. August 26, 2009.
Sweet, Timothy. 1993. "Masculinity and Self-Performance in the Life of Black Hawk." *American Literature* 65: 475–99.
Tarter, Jim. 2000. "'Dreams of Earth': Place, Multiethnicity, and Environmental Justice in Linda Hogan's *Solar Storms.*" *Reading under the Sign of Nature: New Essays in*

Ecocriticism. Ed. John Tallmadge and Henry Harrington. Salt Lake City: University of Utah Press. 128–47.

Thornton, Russell. 1986. *We Shall Live Again: The 1870 and 1890 Ghost Dance Movements as Demographic Revitalization.* Cambridge: Cambridge University Press.

Thrapp, Dan. 1967. *The Conquest of Apacheria.* Norman: University of Oklahoma Press.

Thrush, Coll. 2008. *Native Seattle: Histories from the Crossing-Over Place.* Seattle: University of Washington Press.

Tollefson, Kenneth. 1995. "Potlatching and Political Organization among the Northwest Coast Indians." *Ethnohistory* 34: 53–73.

Tooker, Elizabeth, and Barbara Graymont. 2007. "J. N. B. Hewitt." *History of Anthropology Annual.* Ed. Regna Darnell and Fredric Gleach. Lincoln: University of Nebraska Press. 70–98.

Trask, Kerry. 2006. *Black Hawk: The Battle for the Heart of America.* New York: Henry Holt.

Turrill, Henry Stuart. 1907. "A Vanished Race of Aboriginal Founders." *The New York Society of the Order of the Founders and Patriots of America Publication* no. 18: 5–23.

Two Rivers, E. Donald, ed. [?] 1994. *Skins: Beats from City Streets.* Washington, DC and New York: Barrick and Associates.

Utley, Robert. 1963. *The Last Days of the Sioux Nation.* New Haven, CT: Yale University Press.

Vander, Judith. 1988. *Songprints: The Musical Experience of Five Shoshone Women.* Urbana: University of Illinois Press.

———. 1997. *Shoshone Ghost Dance Religion: Poetry Songs and Great Basin Context.* Urbana: University of Illinois Press.

Vanderwerth, W. C., ed. 1971. *Indian Oratory: Famous Speeches by Noted Indian Chieftains.* Norman: University of Oklahoma Press.

Vaughan, Debbie. Personal communication. November 25, 2009.

Velie, Alan. 1982. *Four American Indian Literary Masters: N. Scott Momaday, James Welch, Leslie Marmon Silko, and Gerald Vizenor.* Norman: University of Oklahoma Press.

Velikova, Roumiana. 2002. "'Philip, King of the Pequots': The History of an Error." *Early American Literature* 37: 311–35.

Venn, George. 1998. "Chief Joseph's 'Surrender Speech' as a Literary Text." *Oregon English Journal* 20: 69–73.

———. 2001. "Brief Chronology of 'Chief Joseph's Surrender Speech,' Versions under Editorial Control of C. E. S. Wood." MS.

———. 2005. "Soldier to Advocate: C. E. S. Wood's 1877 Diary of Alaska and the Nez Perce Conflict." *Oregon Historical Quarterly* 106: 34–75.

———. 2006. *Soldier to Advocate: C. E. S. Wood's 1877 Legacy; A Soldier's Unpublished Diary, Drawings, Poetry, and Letters of Alaska and the Nez Perce Conflict.* LaGrande, OR: Wordcraft of Oregon.

———. Personal communication. July 6, 2010.

Vizenor, Gerald. 1976. "I Know What You Mean, Erdupps MacChurbbs." *Growing Up in Minnesota: Ten Writers Remember Their Childhoods.* Ed. Chester Anderson. Minneapolis: University of Minnesota Press. 79–111.

———. 1987. "Crows Written on the Poplars: Autocritical Autobiographies." *I Tell You Now: Autobiographical Essays by Native American Writers*. Ed. Brian Swann and Arnold Krupat. Lincoln: University of Nebraska Press. 99–110.

———. 1990. *Interior Landscapes: Autobiographical Myths and Metaphors*. Minneapolis: University of Minnesota Press.

———. 1992. *Dead Voices: Natural Agonies in the New World*. Norman: University of Oklahoma Press.

———. 1998. *Fugitive Poses: Native American Indian Scenes of Absence and Presence*. Lincoln: University of Nebraska Press.

———. 2008. "Aesthetics of Survivance: Literary Theory and Practice." *Survivance: Narratives of Presence*. Ed. Gerald Vizenor. Lincoln: University of Nebraska Press. 1–23.

Wakefield, John Allen. 1834. *History of the War between the United States and the Sac and Fox Nations of Indians, and Parts of Other Disaffected Tribes of Indians, in the Years Eighteen Hundred and Twenty-Seven, Thirty-One, and Thirty-Two*. Jacksonville, IL: Goudy.

Walker, Cheryl. 1997. *Indian Nation: Native American Literature and Nineteenth-Century Nationalisms*. Durham, NC: Duke University Press.

Walker, Deward E., Jr. 1969. "New Light on the Prophet Dance Controversy." *Ethnohistory* 16: 245–55.

———. 1998. "Nez Perce." *Handbook of North American Indians*. Vol. 12, *Plateau*. Ed. Deward E. Walker. Washington, DC: U.S. Government Printing Office. 423–38.

Wallace, Anthony F. C. 1956. "Revitalization Movements." *American Anthropologist* 58: 264–81.

———. 1982. "Prelude to Disaster: The Course of Indian-White Relations Which Led to the Black Hawk War of 1832." *Wisconsin Magazine of History* 65 [1970]: 247–88.

———. 1999. *Jefferson and the Indians: The Tragic Fate of the First Americans*. Cambridge, MA: Harvard University Press.

Warren, Robert Penn. 1982. *Chief Joseph of the Nez Perce, Who Called Themselves the Nimipu "The Real People," A Poem*. New York: Random House.

Waterman, T. T. 1973. *Notes on the Ethnology of the Indians of Puget Sound*. Indian Notes and Monographs, no. 59. New York: Museum of the American Indian-Heye Foundation.

Watt, Roberta Frye. 1931. *Four Wagons West: The Story of Seattle*. Portland, OR: Binfords and Mort.

Weaver, Jace. 1997. *That the People Might Live: Native American Literatures and Native American Community*. New York: Oxford University Press.

Weisman, Karen, ed. 2010. *The Oxford Handbook of the Elegy*. New York: Oxford University Press.

Wells, Merle. 1964. "The Nez Perce and Their War." *Pacific Northwest Quarterly* (January): 35–37.

Whitman, Walt. 1876. "A Death-Sonnet for Custer." *New York Daily Tribune*, July 10: 5. Rpt. with slight changes as "From Far Dakota's Canyons" in *Leaves of Grass*, 1881–82 edition.

Whitney, Ellen, ed. 1970–78. *The Black Hawk War, 1831–1832*. Collections of the Illinois State Historical Library, vols. 35–38. Springfield: Illinois State Historical Library.

Whittaker, Gordon. 1998. "The Sauk Language: A First Look." *Papers of the Twenty-Seventh Algonquian Conference*. Ed. David Pentland. Winnipeg: University of Manitoba Press. 362–401.

———. Personal communication. October 29, 2009.

Wilkins, Thurman. 1970. *Cherokee Tragedy: The Story of the Ridge Family and the Decimation of a People*. New York: MacMillan.

Wolfe, Eric A. 2008. "Mourning, Melancholia, and Rhetorical Sovereignty in William Apess' *Eulogy on King Philip*." *Studies in American Indian Literatures* 20: 1–23.

Womack, Craig. 1999. *Red on Red: Native American Literary Separatism*. Minneapolis: University of Minnesota Press.

Wong, Hertha. 1992. *Sending My Heart back across the Years: Tradition and Innovation in Native American Autobiography*. New York: Oxford University Press.

Wood, C. E. S. 1882. "Among the Thlinkits in Alaska." *Century Magazine* 24: 323–39.

———. 1884. "Chief Joseph, the Nez-Perce." *Century Magazine* 6: 135–42.

———. 1893. "Famous Indians: Portraits of Some Chiefs." *Century Magazine* 28: 436–52.

Wood, Erskine. 1978. *Life of Charles Erskine Scott Wood*. Vancouver, WA: Rose Wind Press.

Woodbury, Hanni. 1992. *Concerning the League: The Iroquois League Tradition as Dictated in Onondaga by John Arthur Gibson*. Algonquian and Iroquoian Linguistics, Memoir 9. Winnipeg: Algonquian and Iroquoian Linguistics.

Wright, Mabel. "Prayer for Pyramid Lake." Margaret Wheat Papers, Special Collections, University of Nevada-Reno 83–24 tape, transcribed by Michael Hittman. Courtesy of Professor Hittman.

Wright, Robin, ed. 1991. *A Time of Gathering: Native Heritage in Washington State*. Seattle: University of Washington Press.

Yellow Wolf. 1983. *Yellow Wolf: His Own Story*. Ed. L. V. McWhorter. 1940. Caldwell, ID: Caxton.

Youst, Lionel, and William Seaburg. 2002. *Coquelle Thompson: Athabaskan Witness, a Cultural Biography*. Norman: University of Oklahoma Press.

Index

Aho, 134, 136, 138, 144, 208n7
Akjartoq, 40
Alexie, Sherman, 18, 152, 167–70, 191n69
Algonquians, 113, 146
Allen, Paula Gunn, 162–63
"Among the Savages..." (Salisbury, 2000), 165
animals, elegies for, 18, 147–52, 160, 210n23, 210n28–29
"anniversary poem for the cheyennes who died at sand creek" (Henson, 1976), 155
Aoki, Haruo, 99, 102, 182
Apaches, 2, 9, 15, 41, 59, 66, 68, 87–95, 90–94, 92–93, 198–99n65
Apess, William, 6, 16–17, 109, 122–25, 126, 202n1, 204n25, 205–6n35, 205n31, 205n33
Aquash, Anne Mae Pictou, 157
Arapahos, 47, 51–54, 52, 56–57, 115, 155, 190n55
"At the Burial of a Ball-Player Who Died from Diabetes" (Louis), 162
Auden, W. H., 166, 211n37

autobiography, Indian, 61, 109, 116, 191n3, 202n1, 207n2
Azure, Alice Hatfield, 163–64

Barnes, Jim, 18, 152, 166
Basso, Keith, 2
Bear Sings, 117
Beauchamp, William, 23, 25, 26, 188n40
Beckett, Samuel, 152
Bible, Native American elegy echoing, 64, 66, 72, 92, 127, 193n17, 199n67
Big Foot, Sitanka, 50, 161, 57203n14
Biography and History of the Indians of North America from Its First Discovery (Drake, 1834/1841), 70–72, 173, 194n25
bison ceremony, 118
Black Elk and *Black Elk Speaks* (published 1932), 9, 16, 116–22, 118–20, *119*
Black Fox/Black Coyote, 57
Black Hawk: Catlin's portrait of, *71;* Cochise compared, 92; exile, Native American experience of, 9; *Life* (published 1833),

Index

Black Hawk *(continued)*
16, 70, 72–73, 106, 108–16, 130; "Logan's Lament" and, 66, 67, 68; Sauk lifeways, *Life* as elegy for, 110–11, 114–16; "Surrender Speech" of (1832?), 15, 69–73, 85, 105–6, 108–9, 172–75
Black Hawk War (1832), 15, 69, 70, 113
Black Leggings Society, 143
Black Road, 117
Blaeser, Kimberly, 18, 152, 158–59, 210n29
Bradford, William, 64, 171
Brant, Molly (Tekonwatonti), 156–57
Brown, David, 129, 130
Brown, Mark H., 99, 100–101, 200n74, 201n82
Bryan, William Jennings, 64, 66
Buck, John, 24, 25
Buffalo Bill's Wild West, 118
Buffon, Count de, 65
burial and death, 46, 84–86, 94, 104, 113–14, 130, 156–60, 170, 183n2, 210n30
Bushyhead, Jesse, 131

Camp, Thelma Louise, 165
Captain John, 98, 100, 101, 200n78, 201n84, 201n88, 202n91
Carlson, David, 78
Catlin, George, 71
Cayugas, 21, 24, 62, 63, 67, 185n8, 192n11, 192n14
Ceremony (Silko, 1977), 8
Chaetar, 69, 70, 193n23
Chaleco, Arsenius, 133
Changer or Transformer, in Coast Salish mythology, 81
Changing is Not Vanishing (Parker, 2011), 128, 143–44, 206n38
"Changing is Not Vanishing" (Montezuma, 1916), 206n38
Chapman, Arthur "Ad," 99, 102–4, 182, 190n56
Charles, Abram, 24
Cherokees: exile of (1838), 9, 16–17, 123–25, 129–33, 164, 206n37, 211n33; modern elegiac poetry and, 153, 159, 164; Ridge, John Rollin, and, 128, 206n37; Sauk people and, 110, 111; Sequoyah, poetic memorializations of, 129–30, 165
A Cheyenne Sketchbook (Henson, 1992), 155
Cheyennes, 49–50, 51, 54–55, 139, 155–56, 189–90n55
Chicago, Indian poetry from, 163–64
Chickasaws, 144, 145, 146
Chief Joseph, surrender speech of (1877?), 15, 95–105; authenticity of, 98–105, 106; exile, Native American experience of, 9; historical circumstances of, 95–98; Kershaw's poetic monologue, 132; "Logan's Lament" compared, 66; as message or reply versus speech, 100–105, 200n81, 201n85; modern elegiac poetry on Chief Joseph, 162, 211n34; names of Joseph, 95, 199n70; photograph of Chief Joseph, 97; publication history, 99–105, 201n86; text of speech, 181–82; Turrill and Joseph, 90
Chippewas (Anishinaabe), 147
Chiricahua Apaches, 41, 87, 90–94
Chivington, John, 155
Choctaws, 130, 166
Chokonen people, 91
Christianity and Native American elegy, 64, 66, 80–83, 86, 120, 122–25, 127, 129, 147, 163, 190–91n64, 193n17, 197n54, 204n23
Clinton Duncan, DeWitt, 129, 130, 132–33, 206n45
Cochise, 9, 15, 66, 68, 87–95, 106, 179–81, 198–99n65–66
Coeur d'Alene people, 169
Cogewea (Humishuma, 1927), 201n90
Columbus, Christopher, 8, 168
"Columbus Day" (Durham, 1983), 153–55
Comanches, 51, 139
communal or societal nature of loss in Native American elegy, 4–6, 9–10, 13, 116
communal or societal nature of Native American identity, 109–10, 148–49
"The Contrast, a Splenetic Effusion, March, 1823" (Schoolcraft), 125
cosmopolitan perspective on Native American literature, 11–12
Coyote (mythological figure), 4
Crazy Horse, 50, 162
Cree people, 2, 42–43, 144, 145, 147
Creeks, 112
Cresap, Michael, 63, 67, 172
Crook, George, 87, 90
Crow Foot, 57
Crow people, 96, 98, 200n76
Crow Woman in Cheyenne ritual and ceremony, 54–55
"Crows Written on the Poplars" (Vizenor, 1987), 148–49
Custer, George Armstrong, 57, 167–68

Daklugie, Ace or Asa, 59, 199n65
Dalton, Jessie, 32–37, 188n38
David of Schoharie, 25
Dawes (General Allotment) Act (1887), 76–77
"The Dead Nation" (Duncan), 132–33
Dead Voices (Vizenor, 1992), 147–48, 149, 150–52
death and burial, 46, 84–86, 94, 104, 113–14, 130, 156–60, 170, 183n2, 210n30
"Death Song, My Own" (Salisbury, 2000), 166
Deganawidah, 20, 184n2
Delaware people, 21, 113, 192–93n14
Deloria, Vine, Jr., 6–7, 9, 44, 45, 190n58, 209n16
Demosthenes, 64, 66
Denny, D. T., 78
Deserontyon, John, 25
Diderot, Denis, 62
dogs, ceremonial use of, 111, 118
Drake, Samuel, 70–72, 73, 105–6, 173, 194n25
Dunmore, Lord, 62–64, 105, 171
Durham, Jimmie, 18, 153–55, 156
Duthu, N. Bruce, 7
Duwamish people and language, 73, 79, 83, 85, 194n29, 196n44
Dying Speeches of Several Indians (Eliot, 1685), 60

Eastburn, James Wallis, 124, 204n25
Edmunds, R. David, 112
The Ego and the Id (Freud, 1923), 5
"1838" (Lundgren, 1994), 164
El Cautivo, 91
"elegy for my cowboy" (Azure, 1994), 163–64
"Elegy for My Son" (Allen, 1997), 162–63
"Elegy for One of Us" (Louis), 162
"Elegy for the Forgotten Oldsmobile" (Louis, 1989), 162
"Elegy on the death of my aunt Mrs [sic] Kearny of Kilgobbin Glebe Dublin, Ireland" (Schoolcraft), 127
"Elegy: On the death of my son William Henry, at St. Mary's" (Schoolcraft), 126
Eliot, John, 60
elk ceremony, 118
Elk Creek, Battle of (1874), 139
Ellis, Anderson Nelson, 88–89, 90–91, 92–95, 179–80
Erdrich, Louise, 153
Eskimo mourning songs, 39–41

Eskimo Poems from Canada and Greenland (ed. Lowenstein, 1973), 39
Eulogy on King Philip (Apess, 1836), 6, 16–17, 122–25
Everett, Edward, 123–24, 204n26–28, 205n30
"The Everlasting" (Harjo), 157–58
exile as indigenous condition, 6–9, 44, 45
Extending the Rafters (ed. Foster, Campisi, and Mithun, 1984), 22

"[Far in a Lonely Wood]"/"The Indian's Grave" (Ridge, 1847), 128
"Farewell Song" (Dan Hanna, c. 1964), 38, 41–42
farewell speeches, 15, 60–107; authenticity of, 18, 61–62, 68, 69–70, 78–80, 94–95, 98–107; Black Hawk's "Surrender Speech" (1832?), 15, 69–73, 85, 105–6, 108–9, 172–75; of Cochise (1871 and 1872?), 9, 15, 66, 68, 87–95, 106, 179–81; historiography of, 60–62, 77; "Logan's Lament" (1774?), 15, 62–69, 79, 105, 171–72; as speeches versus messages or replies, 62–64, 100–105, 106, 200n81, 201n85; third-person self-reference in, 66, 67, 72, 94, 202n92; whites, addressed to, 60. *See also* Chief Joseph, surrender speech of; Sealth, farewell speech of
"Farewell to Synthesis" (Louis, 1989), 162
Fee, Chester, 101, 202n91
Fenelon, Jim, 164
Fenton, William, 19, 20–21, 23, 24, 26, 185–86n14, 185n10
"Fire Storm" (Alexie, 1993), 167–68, 170
First Indian on the Moon (Alexie, 1993), 167–69
Fish Lake Valley Paiute, 46–47
Folsom, Israel, 130–31
"For a Shawnee Neighbor" (Salisbury, 1982), 159
"FOR ANNA MAE PICTOU AQUASH…" (Harjo), 157
"For Our Brothers: Blue Jay, Gold Finch, Flicker, Squirrel…" (Ortiz, 1992), 160
"The Forgiven Dead" (Ridge), 128
Francis, Lee, 18, 152, 166–67
Freud, Sigmund, 5–6, 205n33, 208n13
From Sand Creek (Ortiz, 1981), 155

Gaines, Edmund, 109, 114, 202n2
Gall, 90

"The Game between the Jews and the Indians..." (Alexie, 1993), 168
"Genealogical Research" (Rose, 2002), 152
Geronimo, 59, 87, 91, 93
Ghent, Treaty of (1814), 112
Ghost Dance movement, 14–15, 44–59; in *Black Elk Speaks,* 118–20; Christian influences on, 120, 190–91n64; in context of oral and written elegy traditions, 15–16; continuations and revivals after 1890, 47, 59, 191n69; exile, as response to experience of, 6, 9; historical and historiographical context, 44–46; illustration of Arapaho Ghost Dance, 52; Paiute Ghost Dance prophets of 1869 and 1889, 46–47; Pine Ridge meeting and report (1889), 49, 49; spread of movement through Northern Plains tribes, 47–50; whites, belief in eventual disappearance of, 50, 59; Wounded Knee (1890) and, 47, 57–59, 58, 120, 161
The Ghost-Dance Religion and the Sioux Outbreak of 1890 (Mooney, 1896), 44–45, 58
Ghost Dance shirts, 57, 190n61
Ghost Dance songs, 50–57; Black Hawk's *Life* compared, 115; deceased persons, songs about, 54–55; as elegiac, 50–52; recovery or revitalization, as act of, 45, 53; suffering or life-negating conditions, songs about, 53–54; traditional practices, songs about, 56–57
"ghost fright" (ritual avoidance of the dead), 46, 94, 104, 183n2, 210n30
Gibbs, George, 79
Gibson, Hardy, 24
Gibson, General John, 63, 67, 105, 171
Gibson, Chief John Arthur, 23–24, 25, 26
Gibson, Simeon, 24
Gilbert, Sandra, 162, 164
Gillis, Alfred C., 133
Ginsberg, Allen, 13
Girty, Simon, 63, 193n15
Glancy, Diane, 152, 159
Goldenweiser, Alexander, 24, 26
Good Thunder, 118
Gourd Dance Society, 143
"grandfather" (Fenelon, 1994), 164
Granger, Gordon, 87–89, 91, 94, 179, 197–98n59, 198n61
Grant, Frederic, 74, 78
Grant, Ulysses S., 87, 95
Great Depression and Native American situation, 77

Greathouse, Daniel, 63, 67
Gregg, J. Irwin, 88

Hadjo, Hillis (Josiah Francis or Francis the Prophet), 112
Haines, Francis, 104, 201n86
Hale, Horatio, 23, 25, 26, 186n21
Hallam, Arthur Henry, 12
Han, Shinhee, 6, 205n33
Handsome Lake, 113, 202n7, 204n24
Hanna, Dan, 38, 41–42, 188–89n44–45
Harjo, Joy, 152, 157–58
Harrington, M. R., 114
Havasupai people, 38, 41–42, 51, 59
Hayes, Jonah, 102
Hear Me, My Chiefs (McWhorter, 1944), 103, 200n78, 201n90
Henson, Lance, 18, 129, 152, 155–56
Hewitt, J. N. B., 23–26, 29, 185–86n14, 185n10, 188n43
Hiawatha, 20
History of Seattle, Washington (Grant, 1891), 74
Hogan, Linda, 18, 129, 144–47
Holocaust, 157, 168–69
Hopewell, Treaty of (1785), 123
Horse Dance, 117
House Made of Dawn (Momaday, 1968), 134, 209n16
Howard, O. O., 87–88, 90, 91, 94, 96–104, 106, 179, 199–200n73, 199n66, 199n71, 200n79, 200n81
"A Hunting Memory" (Ivaluardjuk, collected c. 1973), 40

"I Know What You Mean, Erdupps MacChurbbs" (Vizenor, 1976), 148, 149
identity, Native American, 109–10, 148–49
"In Memoriam" (Tennyson, 1849), 12–13
"In Memory of a Day Nobody Remembers: 26 September 1874" (Barnes), 157
"In Memory of W. B. Yeats" (Auden, 1939), 166, 211n37
Indian farewells. *See* farewell speeches
Indian Removal Act (1830), 123
Indian Reorganization Act (1934), 77
"The Indian Requiem" (Chaleco), 133
The Indians' Book (Curtis, 1907), 54
"The Indian's Farewell" (Bushyhead), 131
"The Indian's Grave"/"[Far in a Lonely Wood]" (Ridge, 1847), 128

indigenist perspective on Native American literature, 11–12
individualism and individual loss in Western elegy, 4–6
Interior Landscapes (Vizenor, 1990), 148–50
Iroquois Condolence Rites, 7, 14, 19–29; "At the Wood's Edge" or "Near the Thorny Bushes", 21, 26, 185n8–10; Black Hawk's *Life* compared, 115; chiefs of League, association with deaths of, 20–21; "The Council Fire", 28; "Darkness of Grief", 28; deer antlers or horns of authority presented to new chief, 20, 22, 184n6; Eulogy or Roll Call of the Founders, 21, 22; insanity of grief, warnings against, 28; installation of new chief, 22–23, 26, 29; "Logan's Lament" and, 67, 68; "Loss of the Torch", 28–29; moiety divisions of Elder and Younger Brothers and, 21, 185n8; mourning call, 21; name of deceased chief given to new chief, 22–23, 185n7; names for parts of, 185n6; records of, 23–25; recovery or revitalization, as act of, 21, 29, 37; Requickening Address, 21, 22, 25–29, 188n43; Rubbing Antlers (celebration dance), 23; societal or communal aims of, 6; three *bare* or three *rare* words of Requickening, 21–22; Tlingit *koo.'eex'* compared, 29, 30, 31, 33, 36, 184n5, 188n40, 188n42–43; wampum in, 21, 22, 25, 28, 184n6; "Water of Pity", 27–28; wiping away tears and clearing ears and throats of mourners, 21, 22, 25–28, 36
Iroquois League, 19–21, 67
Irving, Washington, 108, 123, 124, 204n25, 205n30
"The Itch: First Notice" (Rose, 2002), 170
Ivaluardjuk, 40

Jackson, Andrew, 16, 109, 123, 129
Jaskoski, Helen, 207n5
Jefferson, Thomas, 15, 62–64, 67, 68, 79, 105, 171, 172, 192n6
Jeffords, Thomas, 87–88, 89, 198n60
John, Peter, 19
Johnson, George H. M., 25
Johnson, John "Smoke," 25
Johnson, Sir William, 156
Jones, Louis, 64, 201n88
Joseph, Hinmatowyalahtquit (Thunder Traveling High). *See* Chief Joseph, surrender speech of

Josephy, Alvin, 98, 202n91
Juh, 59, 199n65
Jung, Patrick, 112

Kadashan, David, 37
"Kaddish" (Ginsberg, 1959), 13
Kaiser, Rudolf, 75
Kan, Sergei, 29, 30, 34, 36, 37
Kau-au-inty, 136
Kazanjian, David, 5, 124, 205n33
Kelly, 83
Kenekuk, 113
Kenny, Maurice, 18, 152, 156–57
Keokuk, 114, 193n23, 203n9
Kershaw, William J., 132
Kickapoos, 113
Kicking Bear, *49,* 49–50, 118, 190n59
Kicking Bird, Tay-nay-angopte, 157, 211n31
King, Edward, 5, 17
King Philip, Metacomet, 8, 16, 122–25, 132, 204n25, 205n31, 205n34
King Philip's War (1676), 8, 122, 204n25
Kiowas, 47, 59, 134–44, *137,* 157, 183n2, 190n56, 190n58, 207n6, 208n8, 208n10. *See also Way to Rainy Mountain*
Kitsap, 194n29
Kuwape, 50
Kwa'wa'ka (formerly Kwakiutl) potlatching, 29
K'ya-been, 157

La Fort, Daniel, 25, 186n18
Lakota, 49–50, 51, 52, 56, 57, 116–22, 190n55, 190n59, 203n21
"Lamentation and Farewell" (Barnes, 1997), 166
land, European versus Native American attitudes toward, 7, 76–77
LeClaire, Antoine, 70, 109, 116, 203n11
Left-Hand, Grant, 54–55, 191n67
Left-hand, Nawat, 54
"Legacy of Bones" (Barnes, 1997), 166
Leschi, 83, 197n52
Lewis and Clark expedition, 95
The Life and Adventures of Joaquin Murieta, the Celebrated California Bandit (Ridge, 1854), 128
Life Is a Fatal Disease (Allen, 1997), 162–63
"That Lightning's Hard to Climb" (Revard), 165

Lincoln, Abraham, 17
"Little Boy's Mourning Song" (Tsimshian people, collected 1979–1981), 38–39
"Lo! The Poor Indian's Hope" (Folsom, c. 1831), 130–31
Logan, James (Tahgahjute), 62, 192n13
Logan, John (Tachnedorus), 62, 192n13
"Logan's Lament" (1774?), 15, 62–69, 79, 105, 171–72
Lone Dog's Winter Count (Glancy, 1991), 159
Lone Wolf, Guipago, 139, *140,* 208n9
Looking Glass, 98, 104, 182, 202n94
Lord Dunmore's War (1774), 15, 62–63, 68, 105
Louis, Adrian, 18, 152, 161–62, 210n30
Lundgren, Mary Little Field, 164
Lushootseed, 75, 79–81, 85, 175, 194n28, 195n34, 195n39, 196n44–46, 197n54
"Lycidas" (Milton, 1638), 5, 12, 17
Lyman, Edward D., 104, 200n80, 201n86, 202n91

MacKenzie, Ranald, 139, 157
Madison, James, 64, 67, 171, 172
Main Poc, Crippled (Withered) Hand (Wenebeset, Crafty One), 112
Maman-ti, the Owl Prophet, 139, 157, 208n9
"Mama's and Daddy's Words" (Ortiz, 1992), 170
Mammedaty, 136, 208n9
"The man twenty feet high..." (Ridge, 1848), 128, 129
Man-yi-ten, Woman's Heart, 139
manifest destiny, 61
Marks, Jim, 31, 32
Matinnecocks, 132
Maya-Ga-Way, Le Magouis or Magovis/The Trout, 113
Mayer, Brantz, 63, 64
McGillycuddy, Valentine T., 58, 191n68
McNickle, D'Arcy (Dahlberg), 206n44
McWhorter, Lucullus Virgil, 103, 104, 200n78, 201n90
Meacham, Albert Benjamin, 103
Mecabkwa, 114
medicine bundles, 110–11, 114, 116, 202–3n8
Medicine Creek Treaty (1854), 74, 83, 197n52
melancholia, concept of, 5–6, 124, 183n6, 205n33
Menominees, 132, 133, 157
Merriam Report (1928), 77

metric sub-structure, presence or absence of, 13, 37–38, 52, 184n17, 188n43
Miles, Nelson, 90, 96, 98–100, 104, 106, 200n77, 200n79
Mills, George, 36
Milton, John, 5, 12, 17
Minneconjou, 50, 57
Mingo people, 62–63, 66, 67, 192–93n14
Mohawks, 20, 21, 25, 26, 156, 185n8, 185n10, 186n18
Mohegans, 126
Mo'ki, Little Woman, 54–55
Momaday, N. Scott, 18, 134, 141–42, 209n16. See also *Way to Rainy Mountain*
Montauketts, 132
Mooney, James, 44, 51–53, *52,* 55–58, 190n56, 211n33
Morning Star, 156
"morning star / the passing of the northern Cheyenne" (Henson, 1976), 156
Moses, Mrs. Agnes, 102–3, 199n72
"Mourning and Melancholia" (Freud, 1917), 5, 205n33
Muk-a-ta-quet, 111
Muscogeans, 113, 129
Muskrat (Bronson), Ruth Margaret, 131–32, 206n44
"My Mother" (Ann Taylor, 1804), 126–27

Na-na-ma-kee, Thunder, 111
names: of Chief Joseph, 95, 199n70; "ghost fright" (refusal to speak names of the dead), 46, 104, 183n2, 210n30; importance of remembering, in modern elegiac poetry, 156–60, 170; Iroquois Condolence Rites, name of deceased chief given to new chief in, 22–23, 185n7; Native American loss of ancestor and place names, 7–8; for parts of Iroquois Condolence Rites, 185n6; redistribution of names among Tsimshian, 188n39
Nanticoke people, 21
naraya songs of Shoshone, 51, 59
Nasheaskuk, Whirling Thunder, 114
nationalist perspective on Native American literature, 11–12
Native American elegy, 1–18; balancing literary analysis with historical and cultural information, 17–18; comparability of European and non-European genres, 1–3; consistency of response to death and loss

across Native nations, 3; exile as indigenous condition, 6–9, 44, 45; methodological considerations, 9–12, 17–18; nationalist, indigenist, and cosmopolitan perspectives on Native American literature, 11–12; societal or communal nature of, 4–6, 9–10, 13, 116; thematic and behavioral characterizations of, 13. *See also* farewell speeches; "Native American Renaissance" and after, elegy from; oral elegy; recovery or revitalization of the people, Native American elegy as act of; religion and spirituality in Native American elegy; written elegy
Native American identity, 109–10, 148–49
"Native American Renaissance" and after, elegy from, 18, 134–70; family elegies, 164–70; names of the dead, poems stressing importance of remembering, 156–60, 170; recovery or revitalization of the people, as act of, 143–44, 147, 152, 155, 157, 159, 160–61, 169, 170; self-elegies, 166. *See also specific authors and works*
Neihardt, John G., 16, 116–22, 203n13, 204n23
Neolin, 113
"New Tidings" movement, 59
Nez Perce (Nimipu), 95–96, 98, 102–5, 106, 162, 183n2, 193–94n72–74, 200n78, 201n90, 202n93
Nez Perce "War" (1877), 96–97, 102, 105, 200n77, 200n79
Niatum, Duane, 162
Nisqually people, 73, 83
"noble savage," concept of, 61, 63, 89–90, 105, 193n19, 193n22
Northern Paiutes, 43–44, 46–50, 51–52, 189n53
Notes on the State of Virginia (Jefferson, 1784), 15, 62, 64, 192n6
nyah songs of Lee Francis, 166–67

Occom, Samson, 126, 184n18, 202n1
Oglalas, 50, 118
Ojibwe language and people, 127, 210n25
Old George, 98, 101, 200n78, 201n84, 201n88, 202n91
"Old Isidore" (McNickle, 1925), 206n44
"Old Woman's Mourning Song" (Tsimshian people, collected 1979–1981), 39
"An Old Woman's Song" (Akjartoq, collected c. 1973), 40

Old Yellow Wolf, 103
Ollokot, 98, 102, 104
On Native Ground (Barnes, 1997), 166
On the Good Red Interstate (Francis, 2002), 166–67
One-Eyed Decorah or Decorri, 69
"One Stick Song" (Alexie, 2000), 169–70
"one tear for Tahlequah" (Lundgren, 1994), 164
Oneidas, 21, 62, 67, 185n8, 192n11, 193n14
Onondagas, 21–26, 185n8, 186n15, 186n18, 186n24, 187n27
oral elegy, 10–11, 13–15; Momaday on oral literature, 141–42; occasional, improvisational elegy, 38–44; presentation of translations of, 184n17; as traditional means of expression, 10. *See also* entries at Ghost Dance; farewell speeches; Iroquois Condolence Rites; Tlingit *ḵoo.'eex'*
Oriole and Airplane songs, 3
Ortiz, Simon, 8, 18, 84, 152, 155, 156, 160, 170, 197n53, 204n22, 211n34, 211n38
Osages, 110, 112, 164–65
Ottawas, 113
"Out of Chaos" (Deloria, 1989), 6–7

"Pabst Blue Ribbon at Wounded Knee" (Louis, 1989), 161
Paiutes (Numu), 46–50, 51–52, 189n53, 210n30
Parker, Robert Dale, 126, 127, 128, 129, 143–44, 206n38
Patterson, John Barton, 16, 61, 70, 109, 110, 115, 118
Pawnee Ghost Dance songs, 51
Pequots, 6, 16, 105–6n35, 109, 122, 126
Perry, David, 96, 102
"Philip of Pokanoket" (Irving, 1819–20), 108, 123, 124, 204n25, 205n30
Phillips, Wendell, 89
Pine Ridge, occupation of (1972), 157
Poems (Ridge, 1868), 128
Point Elliott/Mukilteo treaty convention (1854–1855), 74–77, 80, 83, 86, 175, 195n33–34
Pontiac, 113
Poor Buffalo, Pa-tadal, 139, 157
Pope, Alexander, 130
Porcupine, 49, 50, 190n59
Posey, Alexander, 129, 130, 206n40

Potawatomis, 110, 112, 113
potlaches, 29, 187n30, 194n28. *See also* Tlingit *ƙoo.'eex'*
"Prayer for Pyramid Lake" (Wright, 1998), 43–44
Priber, Christian, 165
Pueblo revolt of 1680, 8
Puget Sound War (1855–56), 83
Puritans and Puritanism, 122–25
Puts Leaves Into Roots, 159
Pye-sa, 111
Pyramid Lake, 43–44

Qernertoq, 39–40

racial memory, concept of, 207–8n7
racism, scientific, 61
raiding in Apache culture, 92–93
Rainbows of Stone (Salisbury, 2000), 165–66
Rains, John, 42–43
Ramazani, Jahan, 6, 161, 164, 183n6
Rea, John, 100
"Recite the Names of All the Suicided Indians" (Blaeser), 158–59
recovery or revitalization of the people, Native American elegy as act of: in Apess's *Eulogy on King Philip*, 125; in *Black Elk Speaks*, 122; in Black Hawk's *Life*, 115–16; in Ghost Dance songs, 45, 53; in Hogan's *Solar Storms* (1995), 147; in Iroquois Condolence Rites, 21, 29, 37; in modern elegiac poetry, 155, 157, 159, 160–61, 169, 170; in Momaday's *The Way to Rainy Mountain* (1969), 143–44; Tlingit *ƙoo.'eex'*, 29–30, 37–38; in Vizenor's elegies for a red squirrel, 152
Red Cloud, 49–50, 90, 191n68
Red River War (1874–75), 139, 157, 208n8, 208n10
red squirrel, Vizenor's prose elegies for, 18, 147–52, 210n23, 210n28–29
"A Refusal to Mourn..." (Thomas, 1945), 4
religion and spirituality in Native American elegy, 5, 12–13; Bible, works echoing, 64, 66, 72, 92, 127, 193n17, 199n67; in *Black Elk Speaks*, 117–22, 204n23; Black Hawk's familiarity with religious resisters to American expansion, 112–13; Christianity and Native American elegy, 64, 66, 80–83, 86, 120, 122–25, 127, 129, 147, 163, 190–91n64, 193n17, 197n54, 204n23; European colonization and destruction of Indian ceremonial life, 7. *See also entries at* Ghost Dance
"Retrieving Osceola's Head" (Rose, 1994), 160
Revard, Carter, 18, 152, 164–65, 211n36
Rich, John, 74, 77, 194n30, 197n50
Ridge, John Rollin (Chees-quat-a-law-ny, Yellow Bird), 10, 11, 17, 127–29, 206n37
Roberts, John, 63
Robinson, Fred, 59
Rock Cree oral narrative genres, 2
Roosevelt, Theodore, 62
Rose, Wendy, 152, 170, 211n36, 211n39
Ross, Joshua, 129

Salisbury, Ralph, 18, 152, 159, 165–66, 211n34, 211n36
Sand Creek massacre (1864), 155, 168
Sands, Robert, 124, 204n25
Satanta (Set-t'ainte), White Bear, 90, 139, *141*, 208n8
Sauk (Sac) people, 9, 69, 109–16
Schofield, George, 139
Scholitza, 73
Schoolcraft, Henry Rowe, 126, 206n36
Schoolcraft, Jane Johnston, 10, 11, 17, 125–27, 163
Schweabe, 73
scientific racism, 61
Sealth, farewell speech of (1854?), 9, 15, 73–87; authenticity of surviving text, 78–80, 106; biographical information about Sealth, 73, 81–83, 194n28–29; Christian influences on Sealth, 80–83, 86, 197n54; the dead, on white versus Native relationship to, 84–86; as elegy, 77–78, 80–87; "Logan's Lament" compared, 66, 79; loose structure of, 196n46; oratorical powers of Sealth, 78–80; original delivery, accounts of, 74–76; physical appearance of Sealth, 78, *82*, 195–96n40–41; Point Elliott/Mukilteo treaty convention (1854–1855), association with, 74–77, 80, 83, 86, 175, 195n33–34; "progressive" chief willing to accommodate white society, Sealth as, 83–84, 86; publication history, 74, 194n30; purposes of, 74, 85; spelling and pronunciation of name, 194n28; texts of speech, 175–78
Seeber, Edward, 64, 66, 192n11
Seekaboo, 112
Senecas, 21, 23, 26, 113, 185n8, 192n14, 206n38
"Sentenced (A Dirge)" (Muskrat), 131–32

Sequoyah, 129–30, 165, 211n33
Shawnees, 112, 159
Shelton, "Gram" Ruth Sehome, 80–81, 83, 196n45–46
Shickellamy, 62, 192n11
Short Bull, Tatanka-Ptecila, 44, 49, *49,* 54, 59, 118
Shoshone *naraya* songs, 51, 59
Silko, Leslie Marmon, 8
"Sittin' on the Dock of the Bay" (Alexie, 1993), 168–69
Sitting Bull (Arapaho), 47, *48,* 51, 190n59
Sitting Bull (Lakota), 49–50, 57, 96, 191n2
The Sixth Grandfather (ed. DeMallie, 1985), 116–17, 120–21, 203n15, 203n17, 203n20, 204n24
Skins: Drum Beats from City Streets (1994), 163–64
Sky, Howard, 24
Sladen, Joseph Alton, 91, 199n66
Slickpoo, Allen, Sr., 200n74, 200n77
Smith, Henry A., 74–80, 81, 85, 87, 175, 196n44, 196n47
societal or communal nature of loss in Native American elegy, 4–6, 9–10, 13, 116
societal or communal nature of Native American identity, 109–10, 148–49
Solar Storms (Hogan, 1995), 18, 144–47
A Son of the Forest (Apess, 1829), 16, 109, 204n25, 205n35
The Song of the Messiah (Neihardt, 1935), 117
"Sonnet" (Schoolcraft), 126
Spier, Leslie, 46
Spokane people, 169
"The Spring of Youth" (Ulivfak, collected c. 1973), 40–41
Steiner, George, 148, 210n23
Stevens, Isaac Ingalls, 74–76, 79–81, 83–85, 95, 175, 196n43
Stevenson, M. Louise, 63–64, 66, 193n19
Stone, John Augustus, 124, 204n25
Street, Joseph M., 15, 69–70, 72, 73, 106, 114, 172–73
Strikeaxe Jump, Josephine, 164
Sun Dance, Kiowa, 47, 136–38, *137,* 190n58, 207n6
Suquamish people, 73–74, 79, 85, 194n28–29, 195n34, 195n40, 196n44
surrender speeches. *See* farewell speeches
Sutherland, Thomas, 99–100, 201n82, 202n91

Swampy Cree, 42–43
"Sweet Willy" (Schoolcraft), 127

Taylor, Ann, 126–27
Taylor, Zachary, 69, 194n26
"Tears of One Hundred Years" (Louis), 162
Tecumseh, 108, 112, 202n7
Tekonwatonti/Molly Brant: Poems of War (Kenny, 1992), 156–57
Tennyson, Alfred, Lord, 12–13
Tenskwatawa, the Open Door (Lalawethika, the Rattle or Noise-Maker), 112–13, 202n7
"These Sacred Names" (Salisbury), 159
third-person self-reference in farewell speeches, 66, 67, 72, 94, 202n92
Thomas, Dylan, 4
Three Eagles, 102
Tlingit *ḵoo.'eex'*, 7, 14, 29–38; *aawe* response of audience, 32–33; ancestral, genealogical, and mythological references in, 33–37; *at.oow,* displays of, 31, 33, 34, 36; Black Hawk's *Life* compared, 115; closing speeches by hosts, 31; "Cry" or "taking up the drum" by hosts, 31; Dalton, Jessie, analysis of "Widow's Cry" speech of, 32–37; drying grief in, 35–37; gathering of Tlingits in ceremonial regalia for 1904 potlach, *32;* Iroquois Condolence Rites compared, 29, 30, 31, 33, 36, 184n5, 188n40, 188n42–43; moiety divisions of Ravens and Eagles, 30, 32, 187n33; purpose of, 29–30; recovery or revitalization, as act of, 29–30, 37–38; societal or communal aims of, 6; "Widow's Cry" speeches by guests, 31–32
"To my ever beloved and lamented Son William Henry" (Schoolcraft), 126
T'ohono akimel (Pima) oral performances, 3
Toohoolhoolzote (Ta-hool-hool-shute, Ta-hool-hool-shoot), 98, 104, 182
"tragic" view of Native American decline, 16, 45, 65–66, 78, 105, 106, 120–21, 124–25, 189n49, 204n25
"Trail of Tears" (exile of Cherokees, 1838), 9, 16–17, 123–25, 129–33, 164, 206n37, 211n33
"The Trail of Tears" (Muskrat), 132
Transformer or Changer, in Coast Salish mythology, 81
tree, elegy for, 165
tribal societies, 3, 5, 10, 13, 148–52
"A Tribute to Chief Joseph" (Niatum), 162
the Trickster, 81, 148

Trimble, Joel, 96
Tshimshian people, 38–39, 185n7
Tuekakas, Old Joseph, 95, 199n69
Tulalip, 80, 196n45–46
Turrill, Henry Stuart, 88–90, 91–92, 95, 179, 180–81
Tuscaroras, 21, 23, 184n4, 185n8
Tutelos, 21
Two Rivers, E. Donald, 163

Ulivfak, 40–41
Umatilla people, 102
"The Unauthorized Autobiography of Me" (Alexie, 2000), 170
The Unnamable (Beckett, 1953), 152
Uvluniaq, 40

Vancouver, George, 83, 197n50
Vizenor, Gerald, 9, 18, 116, 129, 147–52, 184n9, 203n13

Wabokieshiek, White Cloud, 69, 113, 193n23
Walker, Bertrand (Hen-toh), 132
Walker, William, Jr., 131
Wampanoags, 16, 122, 206n35
Wampora, 60
wampum in Iroquois Condolence Rites, 21, 22, 25, 28, 184n6
wanaki, 150, 210n25
War of 1812, 112
Washinawatok, Ingrid, 157
wasna (pemmican), 56
Water, James E. (Wild Pigeon), 132
Watt, Roberta Frye, 74, 75, 77, 194n30, 195n33, 196n44, 197n50, 197n56
The Way to Rainy Mountain (Momaday, 1969), 10, 134–44; continuation of Kiowa culture and, 143–44; on cultural journey of Kiowas, 136–38, *137;* opening and closing poems, 135–36; in oral and Western belles lettres traditions, 11, 140–43; as presumptive initiator of Native American Renaissance, 18, 209n16; rainy day in 1874, analysis of Momaday's focus on, 138–40, *140, 141,* 157
"*Wazhazhe* Grandmother" (Revard), 164–65
Western Apache, narrative genres of, 2
western Shoshone *naraya* songs, 51, 59
"When Lilacs Last in the Dooryard Bloomed" (Whitman, 1865), 5, 17
"Where Sleep the Wintoon Dead" (Gillis), 133

White Bird, 96
"White Clay, Nebraska" (Louis, 1989), 161
Whitman, Walt, 5, 17
Willard, J. P., 88
the Windigo, 146
Winnebagos, 69, 113, 114
Winnemem Wintus, 133
"wo he iv 11/29/90" (Henson, 1990), 155–56
Wodziwob, Fish Lake Joe, 46–47, 202n6
Wood, Charles Erskine Scott, 99–105, 106, 181–82, 200n79, 201n86, 202n91
Wood, Erskine, 105, 201n85–86, 202n94
Wooden Lance, A'piaton, 47
Wounded Knee (1890), 47, 57–59, *58,* 120, 161, 168
Wovoka, Wood Cutter (Jack Wilson), 47–54, 56, 59, 118–20, 189–90n55–56, 189n53, 190n59, 190n61, 190n64, 201n89, 202n6, 203n14, 210n30
Wright, Asher, 23
Wright, Mabel, 43–44
written elegy, 10–11, 16–17, 108–33; Apess's *Eulogy on King Philip* (1836), 6, 16–17, 122–25; *Black Elk Speaks* (published 1932), 16, 116–22; Black Hawk's *Life* (published 1833), 16, 70, 72–73, 106, 108–16, 130; exile of Indians from lands east of Mississippi, poems responding to, 129–33; indigenous adoption of written medium, 10–11; of Ridge, 10, 11, 17, 127–29; of Schoolcraft, 10, 11, 17, 125–27, 163. *See also* "Native American Renaissance" and after, elegy from
Wyandots, 131, 132
"The Wyandot's Farewell" (Walker, 1843), 131

Yellow Bird (Minneconjou medicine person), 57
Yellow Bird, Chees-quat-a-law-ny (John Rollin Ridge), 10, 11, 17, 127–29
Yellow Breast, 118
Yellow Wolf, 98, 103, 199–200n73, 200n77, 201n90
yimaaje Havasupai dance, 51
Young Bear, Ray, 129
Young, Irene, 34
Young Joseph. *See* Chief Joseph, surrender speech of
Young Man Afraid of His Horses, 90
Yumas, 133